"*The Mystic Quest* ma[.....]ticated introduction to Jewish my[.....]paring Jewish mysticism to Chris[.....]g on writers such as William James and Sigmund Freud to define his terms. He then provides a history of Jewish mysticism, starting with Ezekiel's vision of the chariot and working up to the present day, with special attention to the ways that *Kabbalah* has influenced mainstream Judaism. By demonstrating the pervasive mystical dimension of Jewish culture, Ariel gives his Jewish readers the great gift of enlarging their understanding of what they already know, enabling them to find new revelation in the religion that has always guided them.

—Michael Joseph Gross

"The Jewish mystical tradition is unknown to most Jews today, yet for centuries prior to the French Revolution mysticism was an important current in Judaism. Rabbis in second-century Israel practiced visualization, techniques, and meditation. To the early Jewish mystics, God's wisdom (*Hokhmah*) prefigured everything that might come into existence; each person possessed a higher and lower soul; and God's feminine, caring aspect (*Shekhinah*) was locked in holy marriage with his masculine component. Ariel's brilliant study is the first comprehensive history of Jewish mysticism to make its ideas accessible to the nonspecialist. Readers, Jewish or non-Jewish, with an interest in mysticism will find much knowledge here.

—*Publishers Weekly*

"Ariel discusses the nature, history, character, and principles of Jewish mysticism. He also details number symbolism, reference to the feminine aspect of God, the idea of Torah as God's emanation, destiny of the soul, religious life of the mystic, and modern Jewish mysticism. The book is useful for general readers and specialists, but it does not oversimplify. It is an excellent, comprehensive study."

—*Library Journal*

KABBALAH

KABBALAH

The Mystic Quest in Judaism

DAVID ARIEL

ROWMAN & LITTLEFIELD PUBLISHERS, INC.
Lanham • Boulder • New York • Toronto • Oxford

The author gratefully acknowledges permission to reprint excerpts from the following material: *The Varieties of Religious Experience* by William James. Reprinted by
permission of Scribner, an imprint of Simon & Schuster Adult Publishing Group
from *The Varieties of Religious Experience* by William James (New York: Collier
Books, 1961). *Zohar: The Book of Splender* by Gershom Scholem. Copyright © 1949
and renewed 1977 by Schocken Books, used by permission of Schocken Books, a
division of Random House, Inc., New York. *The Sages: Their Beliefs and Opinions*
by Efraim Urbach. English edition, 1975, vol. 1. Reprinted by permission of The
Magnes Press, Jerusalem. *Mishnat ha-Zohar* by Isaiah Tishby, Hebrew edition, vols.
1 and 2. Reprinted by permission of The Bialik Institute, Jerusalem. *Zohar: The
Book of Enlightenment* translated by Daniel Matt. Copyright © 1933 by Daniel Matt.
From the Classics of Western Spirituality Series. Used by permission of Paulist Press,
Ramsey, New Jersey (www.paulistpress.com).

ROWMAN & LITTLEFIELD PUBLISHERS, INC.

Published in the United States of America by Rowman & Littlefield Publishers,
Inc.
A wholly owned subsidiary of The Rowman & Littlefield Publishing Group, Inc.
4501 Forbes Boulevard, Suite 200, Lanham, Maryland 20706
www.rowmanlittlefield.com

PO Box 317
Oxford
OX2 9RU, UK

Copyright © 2006 by Rowman & Littlefield Publishers, Inc.

British Library Cataloguing in Publication Information Available

Library of Congress Cataloging-in-Publication Data

Kabbalah : the mystic quest in Judaism / by David Ariel.
    p.   cm.
Includes bibliographical references and index.
ISBN 0–7425–4565–2 (cloth : alk. paper)—ISBN 0–7425–4564–4 (pbk. :
alk. paper)   1. Mysticism—Judaism.   2. Cabala.   I. Ariel, David S.
BM723.K18   2005
296.7'12—dc22   2005016872

Printed in the United States of America

♾ ™ The paper used in this publication meets the minimum requirements of American
National Standard for Information Sciences—Permanence of Paper for Printed Library
Materials, ANSI/NISO Z39.48–1992.

To
Joshua Rubenstein
and
Peter Geffen
"There are companions to keep one company,
And there is a friend more devoted than a brother."

(*Proverbs* 18:24)

CONTENTS

ACKNOWLEDGMENTS

When I began to study *Kabbalah* in 1968, it was a countercultural statement. I had a traditional Jewish education which seemed increasingly irrelevant in the late sixties—a period of political and social turmoil. I, and many others, found that the major Jewish denominations did not adequately address the questions of peace and social justice that consumed our attention. In my despair at the Vietnam War, the military draft, racial injustice, and the direction of American society, I turned towards Zionism and the study of Jewish mystical texts in the original Hebrew. Zionism, in the aftermath of the Six Day war, provided me with an outlet for my youthful idealism. The study of medieval Jewish mysticism provided me with the intellectual and spiritual home that I could not find in contemporary Judaism. I started a new life in Israel and immersed myself in the academic study of *Kabbalah*.

I would like to thank those who helped me on my journey. Professor Asher Finkel introduced *Kabbalah* to me in 1968 when I was an undergraduate at New York University. My studies continued at the Hebrew University of Jerusalem under the guidance of Professors Rivka Schatz-Uffenheimer, Isaiah Tishby, Yosef Dan, and Efraim Gottlieb and, later, at Brandeis University under the direction of Prof. Alexander Altmann. Professor Marvin Fox of Brandeis University introduced me to a conceptual and philosophical approach to Jewish mysticism, which formed the underlying method of this book. Professor Gershom Scholem, the pioneer in the modern study of Jewish mysticism, whom I served as a teaching assistant at Boston University, helped me immeasurably in my studies.

During several years teaching in the Department of Religion at Wesleyan University, colleagues and friends introduced me to fresh conceptual approaches to the study of religion drawn from the fields of religious studies and psychology. These approaches have informed my thinking about *Kabbalah*.

Siegal College and the Jewish community of Cleveland have provided me with the opportunity and motivation to write about *Kabbalah* and Jewish spirituality. The students at Siegal College have inspired me to write a book that introduces and explains Jewish mysticism. My close colleagues have offered valuable suggestions and criticisms in the course of writing this book. Good friends and colleagues, especially Professors Rachel Elior and Daniel Matt, challenged me with their questions and suggestions along the way.

I could not have written this book had it not been for the support and encouragement of Siegal College's Board of Trustees, particularly its chairman, Lawrence M. Bell. The trustees include: Barbara Amper, Ernest Benchell, Renee Chelm, Morton A. Cohen, Philip M. Cohen, Deedra Dolin, Gail Dolin, Rita Frankel, Rina Frankel, Stuart A. Gertman, Rachelle Goddard, Robert Goldberg, Sharon Guten, Michal Hilman, Terri G. Kline, Margery Kohrman, Teela C. Lelyveld, Ray Leventhal, Fred J. Livingstone, Herb Marcus, Allen Miller, I. Ron Moskowitz, Edward Pelavin, Michael Penzner, Dan Aaron Polster, Eli Reshotko, Ken Rosen, Marc Saltzberg, Mitchell Schneider, Alan Schonberg, David Shifrin, Alvin Siegal, Anita H. Siegal, Marc Alan Silverstein, James C. Spira, Maurice Terkel, Muriel Weber, Jeffrey J. Wild, Larry Wymor, Donna Yanowitz, and Dan Zelman.

The staff of Siegal College enabled me to devote precious and undisturbed time to this book. In particular, I would like to acknowledge my colleagues: Sylvia Abrams, Nili Adler, Brian Amkraut, Moshe Berger, Ronald Brauner, Allan Feldman, Roberta Goodman, Jean Lettofsky, Alan Levenson, Linda Rosen, Carrie Rosenfelt, Lifsa Schachter, Jeffrey Schein, Leonard Steiger, and Yakov Travis. In addition, thanks to Eli Aschkenasy, Penny Kaufman, Rachel Kugelman, Jennifer Morton, and Judy Shafron. Special thanks go to my devoted assistant, Sheryl Hirsh, for her patience and support.

Through his deep personal interest in the subject, Brian Romer, editor of Rowman & Littlefield, has supported me throughout the project with his comments and questions. My literary agent, Jill Grinberg, has been a source of constant and valued guidance.

My children, Judah, Micah, and Aviva, have lived patiently through my writing bouts.

INTRODUCTION

The study of *Kabbalah*, the Jewish mystical tradition, is the path to a deeper understanding of the spiritual resources within Judaism. This book introduces the reader to the breadth and depth of Jewish mysticism. It is intended to make the meaning of Jewish mysticism accessible to a general audience in two ways. First, I have explained the underlying meaning of Jewish mysticism in language that can be understood by an uninitiated reader. Jewish mystics speak in a rich, symbolic language that is incomprehensible without a guide and explanation. Second, I have translated many passages from Jewish mystical literature originally written in Hebrew and Aramaic. I have also drawn upon the growing volume of scholarly literature on the subject, much of which has been written in Hebrew and German. Most works written in English about Jewish mysticism are either too scholarly or too inaccurate to faithfully represent the subject. My task, therefore, has been to serve as a translator in a dual capacity.

This book is concerned primarily with the development and meaning of the *Kabbalah*. *Kabbalah* (pronounced *ka-ba-lah'*), literally the Hebrew word for "tradition," is the name of the Jewish mystical movement that began in southern France and Spain around 1200 and which continued uninterrupted through the nineteenth century. Although at times *Kabbalah* was the dominant religious movement in Judaism, it was largely abandoned by Jews living in Europe and other Western countries in the last two centuries.

In 1988, when I published the first edition of this book, *The Mystic Quest: An Introduction to Jewish Mysticism*, the word *Kabbalah* was too unfamiliar to include in the title. At the time, there were only a handful of scholars in North America engaged in serious research in this area. To my great surprise and, sometimes distress, all this has changed. Today, more than 100 books appear each year with Jewish mysticism, spirituality, or *Kabbalah* in the title. Madonna and the others have made *Kabbalah*, the red string (*bendel*), and "*Kabbalah* water," household words.

By all indications, American Jewry is standing on the brink of a spiritual revival. The evidence for this can be found in the increasing attention to personal Jewish growth, the emergence of serious adult Jewish learning, the resurgence of Jewish countercultural alternatives, the interest in *Kabbalah*—the mystical dimensions of Judaism, the expansion of the market for Jewish books, the rise of the "Jewish Internet," and the strength of the *baal teshuvah* (born-again Jews) movement.

The growing interest in the exploration of one's own personal Jewishness can be seen among those who are engaged in a variety of Jewish "journeys" or who identify themselves as Jewish "Seekers." The rise in the number of people involved in adult Jewish learning and the proliferation of national, regional, and local programs that promote Jewish spiritual growth are sure signs of this phenomenon. The Jewish counterculture that began with the Havurah movement in the late sixties has developed into an eclectic, spiritual movement—Jewish Renewal—that integrates elements of traditional Judaism, ecstatic *Hasidism*, and Buddhist meditation.[1] Jewish meditation groups and courses on *Kabbalah* are now offered within synagogues, temples, and homes. Major trade publishers and Jewish niche publishers are experiencing strong sales of books on Jewish spirituality that are supported by national author tours. Numerous Internet websites offer "Jewish spiritual resources" from varying religious perspectives. Finally, some Jewish adults—the *baalei teshuvah* ("Returnees") continue to embrace Orthodox Judaism and its rigorous lifestyle without any ambivalence or ambiguity.

A growing number of younger Jews, as many as one-third of the adult Jewish population in North America between the ages of twenty-five and fifty, increasingly identify themselves as "Seekers" in pursuit of deeper personal meaning and connectedness.[2] This is documented in several recent demographic studies including Bethamie Horowitz's "Connections and Journeys."[3] Horowitz's research shows that adult Jewish identity changes throughout the course of a lifetime and is just as likely to increase as to decrease. This goes against the widely held assumption that Jewish identity among non-Orthodox Jews is in decline and is reflected in a high rate of assimilation and intermarriage. Still, the overall increase in the importance of being Jewish is accompanied, paradoxically, by a general decrease in traditional ritual observance. "Seekers" may feel very Jewish inwardly but they do not necessarily follow recognizable patterns of Jewish observance. Therefore, the right metaphor for the "Seekers" approach to Jewish practice may be a "salad bar"—choosing, trying, selecting, adding, and discarding Jewish rituals and identities.

Other studies have begun to draw a clearer portrait of the contemporary Jewish landscape. Arnold Eisen and Steven M. Cohen have studied "moderately affiliated Jews," that is, married Jewish adults who belong to at least one Jewish institution but who are not deeply engaged, learned, or pious. This group constitutes 50–60 percent of the American Jewish population that is between the ages of 35 and 50. This "broad middle" has a largely positive relationship to their own Jewishness but it is not necessarily the most significant factor in their lives. The authors differentiate this group from the "core Jews" (20–25 percent) and the "completely uninvolved" (20 percent) at either end of the continuum of Jewish identity.

Their research finds that "the principal authority for contemporary American Jews has become the sovereign self."[4] "The 'first language' is by and large one of profound individualism."[5] Like many of their generation, the quest for personal meaning and the quest for Jewish meaning are extremely important to them. Like many of their contemporaries, they are guided by an internal compass rather than by communal or traditional norms. Personal meaning is the arbiter of their Jewish involvement. Jewish meaning is constructed selectively one experience at a time, is fluid and changing, and is part of an unending journey. This "unprecedented exercise of autonomy among the current generation of Jews when it comes to ritual observance" is the hallmark of this generation: "They aim to make Jewish narratives part of their own personal stories, by picking and choosing among new and inherited practices and texts so as to find the combination they as individuals can authentically affirm."[6]

The authors provide a picture of a wholesale "retreat from public Judaism." "The forces of personalism and privatization and the diminished role of ethnic identification have exerted a major impact upon Jews' engagement with the public sphere in recent years."[7] Moderately affiliated Jews often combine a great concern for spirituality and meaning with severely diminished interest in the organizational life of the Jewish community.[8] They exhibit an "enduring ambivalence toward the organizations, institutions, commitments and norms which constitute Jewish life."[9] Although 48 percent of Jews are affiliated with a synagogue, more than 40 percent responded that Jewish organizations are remote and irrelevant.[10] At the same time, 94 percent agree with the statement that "the Jews are my people" and that "Jews have an especially rich history, one with special meaning for our lives today." They are "even less interested in denominational differences than their parents' generation was, insisting on the right—and fact—of individual autonomy when it comes to deciding the details of Jewish practice."[11] Eisen and Cohen identify these as the characteristics of "postmodern Judaism"—the retreat of public Judaism, the privatization of Jewish meaning, and ritual eclecticism.

Today's "Seekers" view spirituality as the deeply held core of values by which they lead their lives. They search for truths that serve as the unassailable anchor of their personal experience. They want to find corroboration in Judaism for what they know in their hearts to be true. They seek wisdom that can guide their public behavior and their relationships with others. Inwardness becomes the measure of whether their public activities have meaning. They are engaged in a lifelong journey in which various forms of Jewish expression are synthesized into an evolving system of personal identity.

The emergence of personal Jewish expression in all its varieties constitutes a spiritual revival, although this revival is not necessarily unified or coherent. What makes this phenomenon unique is that it is taking place largely outside the purview of institutionalized Jewish life, the major Jewish denominations, and most congregations. It is one of the few truly indigenous developments in American Jewish life. It is a genuinely grassroots movement that started on the periphery of Jewish life but which has recently begun to move into the center.

For the first time in three generations, a growing number of younger Jews are not content with accepting conventional Judaism. They want to know about Judaism for themselves and reject the passivity of vicarious Jewishness, of letting others define Judaism for them. They seek empowerment as Jews to counter the meagerness of the Judaism they were taught in Hebrew school. It is not sufficient for the rabbi to lecture, define, and lead. They want to learn, experience, and understand for themselves. But they do not want to learn *about* Judaism, they want to learn Judaism. They seek immediacy, authenticity, and truth. This puts increasing pressure on the Jewish community to respond to this development positively, seriously, and with additional resources.

Many "Seekers" today view Jewish institutions as more concerned with sustaining membership and preserving an institution for its own sake than with the heart and soul of the individual. Abraham Joshua Heschel's critique of organized Jewish life in the 1950s may have been prophetic. He expressed criticism of the vacuousness of the American Jewish community for not deepening the spiritual and religious life of the individual. He criticized the excessive preoccupation with the communal aspects of Jewish life at the expense of the spiritual dimension of life. In his own words: "The concern for the welfare of the community and its institutions that has dominated Jewish life in America has also diverted our attention from the individual. Jews attend Jewish meetings, belong to Jewish organizations, and contribute to communal and national funds: In seeing the forest, we could not see the trees. In building a strong communal life, we have forgotten the spiritual condition of the individual Jew. The private life of the Jew has become impoverished and is reflected in the spiritual vacuousness of many Jewish homes and synagogues. The concern of the Jewish community should be reversed: Unless the religious spirit of the Jew as an individual is enriched, the life of the community will be a wilderness. If the individual is lost to Judaism in his privacy, the people are in danger of becoming a phantom."[12]

Today's spiritual revival may be a reaction to the situation that Heschel described. But this change may also reflect the growing assertion of the spiritual—the personal, the private, the inward—into the public arena. When institutions such as the family, voluntary organizations, the workplace, religious organizations, and political institutions no longer meet our deeply personal criteria of meaning, we turn to alternative forms of expression that have greater personal meaning. We ask not what we can do for institutions, but what institutions can do for us. Therefore, many of the spiritual expressions of personal Jewish meaning today take place beyond the institutions of Jewish life. But because these are positive expressions of Jewish meaning in the eyes of the "Seekers" themselves, they represent a deepening of personal Jewishness among individuals who were previously less engaged with Judaism.

This awakening reflects the maturation of the growth of Jewish identity that has evolved in the last thirty-five years. What began as growing comfort with the public expression of Jewish identity has matured into a growing concern with the personal meaning of Jewish identity—"the Jew within." It is no longer sufficient to base Jewish identity on the social, public, communal, or organizational forms of Judaism—or on the imperatives of fighting anti-Semitism and defending Jews in Israel and around the world—unless we also understand what this means to us personally.

The recent spiritual awakening is also an inevitable reaction against the trend of assimilation that has resulted in a weak congregational Jewish educational system. Many congregational schools have encouraged Jewish identity but not Jewish knowledge. They have often validated a minimalist form of Judaism and expected little of the student, their parents, or their teachers. With the growth of more intensive Jewish education—day schools, summer camps, youth groups, Israel programs, and congregational family education—the pendulum has swung the other way towards taking Judaism more seriously. And those Jewish adults whose own Jewish education was inadequate, but whose children are involved in more intensive Jewish education, often want to explore and live Judaism on a more intense level.

The Jewish spiritual awakening also reflects the growing acceptance of public religious expression in the United States. It mirrors the penetration of religion into public discourse and political life among many sectors within American society. Spirituality in America is often accompanied by a commitment to societal change rather than a retreat from society.[13] Likewise, many Jewish adults seek ways to express their spirituality in the world rather than withdraw into a private cocoon. At the same time, the spiritual developments within contemporary Judaism echo many forms of expression in contemporary American culture—lifelong adult learning, an increased focus on expanding leisure-time activities, efforts to create intentional communities, the exploration of new age and healing traditions, an openness and eclecticism that blends elements of various traditions, alternative lifestyles, and other nontraditional forms of personal expression.

Jewish "Seekers" see themselves in pursuit of genuine spirituality. They crave, above all, authenticity, which to them means a faith and a way of life that are unambiguous, based on certain authority, and which is not self-conscious or temporizing. They want guides who are authentic and who do not just "talk the talk but also walk the walk." They look for a Judaism that speaks to their hearts and that provides a clear answer to those questions that matter most—how to validate one's own feelings, how to be a good person and lead a moral life, how to relate to other people, how to find balance and perspective between and among the many competing claims on our time, how to create a Jewish home life, and what to believe about the presence of God in our lives. Although they might belong to a congregation, they often reject Orthodox, Conservative, and Reform Judaism, the denominations in which many were raised. They often see their rabbis as lacking spiritual authenticity, as being uncomfortable with their questions, and as preferring to advocate rather than serve as role models. They view mainstream, liberal congregations as too concerned with institutional self-preservation rather than with spirituality. Still, they may draw comfortably on those elements of traditional belief and practice that they can integrate into their lives. They want Judaism to provide an internal compass that guides them across the terrain of life, to provide the basis for religious practice in their home and daily lives, and to lay the foundation of friendships and relationships with other like-minded individuals. They want "intimacy," the clear comfort of a certain identity that is both deeply personal but also connects them to others.

The search for authenticity finds many forms of expression. "Seekers" are not necessarily loyal to institutions but view them instrumentally as vehicles that warrant their affiliation only as long as they serve their needs. Some "Seekers" create or join communities of connectedness outside of institutional Jewish life such as alternative or intentional congregations (*chavurot*), alternative prayer groups (*minyanim*), or create their own circle of friends that get together for Jewish holidays.

Some "Seekers" idealize some of the more open-minded and accepting Orthodox rabbis and teachers as being authentic role models. These rabbis are often youthful "outreach workers" for various Orthodox groups. They are devoted teachers who are often willing to teach anyone, anywhere, and with no financial obligation. Their followers seek genuine Jewish experience even if they are not willing to embrace the lifestyle of their idealized Orthodoxy. Thus, they are drawn to Orthodox teachers but not to Orthodoxy as a way of life. In some ways, they are "tourists within an Orthodox theme park" who are comfortable making a weekly foray into studying with an Orthodox teacher as long as they can go home afterwards.

Authenticity "Seekers" do not necessarily embrace Orthodoxy. Authenticity "Seekers" might pursue a gradual, incremental embrace of Jewish life or they might follow a patchwork of observances that are not necessarily internally consistent. Sometimes "Seekers" adopt particular observances without regard for how a particular ritual fits into a larger context. For example, a woman might study the laws of family purity, be inspired by its notion of holy sexuality, and decide to attend a *mikveh*, the ritual bath, after her monthly menstruation. This same woman may be just as likely to drive to synagogue on the Sabbath. While the practice of *mikveh* has traditionally been limited to Orthodox observance, Sabbath observance is more fundamental to Judaism than *mikveh* and more widely practiced. Within the context of traditional Judaism and its hierarchy of practice, one is more likely to observe Sabbath than attend the *mikveh*. When *mikveh* is taken out of its context, all things are possible. There is often such a contradiction between a seeker's idealization of Orthodoxy and an unwillingness to accept the whole package.

Some authenticity "Seekers" embrace Orthodoxy. These born-again Jews are called "Returnees" (*Baalei Teshuvah*) to indicate that they have returned to the correct path. Many Returnees were raised in assimilated Jewish homes and have often pursued extended spiritual odysseys before returning home to Judaism. Returnees are critical of non-Orthodox Judaism, which they often see as hypocritical, superficial, lacking conviction, relativistic, and spiritually vacuous. Like other authenticity "Seekers," Returnees seek genuine Jewish experience. Unlike other "Seekers," they are not satisfied by anything less than total immersion in Judaism. They are drawn to the various forms of Orthodoxy—modern, *Hasidic*, and fundamentalist—in which they find the overpowering appeal of unambiguous commitment of both heart and body.

The Jewish Renewal movement is the only organized contemporary Jewish spiritual movement. It is an outgrowth of the Havurah ("commune") movement that began in the sixties and combined elements of *Hasidic* ecstasy and communal intimacy in a noninstitutional and egalitarian culture. As the Havurah movement matured, the influence of two master teachers—Rabbi Zalman Schachter-Shalomi and Rabbi Shlomo Carlebach—came to tower above the movement. Schachter-Shalomi's immersion in traditional *Hasidism* and his openness to Buddhist meditation, Sufi chants, and other mystical traditions coalesced into a teaching of inwardness, mindfulness, and soulfulness. Carlebach's neo-*Hasidic* melodies gave this movement a liturgy, a tradition of teaching stories and *niggunim*—Jewish melodies that induce ecstasy and self-transcendence. In recent years, this movement has taken shape as Jewish Renewal, a loose confederations of groups across the country. A spiritual retreat center in upstate New York, *Elat Hayyim*, serves to continuously energize the adherents. A recent decision to ordain Jewish Renewal rabbis is evidence of the movement's aspirations to deepen its impact.

Jewish Renewal promotes authentic Jewish spiritual experience by embracing the mystical traditions of *Hasidism*. Unlike some New Age groups that dabble in *Kabbalah*, the center of gravity of this group is rooted within traditional Judaism even as they emphasize the mystical tradition over other Jewish traditions. They are also eclectic and incorporate elements from Buddhism and other Eastern traditions. Their greatest accomplishment so far is that they have created small communities across the country and have reintroduced elements of ecstasy, sensuality, music, and dance into the

Jewish experience of communal prayer. To Jewish Renewal adherents, Judaism without ecstasy is empty and the support of a community of people connected together by a common spiritual outlook is indispensable.

There is substantial evidence that many Jews have turned away from Jewish life but still seek a spiritual anchor within Judaism. However, for some, Judaism itself carries no greater authority than any other spiritual tradition. These "Seekers" may have been born Jewish, but they have no real familiarity with it. Precisely because Judaism is foreign to them as individuals, Judaism possesses an exotic attraction. They see Judaism as an occult tradition of ancient wisdom and a guide to esoteric practices such as mystical union, soul-travel, reincarnation, healing, and achieving gnosis. These spiritualists are eclectic and draw on a wide range of New Age and other spiritual paths—especially Native American and Buddhist practices—as effortlessly as they draw on Judaism. They seek to find a spiritual path by combining whatever spiritual elements appeal to them from various traditions. They are drawn, in particular, to *Kabbalah*, the Jewish mystical tradition. However, they rely on New Age interpretations of *Kabbalah*, most of which bear little or no relation to actual *Kabbalah*. This group is largely peripheral to Jewish life even if the significance of this phenomenon is greater than meets the eye.

The present revival may reflect the perennial spark of Jewishness that resides in every Jewish soul waiting to be ignited. In every generation, there is a yearning to discover the mystery of Jewish existence that inspired and nourished earlier generations. It is not a legacy that one would want to relinquish easily. The yearning today, however, manifests itself not as a simple return to the innocence of traditional Jewish life that defines and directs all aspects of life. Rather, it can be described as a "second innocence," a Jewish yearning to return to the innocence and faith of earlier generations while preserving the "Seekers" autonomy, freedom, and modernity—not by returning to the lifestyle of the past but rather by invigorating the Jewish legacy with new vitality. Throughout Jewish history, Judaism retreats from the precipice of near-extinction and miraculously gains power, endurance, and vitality.

A NOTE TO THE READER

I have employed certain conventions that may be unfamiliar to many readers. Dates according to the Gregorian calendar are usually indicated by B.C. (Before Christ) and A.D. (Anno Domini, Latin for "in the year of our Lord"). Since these conventions reflect a Christian concept of history, they are generally regarded as inappropriate among historians of Judaism. The terms B.C.E. (Before the Common Era) and C.E. (Common Era) are used when writing Jewish history. I have employed these terms throughout this book in reference to dates according to the Gregorian calendar.

There are several common systems employed in transliterating Hebrew terms. The most popular form is the phonetic system that is in standard usage in popular books, magazines, and newspapers. The disadvantage of this system is that it does not accurately correlate with the original Hebrew. I have adopted the less familiar system of transliteration employed in modern scholarly literature. It is a modified version of the transliteration rules of the *Encyclopedia Judaica*. Certain common spellings have been maintained, such as "Kabbalah," for terms that have generally entered common English usage.

All translations in this work are my own, except where otherwise noted as quoted from another source.

All passages from the Hebrew Bible have been cited in the translation of the Jewish Publication Society.

א	–	ל	l
בּ	b	מ	m
ב	v	נ	n
ג	g	ס	s
ד	d	ע	–
ח	h	פּ	p
ו	v	פ	f
ז	z	צ	tz
ח	h	ק	k
ט	t	ר	r
י	y, i at the end of a word	שׁ	sh
כּ	k	שׂ	s
כ	kh	ת	t

I

SEEKERS OF UNITY

The Nature of Mysticism

What is mysticism? The *Oxford English Dictionary* defines mysticism as follows:

> The opinions, mental tendencies, or habits of thought and feeling, character-istic of mystics; mystical doctrines or spirit; belief in the possibility of union with the Divine nature by means of ecstatic contemplation; reliance on spiri-tual intuition or exalted feeling as the means of acquiring knowledge of mys-teries inaccessible to intellectual apprehension.

The earliest usage of the root word *myein*, from which the term mysticism derives, occurs among the ancient Greeks who coined the term *mystikos* to describe a ritual in which one shuts one's eyes in order to close off the world and experience other realities.[1] In the seventh century B.C.E., for example, practitioners (*mystes*) of the mystery cult at Eleusis would detach themselves from mundane stimuli during the festivals celebrating the sowing, sprouting, and reaping of grain harvests. The *mystes* would participate in secret rituals that dramatized the myth of the mother goddess, Demeter, the goddess of grain, and her daughter, Persephone, who was captured by Hades, god of the dead. Although no account of the actual practices exists, some records indicate that the rituals of the Eleusinian cults involved elaborate initiation ceremonies consisting of eating, drinking, singing, ritual bathing, and medi-tative trances that culminated in symbolic marriages with the gods.[2]

Mysticism today has come to mean something other than the technique of initiation into mystery cults. William James (1842–1910), brother of novelist Henry James, describes the characteristics of mysticism in his book *The Varieties of Religious Experience: A Study in Human Nature*. When he wrote this book in 1902, he was an American pioneer exploring the psychology of religion, a field that had not yet been touched by the theories of Sigmund Freud. James attempted to understand the psychology of religious experiences, feelings, and impulses. He drew his evidence from literature, especially works written in English by Christian authors, and case histories.

According to James, *mysticism* is the term used to characterize ineffable and indescribable religious experiences. Mysticism is at the core of religion, he states, because "personal religious experience has its root and center in mystical states of consciousness."[3] Mysticism, in his view, refers to the essence of a particular human experience rather than to the specific technique by which such an experience is induced. No description of the substance of a mystical experience can adequately be expressed in words. Many people who have had mystical experiences describe them as fleeting, unanticipated occurrences that produce altered states of consciousness. James cites one such experience as an example of a mystical testimony:

> Suddenly, and always, I think, when my muscles were at rest, I felt the approach of the mood. Irresistibly, it took possession of my mind and will, lasted what seemed an eternity, and disappeared in a series of rapid sensations which resembled the awakening from anesthetic influence. One reason why I disliked this kind of trance was that I could not describe it to myself. I cannot even now find words to render it intelligible. It consisted in a gradual but swiftly progressive obliteration of space, time, sensation and the multitudinous factors of experience which seem to qualify what we are pleased to call our Self.[4]

This experience has no connection with initiation into a specific religion or cult. It is a highly individual experience with no reference to a particular content. There is no preparation, training, or initiation process prior to the advent of the experience. It occurs passively and involuntarily in a state of rest and repose rather than being actively induced through initiation, ceremony, or ritual. Members of the Eleusinian mystery cult experience contact with the gods and can describe the experience but choose not to. James' respondent, however, cannot put his experience into words. The account, moreover, relates a feeling of unpleasantness rather than the elation characteristic of some of the earlier mystery cults.

This account, however, includes several features that are common to many forms of mysticism. The experience produces an altered state of consciousness. Conscious awareness of mundane reality recedes, changing the physiological responses to external stimuli and a hypnotic or other trance-like state is entered. The perception of time and space and orientation to the world change in ways that cannot be described. The mystic experiences this as a change in consciousness and a new awareness of other levels of reality that are not accessible to normal consciousness. The experience leads to a change in his orientation to himself and to the world. Although the experience itself is transitory and cannot be sustained, the mystic remains changed by the experience. All subsequent experiences may be understood in light of this new awareness.

Many of James' subjects describe a mystical experience as more than just an emotional state. Their encounters have a *noetic* quality—an element of insight, knowledge, intuition, or revelation not normally acquired through rational means. Such knowledge, they testify, has an authority that endures and influences their lives long after the event itself has passed. R. M. Bucke, author of *Cosmic Consciousness*, an early twentieth-century classic of futurist inspiration and mystical investigation, recounts one such experience after a quiet evening with friends discussing poetry and philosophy:

> My mind, deeply under the influence of the ideas, images and emotions called up by the reading and talk, was calm and peaceful. I was in a state of quiet, almost passive enjoyment, not actually thinking, but letting ideas, images, and emotions flow of themselves, as it were, through my mind. All at once, without warning of any kind, I found myself wrapped in a flame-colored cloud. For an instant I thought of fire, an immense conflagration somewhere close by in that great city; the next, I knew that the fire was within myself. Directly afterward there came upon me a sense of exultation, of immense joyousness accompanied or immediately followed by an intellectual illumination impossible to describe. Among other things, I did not merely come to believe, but I saw that the universe is not composed of dead matter, but is, on the contrary, a living Presence. I became conscious in myself of eternal life. It was not a conviction that I would have eternal life, but a consciousness that I possessed eternal life then; I saw that all men are immortal; that the cosmic order is such that . . . all things work together for the good of each and all; that the foundation principle of the world, of all the worlds, is what we call love, and that the happiness of each and all is in the long run absolutely certain. The vision lasted a few seconds and was gone but the memory of it and the sense of the reality of what it taught have remained during the quarter of a century which has since elapsed.[5]

This testimony introduces several important additional factors present in many accounts of mystical experiences. Some individuals may be predisposed to having mystical experiences by virtue of their personality and training. The scene described in this passage attests to the aesthetic and contemplative inclinations of the respondent. He is a person deeply moved by sublime thoughts and emotions and is, evidently, meditative and contemplative by nature. He also practices a form of attentional meditation that involves the restful visualization of and attention to the sequence of ideas and images that enter his consciousness. He turns his attention away from the external stimuli of the senses towards his own internal consciousness. There is a logical transition from the technique of visualization to the visual experience that soon overcomes him. In this case the nature of the experience is conditioned by the steps that he takes leading up to it. Like many visualizing mystics, he sees himself bathed in a luminous glow. Fire and light frequently form the visual frame for mystical experiences.

The mystical mode of knowing is characteristically paradoxical. The subject describes his experience in paradoxical terms. Since philosophic thinking and visualization are the techniques that lead to this particular encounter, it is not surprising that the subject achieves a type of visual knowledge. He does not merely know things acutely—he sees what he knows. This paradoxical "seeing thought" carries with it a deep conviction of the truth of his discovery because of the specific sensual awareness of what is essentially abstract.

The content of the noetic experience within mysticism is often described as an "oceanic feeling"—a sense that the mystic is undifferentiated from the rest of reality. A mystical experience frequently culminates in the disintegration of the boundaries of individuality and the self and results in a sense of the "oneness" of the universe. Usually this awareness is transient, allowing the mystic to return to routine consciousness and to continue to function in the world. Some mystics, however, cannot shed this "oceanic feeling" and continue to feel undifferentiated. Such individuals who cannot sustain routine consciousness frequently suffer from psychotic delusions. The difference, perhaps, between the mystic and the psychotic is that whereas both have oceanic experiences, the mystic is able to return to the world of mundane reality. Phenomenologically, mysticism may be indistinguishable from a form of temporary insanity. Although the mystic might not be psychotic, he is, nevertheless, transformed by his experience.

This fleeting experience, common to many people during the course of a lifetime, is often called a "peak experience." It is frequently accompanied by the sense that one is communicating with something other than the normal everyday world. The mystic often feels that he has transcended the world of the senses and has peered behind the veil separating this world from the reality beyond.

Transcendent experiences are, according to many, at the core of all religious experience. In religious contexts these experiences may assume a specific character. Sometimes they involve "out-of-body experiences," a visual sense of the entire self separating from and rising above the body. At other times the subject experiences an inner change in consciousness alone. The following example from the *New Testament* illustrates the ambiguity of outward, as opposed to inner, transcendence:

> I know a man in Christ (i.e., a Christian) who fourteen years ago was caught up to the third heaven—whether in the body or out of the body I do not know. God knows. And I know that this man was caught up into Paradise— whether in the body or out of the body I do not know. God knows. And he heard things which cannot be told, which man may not utter.[6]

These examples, which are only several among many recorded mystical testimonies in world literature, exhibit some of the primary characteristics of mystical experiences. Mystical experiences are frequently ineffable and indescribable states of altered consciousness involving a reordering of consciousness or disruption of normal perceptual modes. This phenomenon is also known as "deautomatization," the production of changes in the usual physiological responses to external stimuli. They may be brought about actively through training and preparation or passively as the result of an individual's predisposition. The experiences themselves usually have an emotional content of either serenity or overwhelming awe. They often have noetic content involving the perception of oneness and unity. This frequently manifests as either an "oceanic feeling" of undifferentiatedness of the individual from the rest of the world, a specific perception of contradictory or paradoxical phenomena, or an intense intellectual discovery of transcendence. All mystical experiences are transformative, and many produce significant changes in a person's orientation to the world. Mysticism frequently involves some, but not all, of these characteristics at the same time.

It is still difficult to define mysticism precisely. Some argue that it is a fundamental category of human experience because it is known to occur to a wide range of individuals in widely diverse cultures. One scholar, J. N. Findlay, author of *Ascent to the Absolute*, describes it this way:

The mystical way of looking at things enters into the experience of most men at many times. The so-called great mystics are merely people who carry to the point of genius an absolutely normal, ordinary, indispensable side of human experience.[7]

Sigmund Freud, no admirer of mysticism, describes the "oceanic feeling" as "a sensation of eternity, a feeling as of something limitless, unbounded—as it were, oceanic, . . . (a) feeling of an indissoluble bond, of being one with the external world as a whole."[8] He relates this not to objective reality but to a state of ego-regression. An infant cannot differentiate between himself and objects, and so his ego includes everything. Later he separates the external world from himself. The "oceanic feeling," in Freud's view, is the result of regression to the infantile state or the primitive persistence of this feeling in later life. In either case Freud considers this mystical and "oceanic feeling" to be a psychological state and not objective experience.

Freud explains that there is only one state, other than psychosis, in which the clean, sharp lines of demarcation between the ego and everything else melt away: love. It is not surprising, then, that love should engender a feeling of mysticism or that mystical experiences should involve the sensation of love.

The absolute conviction that one has achieved a type of unification is the most common feature of all mystical experiences. As William James defined it:

This overcoming of the usual barriers between the individual and the Absolute is the great mystic achievement. In mystic states we both become one with the Absolute and we become aware of our oneness. This is the everlasting and triumphant mystical tradition, hardly altered by difference of clime or creed. . . . There is about mystical utterances an eternal unanimity which ought to make a critic stop and think.[9]

In the appendix to W. R. Inge's *Mysticism in Religion* appear a variety of definitions of mysticism. These examples illustrate the extent to which mysticism is a form of unification. At the same time they are emblematic of the different interpretations of the term "unity":

That we bear the image of God is the starting point, one might say the postulate, of all mysticism. The complete union of the soul with God is the goal of all mysticism.[10]

This definition might appear to be valid for practitioners of religions such as Judaism and Christianity in its assumption of the existence of a transcendent God and the human soul. It would not apply to religions that are not based on the Hebrew Bible from which the idea of the "image of God" originated. Moreover, this definition would apply only in those circumstances where "complete union with God" is deemed possible and not in those cases where it is generally regarded as improbable.

Other attempts to offer a broader definition of mysticism often leave the question of how to differentiate between religion and mysticism unanswered, as in the following example:

> Mysticism is the immediate feeling of the unity of the self with God; it is nothing, therefore, but the fundamental feeling of religion, the religious life at its very heart and center.[11]

Mysticism is closely associated with a sense of unity and unification. It is equally apparent that the meaning of unity is not uniform and can mean different things to different people in different cultures. William James is mistaken in his belief that mysticism is a universal phenomenon of union because the notion of the "Absolute," the object of the union, differs from culture to culture. The notion that all mystical experiences are essentially the same in character despite the different ways they are described is misleading. Recent studies have shown that the specific cultural and religious norms in which a mystic's consciousness is shaped make his experience culturally specific. Steven Katz argues against cross-cultural phenomenological accounts of mystical experience as reductive and inflexible, "forcing multifarious and extremely variegated forms of mystical experience into improper interpretative categories which lose sight of the fundamentally important differences between the data studies."[12] He offers a thorough critique of the various methodological approaches to the study of mysticism using examples of Jewish mysticism as illustrations and, at times, counterevidence to commonly accepted notions about mysticism. Although many mystics use similar language, a thorough analysis of their experiences reveals that the meaning of oneness is not the same in each account.

Earlier scholars of mysticism, including William James, Aldous Huxley, and Fritjof Schuuon, have argued that all mystical experiences are essentially identical in content regardless of differences in culture and religion.[13] In their view, Jewish, Islamic, Christian, and Buddhist mysticism are all similar expressions of a universal phenomenon.

One school of thought, represented by Rudolph Otto and Evelyn Underhill, maintains that while all mystical experiences are similar in content, they are expressed in culture-specific expressions. The differences between various forms of mysticism arise out of the different cultural contexts in which the experience occurs.[14] The difference between Jewish, Islamic, Christian, and Buddhist mysticism, in this approach, is that each mystic describes his experience in the language of his respective culture.

Another school of thought, associated with R. C. Zaehner, W. T. Stace, and Ninian Smart, maintains that there is no universal phenomenon of mysticism.[15] As is evident from the survey of popular definitions of mysticism, there is little agreement in what constitutes mysticism. Moreover, as we shall see, there are a variety of distinct types of mysticism that differ experientially and phenomenologically from each other. Not only is there more than one type of mysticism, but the various types might appear in greatly different cultures. Therefore, mysticism is not necessarily culturally specific. It is often difficult, however, to identify the main types of mysticism that cut across cultural boundaries because the descriptions of mysticism are culturally specific and so their components must be analyzed.

Steven Katz has shown the complexities inherent in analyzing and defining mysticism. In his view the categorization of various types of mysticism is helpful, but it must take into account the fact that the culture in which a mystic lives shapes his consciousness and helps to determine the kind of experiences that he might have. Therefore, even the classification of various types of mysticism must take into account the complexities of culturally specific experiences.[16]

It is impossible to define mysticism broadly except perhaps within a specific culture. It is possible, however, to describe various types of mysticism that cut across cultural lines. One type of mysticism involves what many have called the sense of unity. The meaning of unity can involve different and conflicting elements. As is evident in several of the definitions of mysticism, some mystics experience oneness with God, whereas others experience a sense of the oneness of nature. There are mystics who experience an awareness of integration within themselves and others who have the "oceanic feeling" of the unity of all beings. Each of these, as we shall see, is a fundamentally different type of mystical experience. For example, Wordsworth, the English poet, offers a wonderful testimony of mystical oneness with nature in his famous poem, "Tintern Abbey":

> And I have felt
> A presence that disturbs me with the joy

Of elevated thoughts; a sense sublime
Of something far more deeply interfused,
Whose dwelling is the light of setting suns,
And the round ocean, and the living air,
And the blue sky, and the mind of man:
A motion and a spirit, that impels
All thinking things, all objects of all thought,
And rolls through all things.[17]

For Wordsworth, mysticism is the feeling of the presence of "motion and a spirit," a power that infuses all of nature with its presence. He never mentions God because his unity is the pervasive spirit of nature, the presence of something that others might call "God in nature." This idea that nature is united and contains something absolute beyond the entities that make up the physical universe is called "pantheism."

Meister Eckhart, a medieval Christian mystic, also expresses a pantheistic view of the oneness of nature:

> All that a man has here externally in multiplicity is intrinsically One. Here, all blades of grass, wood, and stone, all things are One. This is the deepest depth.[18]

This example illustrates the inadequacy of William James' definition of mysticism. For Eckhart, mysticism is not "union with the Absolute" but the awareness of the inherent unity of all being. Not all mysticism involves union with an absolute or transcendent being. Frequently, nature mysticism is the awareness of the oneness of all things and the inherent unity within nature. In other religions, however, accounts of mystical experiences suggest that the world and nature are illusions. A deeper unity is achieved by annihilating one's awareness of and connection to the world. This is known as "acosmic" or world-negating mysticism and is found in the *Upanishads*, the classic text of Hindu mysticism:

> It is pure, unitary consciousness wherein awareness of the world and of multiplicity is completely obliterated. It is ineffable peace. It is the Supreme Good. It is One without a second. It is the Self.[19]

This passage suggests that consciousness is the "oceanic feeling" of undifferentiatedness. This strongly acosmist declaration suggests that the Self is not the differentiated and individual ego. Paradoxically, the true Self is achieved through the annihilation of self-consciousness and awareness.

Pantheistic mysticism and acosmist mysticism appear in Judaism, particularly among ecstatic *Kabbalists* and *Hasidic* mystics of the eighteenth century. Judaism is a religion based on the idea of the existence of one transcendent God whose being transcends, and is separate from, that of the world. God creates and governs nature, but He also stands above it. The pantheistic idea that God is synonymous with nature, or the acosmic idea that the world is not real is not consistent with the Hebrew biblical worldview. But Jewish mysticism starts from the premise that God and the universe are not fundamentally different.

Judaism is generally "theistic," which means that God is a separate and distinct being whose nature is different from that of the world. It involves a supreme being who transcends and rules over nature. But mysticism may assume a variety of forms. Sometimes Jewish mysticism may strive for the union of two beings who remain essentially distinct even in their unity. A good example of this "nonabsorptive" mysticism can be found in a parable of the Baal Shem Tov, the founder of *Hasidism*, an eighteenth-century mystical movement:

> A king had built a glorious palace full of corridors and partitions, but he himself lived in the innermost room. When the palace was completed and his servants came to pay him homage, they found that they could not approach the king because of the devious maze. While they stood and wondered, the king's son came and showed them that those were not real partitions, but only magical illusions, and that the king, in truth, was easily accessible. Push forward bravely and you shall find no obstacle![20]

In this testimony, union with God is a feature of acquiring the realization that the obstacles to union exist only in consciousness and not in reality. A transformed mystical consciousness is necessary in order to permit the subject to peer behind the veil or to bridge the abyss between himself and the supposedly unknowable and unreachable God. It assumes that God and man can never become one, but the obstacles that prevent the drawing together of God and man are only illusory. In other instances, particularly in acosmist *Hasidic* mysticism, do Jewish mystics suggest that the actual union of man and God is possible. As one early *Hasidic* writer said:

> If we achieve this union, we will think about ourselves as well that we are nothing other than God who gives us life. He alone exists and there is nothing other than Him. . . . And when we realize this, that we are like nothing-

ness in truth and nothing exists in the world but God, just as before creation, He, as it were, takes genuine pleasure.[21]

Traditional Jewish theology gives little support to the idea that man and God can be identical. But a Muslim author, al-Ghazali, describes a type of "absorptive" mysticism not entirely foreign to *Hasidism* in which the ego of the mystic becomes submerged and indistinguishable from God, the object of his devotions. In such a case the individual not only achieves unity but becomes one with God:

> When the worshipper thinks no longer of his worship or himself, but is altogether absorbed in Him whom he worships, that state is called the passing away of mortality (*fana*), when a person so passed away from himself feels nothing of his bodily members, nor of what is passing without, nor what passes in his own mind . . . He is journeying first to his Lord, and then at the end, in his Lord. Perfect absorption means that he is unconscious not only of himself, but of his absorption.[22]

In Judaism, the goal of the mystic quest is often the attainment of nonabsorptive unity with the transcendent deity. Abraham Joshua Heschel, the Jewish theologian, describes Jewish mysticism as a theory of divine transcendence and a method for attaining transcendence.[23] This means that Jewish mysticism involves the experience of overcoming the barriers that apparently separate the world of God from the world of man.

In recent years, Moshe Idel, a leading academic researcher of Jewish mysticism, has proposed a new understanding of the Jewish mystical tradition.[24] He argues that, within Judaism, there are two distinct types of mystical phenomena. The first is characterized by ecstatic experiences in which the mystic seeks to be one with God. This ecstatic mysticism results in a transformation of the individual and a direct relationship, even union, with God. It is highly individualistic, indifferent to societal expectations of religious conformity, and often entails occult and magical practices. Idel has also argued that the Jewish mystical tradition is replete with examples of absorptive mysticism in which the mystic becomes one with, absorbed in, and inseparable from God. Abraham Abulafia, a thirteenth-century Jewish mystic from Spain, asserted that, through ecstatic mysticism, the mystic and God become "one permanent and everlasting entity."[25] Within Jewish mysticism, man and God can become identical. The second type of mysticism is characterized by a "cleaving" to God that results in an understanding of the inner workings of the divine. As a result of this acquired mystical awareness, also called "theosophy," the individual does not so much unite with God as he acquires the ability to influence the divine from a distance. This form of mysticism often embraces the rituals and symbols of the Jewish tradition as a conduit for expressing the practitioner's mystical devotion.

Frequently, the most incisive definitions of mysticism are offered by mystics themselves or those with first-hand experience with mystical traditions. In his own spiritual autobiography, Isaac Bashevis Singer, the Yiddish writer who won the Nobel Prize for Literature in 1978, offers the following observations on Jewish mysticism:

> Mysticism isn't a line of thought separated from religion. They both share a basis in the human soul—the feeling that the world is no accident or blind force and that the human spirit and body are closely linked with the universe and its Creator. If there is a difference between religion and mysticism, it consists of the fact that religion is almost completely dependent upon revelation. All religions have preached that God revealed Himself to a prophet and communicated His demands through him. Religion never remained the property of a single individual. It appealed to a group. It often tended to proliferate and take in whole tribes and nations. Religious leaders often forced obeisance to their faith with the sword. Because of this, religion tended in time to become routine and closely linked with social systems. Mysticism, on the other hand, is individualistic. True mysticism has always belonged to one person or to a small group. It was and it has remained esoteric. The mystic never completely relied upon the revelations of others but sought God in his own fashion. The mystic often assumed the religion of his environment, but he tried to extend it by coupling it with the higher powers; actually to become a prophet himself. My personal definition of religion is a mysticism that has been transformed into a discipline, a mass experience, and thus grown partially diluted and often worldly. The more successful a religion is, the stronger its influence, the further it recedes from its mystical origin.[26]

Singer points out that mysticism is the attempt to overcome routinized religion by reasserting the primacy of individual religious experience. With the passage of time and the growth of religious institutions, individual religious experience is not necessarily the concern of an established religion. Mysticism, representing a strong strain of individualism, may be linked to anti-institutional tendencies in formal religion or it may lead the individual to embrace the rituals and practices of his religion to express something deeper. Therefore, mysticism serves an important function by bringing religious movements back in contact with the powerful experiential impulses that were part of their origins.

Mystical and religious experiences are not necessarily identical. Before there is mysticism, there is religion. Mysticism is a type of religious experience, but not all religious experiences are mystical. Rudolf Otto (1869–1937), the theologian, explained that a religious experience is characterized by the experience of that which is beyond rational knowledge and which has been called variously "the wholly (or holy) other," or "the terrifying awesome majesty," not describable in common language.[27] Religion is associated with the feelings engendered by the experience and with the attempt to communicate that experience and elaborate it through ritual. The Jewish religion may, therefore, be understood as the human response to the experience of the supreme reality of God whose being is beyond rational conception.

Mysticism is a specific theory and practice of how to intensify the religious experience. It involves the transformation of the religious experience into an intense relationship with the supreme reality. It is a more intense form of religion than is generally sanctioned within formal religions. Mysticism, in many religions, is also an esoteric phenomenon restricted to, or practiced by, select individuals rather than by the masses. Jewish mysticism is, therefore, a more intense form of religious experience than is generally found in normative, rabbinic Judaism.

It is important to distinguish between mysticism and spirituality. If mysticism is the search for unity beyond the self, spirituality is a highly personal outlook about what is sacred to the individual, the expression of his most deeply held values, and that sense of higher purpose that guides his daily life. Spirituality is not an otherworldly approach or a retreat into the occult. It is what a person knows in his heart to be true—"heart-knowledge." Jewish mysticism is often about transcendence, while spirituality is concerned with inwardness.

The mystic quest is often a search to return to or to repeat the religious experience upon which a religion was founded. The content of the Jewish mystical experience often takes the form of a revelatory experience, an experience akin to what Moses experienced at Sinai. The varieties of mystical experiences are as diverse as the range of human experiences across different cultures and periods. "Mysticism" refers to a specific category of human experiences associated with certain characteristics. However, these characteristics often differ from one culture to another. It is impossible to define precisely what mysticism is except within a specific culture at a particular moment. A precise, universal definition of mysticism is not possible. Therefore, in order to understand mysticism, it is necessary to comprehend specific types of mystical experiences. That, within the context of Judaism, is the subject of this book.

Kabbalah is the Hebrew name adopted by practitioners of the medieval Jewish mystical tradition. But what is mystical about *Kabbalah*? *Kabbalah* is generally theistic, nonabsorptive mysticism although some devotees practiced a form of absorptive mysticism. Some *Kabbalists* practiced magical and mystical techniques of union with God while others achieved oneness or even dissolution within God. All *Kabbalists*, however, shared a mystical bond: they believed in the continuous and ongoing revelation of divine mysteries that lead to an understanding of the inner workings of God and the universe and a theory and practice of influencing the divine through ritual actions.

The common characteristics that integrated the various *Kabbalistic* traditions were typical of other mystical traditions. Although Jewish mystics often described their experiences as inneffable, transient, and transformative, they emphasized the noetic quality of acquiring new mystical knowledge that was often esoteric, paradoxical, visual, luminous, and provided a deeper level of religious experience that often challenged existing religious teachings. Their experiences included a range of sometimes contradictory expressions including the "oceanic feeling," pantheistic notions that God dwells within all, and panentheistic views that all exists within God or that all is God.

But to truly understand *Kabbalah*, it is helpful to develop a framework that will help illuminate the *Kabbalists'* often abstract and arcane expressions. In order to provide that framework, this chapter will propose that *Kabbalah* can best be understood in light of seven basic principles. These principles were never formally articulated as such by the *Kabbalists*. They are, however, the assumptions that all *Kabbalists* shared and which serve as the unspoken foundation of *Kabbalah*. They are, also, contemporary articulations of the basic tenets of *Kabbalah*. In order to provide a certain degree of symmetry with the *Kabbalists* fondness for reducing their basic principles to an ideal number, including the number "seven," I have organized my restatement of the foundational principles of *Kabbalah* to seven basic tenets.

1. THE DIVINE MYSTERY

God is a mystery beyond any conception of which we are capable. The *Kabbalists* believed that God is ultimately unknowable, unreachable, and indescribable. God cannot be described as He, She, Father, Mother, King, or Judge because God is beyond any conception of which humans are capable. God can only be referred to in sublime, neutral, terms such as "That Which is Without End" or "*The Infinite*." At the same time, the *Kabbalists* believed, there is an inexorable connection between God and the universe. God generated the universe although we cannot comprehend how it occurred. We see evidence of God's activity within the world and within human experience so that we assume a connectedness. And, at rare moments, humans can experience mystical oneness with God even if we cannot articulate the mysterious being and nature of the divine. Although we cannot know God, we can experience mystical oneness with God and feel the divine presence everywhere in the world around us.

2. WHATEVER EXISTS IN THE WORLD FIRST EXISTS WITHIN GOD

Whatever exists in the world first exists within God. Every human characteristic, every human emotion, every experience, and every physical phenomenon is a manifestation of God. *Kabbalah* does not teach that God is only the creator of every thing we experience, but rather that everything we experience is the expression of one or another dimension of God. God has multiple aspects, attributes, and perfections that are idealized versions of those aspects, attributes, and perfections that are part of the realm of human experience. For *Kabbalah*, God is the totality of all possibility and the perfect blueprint of all possibilities that come to exist in the world.

Our world is a pale mirror image of the amalgam of divine aspects, attributes, and perfections. But the roots of everything in our universe are to be found within God where they exist in perfect, ideal form. The universe is nothing less than an extension of God's own being in descending gradation from the divine source. In *Kabbalistic* language, everything that we encounter in human experience "points to" or is "the likeness of" something divine. The only difference is that what we perceive is imperfect whereas the source of what we experience is a quality that exists within God in its most perfect and pure form. The universe, and everything in it, is the vehicle for discovering or uncovering the hidden traces of God. At the same time, what we perceive in the universe is only a fleeting shadow of the divine perfections towards which we strive. The mystic quest in Judaism is the search to discover the divine perfections that reside within our world, the challenge to trace these perfections back to their source, and the mission to embrace and unite with the source itself.

Kabbalah teaches that God is the sum of all perfections including all human intellectual, emotional, sexual, spiritual, and ethical qualities. At the same time, for reasons we shall soon explain, *Kabbalah* identified and reduced the total number of these divine perfections to ten identifiable qualities. In other words, everything in the world can be reduced to ten basic building blocks. These include three intellectual principles (thought, wisdom, and understanding) two emotional principles (an overabundance of love and a just withholding of love, i.e., justice or severity), two sexual principles (maleness and femaleness), and three ethical or spiritual principles (prophecy, providence, and the covenant with Israel).

There are many shocking implications of this *Kabbalistic* teaching. If whatever exists within the world first exists within God, even human sexuality is rooted in divine sexuality. If maleness and femaleness are the fundamental gender characteristics of conventional human sexuality—and the *Kabbalists* lived within a traditional social system—then maleness and femaleness must first exist as divine characteristics. The *Kabbalists* indeed taught that the greatest mystery of human experience—sexuality and relationships—has, as its root, the male and female dimensions of God. God has both male and female characteristics that are at the root of human sexuality and the drama of human relationships. In order to understand the mysteries of human sexuality and relationships, the *Kabbalists* say we need to understand the male and female aspects of God as the source of this mystery.

3. WHATEVER EXISTS WITHIN GOD
EVENTUALLY COMES TO EXIST
IN THE WORLD

As a corollary to the first principle, the *Kabbalists* teach that whatever exists within God eventually comes to exist in the world. With a spare ecology of divine perfection, the *Kabbalists* teach that God's being overflows into the world, which serves as a vessel for containing the fullness of God's beings. As a result, the ten divine perfections are distributed throughout the universe and concentrated especially within human beings. There is nothing in the universe that is not filled with the essence of God, no matter how diluted or remote from the source it might be. Nor is there any dimension of the ten divine perfections that are not somehow present in the universe.

God, in all its dimensions, is accessible to us and can be found through everyday experiences. We do not need to look outside our own lives to find God. The *Kabbalists* reiterate that "there is no place empty of God" and "everything contains sparks of holiness." When one Jewish mystic asks rhetorically, "Where is God to be found?" he answers his own question by answering, "Wherever He is allowed to enter." *Kabbalists* believe the only real obstacle to recognizing the embodiment of God in every human individual, phenomenon, experience, action, and relationship is our limited consciousness. *Kabbalah* is the guide to achieving an expanded consciousness of the hidden presence of the divine in everything around and within us. God can be found not only through following the Jewish ritual actions, but through making each and every human action a sacrament for recognizing the presence of the sparks of divine holiness scattered throughout the universe.

Kabbalists believe that the Torah is the most powerful tool we possess for uncovering the hidden presence of God. Since they believe the Hebrew letters of the Torah are direct expressions of the divine perfections, they concluded that the divine being is uniquely and magically accessible in the Hebrew letters of Torah. But they also believe that God is expressed in the world through human action and experience. They taught that God expresses Himself by transmitting and communicating the divine perfections into the world. The universe can then be seen as a form of divine speech and the ten perfections can, therefore, be considered as God's "vocabulary." This is perhaps what Isaac Bashevis Singer had in mind when he said that "God speaks in deeds and His vocabulary is the universe."

4. GOD DEPENDS ON US

Everything within God ultimately finds its place within our universe. Since pairs of the divine perfections that find their expression in the world can be regarded as antitheses—such as "maleness" and "femaleness" or "an overabundance of love" and "a just withholding of love"—*Kabbalah* explains that even the seeds of human tension and conflict are rooted in the divine perfections. Tension between men and women or between "an overabundance of love" and "a just withholding of love" are seen as necessary within the human context when these perfections are taken out of their divine context. Within God, they are part of a balanced and harmonious ecology in which "maleness" and "femaleness" or "an overabundance of love" and "a just withholding of love" are harmonized.

The *Kabbalistic* God is a being of perfect harmony and union of all the divine qualities. God is both male and female joined together in harmony. God is capable of "an overabundance of love" and "a just withholding of love" as circumstances warrant without ever being excessive or withholding. The human condition, however, is less disposed towards the synthesis of contradictory tendencies such as "maleness" and "femaleness" or "an overabundance of love" and "a just withholding of love." We may easily tend towards polarization and opposition in human relationships and behavior, thus accentuating the tension between man and woman or between acting with love as opposed to withholding love judiciously when the situation requires justice. In fact, *Kabbalah* teaches that tension, conflict, and polarization in the human arena can produce disharmony and isolation among the pairs of divine perfections, especially "maleness" and "femaleness." At the same time, humans have the capacity to restore harmony among the pairs of divine perfections through creating harmony and union through correct religious and ethical behavior and the proper conduct of human sexual relationships. As the *Kabbalists* say, "the lower awakening brings on the higher awakening." We unite God and God, therefore, depends on us. As much as we are in search of God, God is in search of us. When we reach out to God, God reaches out to us.

God does not answer man's prayer or reward him for his actions directly. Rather, human actions such as prayer and the *mitzvot* directed towards God actually cause God to respond involuntarily. God responds by either accelerating towards greater alignment or greater disalignment within God. These responses then produce reverberations that rebound from God to man. If we cause the alignment of God, divine grace will flow into the world. If we cause the disalignment of God, His grace is withheld from the world.

The dialectical influences of God and man imply a new mode of thinking in Judaism about the relationship between them. The novel element in *Kabbalistic* thinking about God and man is their mutual and reciprocal interdependence. God is not complete by Himself. He cannot be complete and perfect except when made so by human action. The unity of the various aspects of God's being depends on human actions. Humans do not benefit except when God's grace flows upon the world. Neither God nor man can act or be fulfilled except through the other.

5. A HUMAN BEING IS A LADDER PLACED
ON EARTH WHOSE TOP REACHES HEAVEN

A human being is a ladder placed on earth whose top reaches heaven. This image, taken from the biblical narrative of Jacob's dream, views the soul as the essence of a human being and as the ladder that bridges heaven and earth. Through the soul, the individual is able to live in the world and find the sparks of holiness scattered there while, at the same time, having the capacity for transcending the mundane and achieving oneness with one or another of the divine perfections.

The true essence of a human being is the soul that is itself an emanation of God that comes to reside within the human body. The soul is from God and the body is from the earthly elements. The human soul is the spark of divinity, which connects the individual to God, its source. By virtue of the soul, the individual can find holiness in the world and unite with the divine source of that holiness. The human soul is the deepest expression of divinity in the world.

The life of the soul is far more significant, for a Jewish mystic, than the life of the body. But the life of the body is both a reflection of and an indispensable platform for living the life of the soul. The needs of the body are material expressions of the divine qualities. Human sexuality, for example, is a reflection of the fact that the male and female divine qualities find their fullest expression in male and female human sexuality. The food we consume contains the sparks of divinity that are found in all organic matter and eating then becomes a ritual of uniting with those divine sparks. But Jewish mysticism also provides an understanding of human life as a voyage of the soul from its heavenly origin before it enters the body, through birth, life, death, and the afterlife. The soul has an independent existence before, during, and after it inhabits the human body.

6. TORAH SPEAKS OF WORLDLY THINGS,
BUT HINTS AT THE DIVINE

The *Kabbalists* believe that revelation did not end at Sinai when Moses received the Torah. They believe, rather, that the continuing revelation of the divine mysteries could be uncovered through individual mystical inspiration and through finding new depths of meaning in the biblical texts. A *Kabbalist* once wrote: "All the words of Torah hint at the divine mystery: If all the oceans were ink, all people were scribes, and the heavens and earth were parchment, we would still be incapable of writing even one iota of what could be said about each and every verse of Torah." Each verse of Torah speaks of worldly things, but hints at the divine. The *Kabbalists* teach that we should not read the Torah literally as stories about human events but as mysterious and veiled hints about the inner workings of God and the relationship of the divine to the world. As the *Zohar* warns: "Woe to the person who says that Torah presents us mere stories with ordinary words! If it were so, we could compose an even better Torah today. Ah, but all the words of Torah are sublime and mysterious."

The sublime mysteries of Torah are the faces of Torah that each one of us must uncover for ourselves. Each one of us has our own path to Torah that is different from everyone else's. The spiritual challenge for each of us is to find our own personal connection to Torah that is ours and no one else's. Torah can touch our soul and speak to each of us directly when we no longer see Torah as mere stories and ordinary words, but as the voice that speaks directly to our own soul. *Kabbalah* is a spiritual discipline that teaches its adherents to hear the voice of God in the received text. *Kabbalah* also tries to uncover the original experience behind the recorded text and helps us place ourselves at Sinai alongside the 600,000 and more Israelites who stood there. It is an attempt to overcome the barriers of time and place that separate us from the immediacy of Sinai. It is an effort to reach across time and fathom the timeless. The divine voice is the voice we can uncover in the text of Torah, a path that guides us to hear the voice of God and recognize the sparks of holiness in the everyday world. Torah is not just the biblical text, but the inner meaning, the voice within the text.

7. THE MYSTIC QUEST

The power of the human soul to bring about harmony within the divine realm is a central tenet of *Kabbalah*. A human being can bring about harmony in the divine realm through understanding the ways in which the divine qualities are affected by human actions and by acting in ways that influence these qualities and bring them into harmony with each other. When we influence the divine, we connect our souls to their source and achieve mystical union. The mystic quest is the effort to understand the divine patterns within the universe, to align these patterns into a configuration that reflects their ideal blueprint, and through this, to unite with the divine source from which all earthly design originates. This is referred to as "raising the sparks," "effecting unities," and "cleaving to God." This is the ultimate mystic goal.

This mystical achievement can occur in a variety of ways. It can be achieved when two souls overcome the barriers to a harmonious relationship. When a man and woman are united in love and marriage, their harmony is both a reflection of divine unity and strengthens that very unity above. When a person prays, he releases the vitality inherent in the Hebrew letters and influences the divine qualities above from which the vitality originates. When a person performs the prescribed Jewish rituals, he manipulates the divine qualities and aligns those qualities in such a way that he creates harmony within the divine realm. At the same time, conflict within the human realm, prayer without devotion, and improper performance of the rituals causes misalignment in the divine realm or, worse, releases destructive forces in the universe.

Kabbalah seeks to infuse unbounded consciousness within an individual by making it possible to live in the finite world while being transported, on a mental level, to the realm where everything is without limit. The *Kabbalist* lives in a universe of worldly matters, all of which point to the divine blueprint of which this world is the embodiment. Without turning his back on this world, the *Kabbalist* seeks to focus his awareness on the blueprint, not just the physical world.

It is important to note that while Jewish mystics are concerned with achieving unbounded awareness, they do not view the mystic quest as a solitary pursuit. Jewish mystics believe that Judaism—its sacred texts and rituals—are the expressions of the divine qualities. Judaism is the embodiment of the divine principles and the roadmap to unbounded awareness. Moreover, they see the totality of the Jewish way of life as an organic whole and the embodiment of the divine qualities. They view the communal dimensions of Judaism—the structures of family, prayer quorums, and community—as an indispensable reflection of the divine qualities. Therefore, Jewish mystics do not engage in their quest as an individual or solitary pursuit. Rather, Jewish mysticism is pursued as the individual prays, studies Torah, marries, raises a family, and participates in the life of the congregation and community. Jewish mysticism develops within the context of daily life by raising the ordinary to a higher plane—taking everything back to its source.

2

VISIONARIES, MYSTICS, AND *KABBALISTS*

The History of Jewish Mysticism

Nebuchadnezzar, the Chaldean king of Babylon, the most powerful nation in the region, defeated the Judean king, Yehoyachin of Jerusalem, in March of 597 B.C.E.[1] When Nebuchadnezzar conquered Jerusalem, he deported a large number of the city's aristocracy to his realm. Among them was Ezekiel, a widowed priest and aristocrat with a powerful devotion to Jerusalem. Ezekiel settled in the valley around Tel Aviv—not today's city by the same name—along the Khabur River, a tributary of the Euphrates in present-day Iraq. Eleven years later, the Babylonian commander Nebuzaradan laid siege and destroyed Solomon's Temple.

Ezekiel was consumed by remorse for the condition of the dispersed Jerusalemites. He was wracked by a powerful sense that his people's infidelity to God's covenant had brought on this disaster. Ezekiel portrayed the terrible national consequences of the exile in starkly imaginative and baroque terms. He prophesied the doom and desolation of Jerusalem to be followed by the eventual physical restoration and moral renewal of Israel.

In the summer of 592 B.C.E., he was suddenly gripped by an unexpected and startling event in which a stunning apparition appeared to be moving toward him. Ezekiel saw a rumbling storm cloud of fire surrounded by a glow. Within the cloud there appeared to be a lustrous and metallic shell containing a vivid and dramatic scene. The shell seemed to contain four bizarre creatures made of metallic bronze. Each had the torso of a man, and each bore the face of man and a lion on the right side, and the face of an eagle and an ox on the left. Each creature had four wings, and under each wing was a hand and bovine hooves with circular soles. The creatures moved as one toward Ezekiel, each one's wings touching those of the adjacent figure, forming a square with their bodies. Their movement was accompanied by fire and lightning.

As the creatures approached him, Ezekiel saw another set of figures within the apparition. Next to each of the creatures were spinning wheels within wheels. On the rim of each wheel were countless eyes. The whole mechanism sparkled like topaz. The creatures and the wheels moved together, sometimes rising into the air, sometimes rolling on the ground, all the while moving toward Ezekiel with a roar.

Looking up, Ezekiel saw within the fiery storm cloud another apparition. Above the heads of the creatures, shrouded in fire and light, was a crystalline vault. Inside the vault was a luminous and radiant throne. Sitting upon the throne was a humanoid figure whose lower torso was fiery and whose upper torso looked like molten brass. The whole mechanism appeared to be rolling toward him rapidly, accompanied by thunder and lightning. Ezekiel took this figure on the throne to be God. He threw himself down on the ground to avoid being crushed by the storm cloud. When he recovered from this event, Ezekiel was fortified, and he proceeded to warn the community of exiles of the impending catastrophic destruction of Jerusalem.[2]

Ezekiel's account may be the first Jewish testimony of a direct visual and mystical encounter with God. His account is reminiscent of those mystics who, like R. M. Bucke, have unanticipated mystical experiences while in a state of repose and attentiveness. Water, in this case the nearby river, often induces a meditative, contemplative state conducive to mysticism. Like other encounters, Ezekiel's experience is visual and contains a strong luminous quality. This event appears to be a wholly spontaneous encounter that is all the more powerful for its unpredictability. Ezekiel, of course, was transformed into a prophet by this gripping and obviously unpleasant experience.

The form of this encounter is especially shocking since it occurs in a state of wakefulness, not in a dream. The figures that he sees are phantasmagoric hybrids of humans and animals. The appearance of beings whose shapes are contradictory and counter to nature make the experience that much more terrifying. The apparition is antithetical to what his consciousness tells him is real. Yet, Ezekiel, like all mystics, has no doubt that what he experienced is real. He is so gripped by the experience that he has no reservations about its authenticity, and will not be persuaded to doubt what his own eyes saw.

This vision is all-encompassing and squeezes out all of the normal, familiar signposts to reality. As a result, Ezekiel is gripped by the power, mystery, and awe of this vision and submits to it. He cowers in fear until a voice from within the apparition calls to him, charging him to become a prophet and to deliver God's message to the other exiles. He is ready to do whatever the voice commands.

As Rachel Elior, the noted scholar of Jewish mysticism has explained, the earliest Jewish mystics saw Ezekiel's heavenly Temple as a microcosm of the heavenly divine order, the "earthly embodiment of cosmic order."[3] Ezekiel's *Merkavah* (Chariot) was seen as a bridge between the divine and human realm whose material features represented heavenly structures. Each element in Ezekiel's *Merkavah* was seen as a heavenly phenomenon that could help the mystic uncover secrets about the topography of the heavens and establish his relationship to the world above.

Ezekiel's *Merkavah* was seen as a heavenly representation of the Jerusalem Temple. Each of the elements in Ezekiel's vision was understood as symbolizing sacred place—(the Temple and the Holy of Holies), sacred time (the calendar of festivals and priestly sacrifices), and sacred rituals (chants, hymns, songs, and prayers). According to Elior, Ezekiel's *Merkavah* was embraced by secessionist priests during the Second Temple period— especially in the two centuries preceding its destruction in 70 c.e. They saw the contemporary priesthood as corrupt and the Temple as defiled. For them, the corrupt priests who presided over the Second Temple turned it into an abomination and made it the equivalent of the destroyed Temple of Ezekiel's time. These secessionist priests, including the authors of many of the Dead Sea Scrolls, focused on the *Merkavah* as the divine prototype of sacred place, time, and ritual because they believed the earthly Temple no longer functioned in this way. They transformed the "defiled" and "corrupted" Temple into the heavenly Temple. They discovered in the *Merkavah* "a whole system of correlations between the ideal picture of the destroyed earthly Temple and the visionary Temple (of Ezekiel) revealed in heaven."[4] The literature composed by these secessionist priests, and preserved in the Dead Sea Scrolls and other writings, elaborated Ezekiel's vision. These texts describe further revelations and visions of the heavenly Temple where angels serve as heavenly counterparts of the earthly priests, preside over heavenly rituals, and chant hymns and prayers in a divine liturgy. This projection of a "mythical space" in which a corrupt earthly order is restored by an idealized heavenly realm was a "source of strength for those (i.e., the secessionist priests) who have no power in earthly existence."[5]

Although the literature of the secessionist priests was almost completely suppressed by the "normative" rabbinic tradition, the early *Merkavah* mystics helped establish some of the principles that have characterized Jewish mysticism ever since. Their belief that heavenly revelations are ongoing encouraged those Jewish mystics who sought prophetic illumination, the influence of the Holy Spirit, and secret heavenly knowledge conveyed by angelic beings. Although much of their contribution was suppressed by the rabbinic tradition, the mystical experiences of these secessionist priests validated the mystic quest in Judaism and generated a rich literature that inspired later Jewish mystics.

Ezekiel was also seen by later Jewish mystics as the prototype of a Jewish mystic. Ezekiel's successors attempted to imitate his experience through rigorous and disciplined training. The earliest recorded attempts at consciously pursuing mystical, visionary, and ecstatic states appear in the second century C.E. Most of the evidence of this early phase of Jewish mysticism has not been preserved, although traces of it appear occasionally in the writings from that period.[6]

Rabbi Akiva ben Yosef (50–135 C.E.), the leader of second-century rabbinic society in Israel, was the master of a small group of practitioners of mysticism. They practiced an ecstatic and visionary form of mystical experience in which each rabbi prepared himself for his ascent to the celestial world through asceticism and rituals of purification. They visualized themselves ascending through seven heavens and through the seven palaces in the highest heaven, the *aravot*. Along the way, they gained admission to each heaven and palace by presenting the correct password to the angelic gatekeeper. These passwords consisted of magical formulae and secret names of God or His angels. They traversed bridges across rivers of fire and had to pass a host of terrible creatures seeking to thwart their passage. They were mesmerized by the hymns of the angels in the highest heaven as they praised a figure sitting on the throne in the highest palace. Often, the figure on the throne was concealed by a curtain. But on those occasions when they were permitted to see behind the curtain, they saw themselves standing face to face with God's celestial throne, and they spontaneously composed and uttered hymns to God. Some of these hymns have made their way into the standard synagogue liturgy (e.g., the Sabbath hymn, *El Adon*; the morning *kedushah*; and various *ofannim*, *sillukim*, and *kedushot*).[7] Some of these mystics believed that the celestial throne that they visualized was identical with the luminous throne described by Ezekiel.

Rabbi Akiva, who frequently engaged in these practices with three colleagues, probably began his study of Jewish law as an adult. Although legend describes him as first having learned the Hebrew alphabet together with his young son,[8] he was soon almost universally recognized as a prodigious and exceptional scholar. He was opposed by Elisha ben Avuyah who resented the intrusion of this neophyte into the rabbinic elite. Eventually, however, Elisha acceded to Rabbi Akiva's leadership and accepted him as a colleague.

Elisha and Rabbi Akiva were joined by Shimon Ben Azzai, his son-in-law, and Shimon ben Zoma in a secret society devoted to mystical meditation. According to legend, the results of their attempts to achieve the visionary ascent were fraught with danger. This effort, described metaphorically as "entering a garden," is described in the *Talmud* as follows:

> Four entered a garden and these are: Ben Azzai, Ben Zoma, Aher (i.e., Elisha ben Avuyah), and Rabbi Akiva. Rabbi Akiva said to them: When you come to the stones of pure marble, do not say: "Water, water!" For it is said: "He who speaks untruth shall not stand before my eyes" (*Ps.* 101:7). Ben Azzai gazed and died. Of him the Torah says: "The death of his faithful ones is grievous in the Lord's sight" (*Ps.* 116:15). Ben Zoma gazed and was stricken. Of him the Torah says: "If you find honey, eat only what you need, lest, surfeiting yourself, you throw it up" (*Prov.* 25:16). Aher cut down the shoots. Rabbi Akiva departed in peace.[9]

Rabbi Akiva and his companions in this enterprise preferred to keep their activity secret. They recognized the deep psychological and religious dangers inherent in this system of meditation and trance inducement. Akiva warned his colleagues that when they achieve a vision of the entranceway to the sixth palace, they are likely to be deceived: "When you come to the stones of pure marble, do not say, 'Water, water!'" Rabbi Akiva said this to warn his colleagues that they should respect the limits to which the mystical imagination can reach. In their visionary state they might see great boulders obstructing the entrance to the chamber of the king. Rabbi Akiva admonished them not to trust their imagination for it might deceive them into believing that these awesome obstacles to the last palace are really fluid and not solid barriers. He warned them not to proceed beyond these limits and not to enter where they are not permitted.

Rabbi Akiva's warning was intended to foster respect for the limits of mystical achievement. Visionary ascent was permitted, even encouraged, reaching as high as to the highest palace. But he cautioned them against going directly from the anteroom into the presence of the king. He warned them strictly against attempting to see God directly in such a vision.

Apparently the results justified the warning. The visionary experience was so powerful that Ben Azzai is reported to have died in an ecstatic trance, and Ben Zoma was overwhelmed by his encounter and lost his mental equilibrium. Elisha ben Avuyah is known to have defected from Judaism to the Roman camp during the war with Rome (132–135 C.E.) and to have gone on to oppress his former co-religionists. Therefore, he was subsequently known as *Aher*, "the Alien." He persecuted Jewish youth and aided the Romans in closing Jewish schools.[10] This became known euphemistically as "cutting down the shoots." His apostasy is regarded as a consequence of his mystical experience and, by implication, to the distortion and error of which Rabbi Akiva warned.

Ezekiel's experience served as a model and paradigm for Rabbi Akiva and other Jewish mystics. The practice of attempting to ascend through the heavens and palaces was seen as an effort to replicate intentionally what had occurred spontaneously for Ezekiel. This became known as "palace" (*Heikhalot*) or "chariot" (*Merkavah*) mysticism or, alternately, as "the visions of Ezekiel" (*Mar'ot Yehezkel*). Akiva's successors debated whether they actually ascended through the heavens on a celestial journey or whether it merely seemed so to them.[11] There is little doubt that the reality of the ascent was certain in their own eyes.

On the other hand, Ezekiel's experience was seen as an act fraught with dangerous possibilities. Because mysticism itself was seen as inherently dangerous, strict warnings against intentionally attempting to replicate Ezekiel's experience appear in Jewish law.[12] Apparently, even the public reading of the biblical account of Ezekiel's vision was banned except on the holiday of *Shavuot*.[13] Later commentators even criticized Ezekiel for not being more reticent about relating what occurred to him.[14]

The techniques of visionary mysticism were practiced throughout the next eight hundred years. As late as the time of Hai Gaon (939–1038), the leader of Babylonian Jewry, these techniques were practiced among circles of Jewish mystical devotees. Hai Gaon recorded the techniques that were employed in order to induce this visionary state:

> You may perhaps know that many of the Sages hold that when a man is worthy and blessed with certain qualities and he wishes to gaze at the heav-

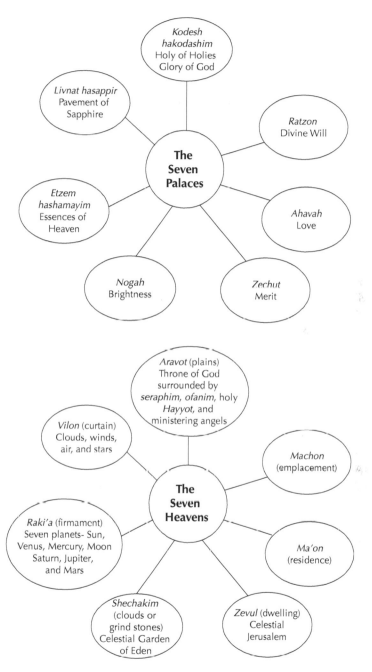

Figure 2.1   The Seven Palaces and Heavens

enly chariot and the halls of the angels on high, he must follow certain exercises. He must fast for a specified number of days, he must place his head
between his knees whispering softly to himself certain praises of God with
his face towards the ground. As a result, he will gaze in the innermost
recesses of his heart. It will seem as if he saw the seven halls with his own
eyes, moving from hall to hall to observe that which is therein to be found.[15]

According to Hai Gaon, this experience is an inner journey to "the innermost recesses of the heart." It is not meant to be an actual celestial journey
of the soul through the heavens, nor does it have any elements characteristic
of "out-of-body" experiences. The techniques employed here lead to
changes in the usual physiological responses to external stimuli and produce
a reordering of consciousness. This state, known as "deautomatization," is
a purposefully contrived effort to induce hypnotic and other trancelike
states. It is common to many *Merkavah* experiences.

Thus, two types of mystical experiences are common in the period of
rabbinic Judaism. First, Rabbi Akiva's experience is representative of "transportation" mysticism in which the subject experiences his whole being traveling on a celestial journey. A variation on this is the "out-of-body"
experience in which the consciousness or soul of the mystic, but not the
physical self, embarks on the celestial journey. Second, Hai Gaon's experience is representative of "penetration" mysticism in which the subject
experiences an inner voyage, a "journey into the heart," achieved through
visualization techniques that are centered within the consciousness of the
mystic. The difference between these two types of experiences in rabbinic
Judaism is whether the encounter is understood by the mystic to occur
externally or internally.

From the time of Islam's birth in the seventh century until the rise of
the Mamluk Dynasty in the thirteenth century, Jewish mysticism flourished
within the Islamic realm. In fact, the relationship between Judaism and Islam
in this period was pivotal in the history of both religions. The prophet
Muhammad was undoubtedly well acquainted with Jewish oral lore based
on biblical and rabbinic legends as well as with some of the forms of Jewish
practice common to Jewish tribes living in the Arabian Peninsula during the
seventh century. Muhammad may, in fact, have drawn inspiration for his
understanding of personal piety and religious justice from tales concerning
the exemplary lives of the Hebrew prophets that were told to him by Jews.[16]

Muhammad wished to bring about the conversion of the Arabian Jewish tribes. He believed that Islam was the legitimate heir to the biblical call-

ing and the fulfillment of the Hebrew monotheistic mission.[17] His earlier, favorable attitude towards Judaism changed when these powerful Jewish tribes rejected his efforts to consolidate them under his leadership. Consequently, Muhammad's disappointment with the Jews is reflected in the Koran's many pronouncements about the moral perversities, treacheries, evasions, and idolatries of the Jewish people. At the same time, the Koran expresses indebtedness to Hebrew prophecy as the original monotheistic tradition.[18]

The ambivalence of the early Koranic attitude served to complicate the later status of Jews living under Islam. The Jews' virtue derived from the fact that they were "the People of the Book," an appellation that was coined by the Koran itself and adopted later by the Jews. They were treated as a protected minority with property and religious rights under Islamic rule. However, they did not share in any of the political rights and other prerogatives of the members of "the community of the faithful," and they were the victims of occasional anti-Jewish outbursts.

The Jews often willingly accepted their status under Islam because it, in fact, offered a greater degree of legal security than did Christianity. From the time of the destruction of the second Jerusalem Temple in 70 C.E. and the transfer of Judaism's spiritual hub to the rabbinic academies, Jews saw themselves as a minority people living under the authority of foreign, dominant political regimes. They eschewed pretensions of political sovereignty for themselves as long as they were guaranteed a measure of self-government and religious tolerance. This important strategy for diasporan living made it possible for Jews to adapt to their status as a protected minority within the Islamic world while preserving their own particular religious institutions and traditions.

The area around Baghdad, Kufa, and Basra provided an especially fertile ground for Jewish life between 635 and 1258 C.E. Baghdad, the seat of the Islamic Abbasid Califate, was the thriving center of Islamic culture during this period. Under Abbasid rule, the institution of the exilarch (*resh galuta*), the lay leader of the Babylonian Jewish community, grew. Islamic authorities vested the exilarch with the power to assess and collect taxes, dispense justice, and supervise the charitable funds of the community. The famous rabbinic academies at Sura and Pumbedita were located near Baghdad. They were presided over by the Geonim ("the Pride of Jacob"), the religious and intellectual leaders of Babylonian Jewry whose authority was recognized throughout the Jewish world. During this period the forty thousand Jews of Baghdad enjoyed a high degree of religious tolerance, integration within Islamic society, autonomous self-government, and religious interaction with Muslims.[19]

Jewish mysticism also flourished in the Islamic Empire especially in the area known throughout Jewish history as Babylonia, which is present-day Iraq.[20] Over the centuries this region, which included the city of Baghdad, produced such diverse personalities as Ezekiel and Hai Gaon. Muslim and Jewish mystics in and around Baghdad and Damascus had close contacts with each other. Some even shared an "interconfessional outlook"—a belief that Judaism and Islam were different but equally valid paths to achieving mystical union with God. There are known instances of Muslims who visibly wore the traditional Jewish headcovering under their turbans and professed belief in a universal religion. When one such Muslim sage was asked by a student for spiritual guidance, he responded, "Upon which road, the Jewish, Christian, or Muslim?"[21]

Jewish and Islamic mystics probably shared meditative techniques and other methods for achieving visionary and ecstatic mystical encounters. For example, in Hai Gaon's attempt to replicate the prophet Ezekiel's ascent to the heavenly chariot, he probably utilized amulets inscribed with magical names of God as passwords and immunization devices in the mystic climb from heaven to heaven.[22] It is likely that Hai Gaon borrowed the technique of mystical amulets from Muslim magical and mystical calligraphy.[23]

Beyond the techniques of mystical ascent and "throne mysticism," little is actually known about the practice of Jewish mysticism in the Islamic world. In the latter half of the twelfth century, the center of Jewish mystical activity shifted from the area around Baghdad to Germany and Provence in southern France. The eleventh century Hebrew travelogue, *The Chronicle of Ahimaaz*, explains that Jewish mysticism was imported to Italy by way of a Jewish mystic from Baghdad, Abu Aharon. Other chronicles identify additional figures who brought Jewish mysticism from "the east" (Baghdad) to "the west" (Europe).[24]

Jewish mysticism in western Europe sank its deepest roots in Germany and Provence and, subsequently, in Spain. Some of the mystical ideas concerning Ezekiel's "Account of the Chariot" were transmitted to European Jewry by the members of the Kalonymide family who learned them ostensibly from Abu Aharon of Baghdad. The Kalonymide family belonged to the twelfth-century religious aristocracy of German Jewry, and they were the acknowledged masters of a spiritual movement known as German *Hasidim* (Pietists). (German *Hasidism* should not be confused with Polish-Lithuanian *Hasidism*, which originated in the eighteenth century.) Many of their ideas, in turn, were conveyed to Provence and Spain by their adherents in the last quarter of the twelfth century.

German *Hasidism* promoted a new religious ideal of spiritual equanimity. The *Hasid*, or truly pious individual, was one who could be indifferent to all the sufferings and temptations of the world. He would turn away both from physical pain and the joys of the physical world and absorb himself exclusively in the contemplation of God. The *Hasid* consciously attempted to inure himself to his passions and physical desires by avoiding their pleasures. He also wittingly faced and accepted scorn and suffering as a means of sharpening his ability to respond to all worldly stimuli with indifference. The *Hasid* was a solitary figure removed from the world and devoted exclusively to God.[25]

The mysticism of the rabbinic practitioners was replaced by a new understanding of meditative prayer among German *Hasidim*. No longer was the emphasis on the ascent to the highest palace of the God who remained inaccessible despite the abundant hymns of the mystics. The emphasis in German *Hasidism* shifted to the paradox of God's absolute uniqueness and remoteness, on one hand, and his accessibility and immanence, on the other hand. The earlier *Merkavah* mystical prayers were spontaneous and uncensored outpourings of praise for the hidden glory on the throne. German *Hasidim* understood prayer as the means of uniting the soul with the omnipresence of the divine.

The German *Hasidim* differentiated between the hidden God and His manifestation which was visible to Moses and to other prophets. The visible manifestation of God, called alternately *Shekhinah* (Divine Presence), *Keruv* (Cherub), *Kavod* (Glory), and *Gedulah* (Greatness), is the relational aspect of God which is revealed to the prophets and mystics. In fact, the *Shekhinah*, in their view, can assume a visible form in the guise of fire and clouds. The German *Hasidim* went farther than the *Merkavah* mystics by positing activity rather than passivity on the part of God. It is not the mystic who ascends through the palaces, but the relational aspect of God that descends to man.

German *Hasidism* integrated elements of "throne mysticism" within a new theology according to which God can be made manifest in the world through prayer. By differentiating between the hidden and the revealed aspects of God, they introduced a new approach to the problem of divine unity. God is one and unique, yet He can create occasional representations of Himself that can appear in a visible form in the world. Despite the problems inherent in saying that God has a created representation on earth, the

German *Hasidim* were able to preserve both the concepts of God's absolute uniqueness and His accessibility to humanity.

The turn of the thirteenth century marked the beginning of one of the most fertile periods in the history of Jewish mysticism. At about the same time as *Hasidism* emerged in Germany, the most important of the medieval Jewish mystical movements was beginning to emerge in Provence. Provence, in the late twelfth century, was the intellectual capital of European Jewry.[26] Closely tied to Spanish Jewry, Provence was emerging as the crossroads between two great cultures—Arab and Christian. Under Arab rule, the Jews in Spain had produced an intellectual and literary renaissance that lasted from the tenth to the twelfth century.

Andalusia, or *Sefarad*, as Spain was called by Muslims and Jews respectively, became the new arena of cultural interaction between these two peoples. From 711 C.E., when Muslim forces under the command of Tarik ibn Ziyyad landed at Gibraltar (named after him in Arabic, *jabl al-tarik* (the mountain of Tarik)), until 1145, when the fundamentalist Almohade movement sought to enforce religious conformity throughout the Iberian Peninsula, Muslim and Jewish scientists, philosophers, statesmen, and physicians served side by side in the Andalusian courts and contributed to a renaissance of learning which later spread inland from Spain to the rest of Europe.

The cultivation and refinement of Arabic prose, poetry, grammar, and philosophy and their influences upon the Jews produced a lasting transformation in Jewish and Hebrew culture. The activities of Muslims and Jews in Spain produced a rich tapestry of cultural accomplishments which exhibit in bold relief how advanced Muslim society became during this "Golden Age" when compared to the "Dark Ages" of contemporary Christian Europe.

Muslim Spain proved fertile soil for a Jewish intellectual and literary renaissance. Shmuel ha-Nagid (993–1055), the preeminent leader of Andalusian Jewry, gained prominence, even among the Muslims, as a poet, statesman, and military commander. Shlomo ibn Gabirol (1020– c. 1057) composed secular, even erotic, poetry as well as deeply inspired religious poetry and important philosophic works. Bahya ibn Pakuda (late eleventh century) introduced the notion that the "duties of the heart," the spiritual and inner dimensions of human life, are as important and obligatory for a Jew as the overt actions prescribed by Jewish law. Yehudah ha-Levi (c. 1075–1141) was the author of *Sefer ha-Kuzari*, an original and compelling conception of Judaism which, as much as the Bible and *Talmud*, articulates popular Jewish belief in its time. The brightest luminary of the period, however, was Rabbi Moshe ben Maimon, Maimonides (1135–1204), the brilliant Jewish philosopher and legal scholar whose ideas and decisions have shaped all of subsequent Jewish thought and jurisprudence.

The accomplishments of the "Golden Age" of Muslim Spain are those of an elite class of courtiers, artists, and intellectuals who lived within a society that imposed strict religious conformity upon Muslims but that was relatively free of dogmatic attitudes regarding non-Muslims. The remoteness of Andalusia, an Umayyad Califate until the eleventh century, from Baghdad, the seat of the Abbasid dynasty, contributed to the Andalusian sense of cultural autonomy. The prosperity of the Andalusian courts made it possible to promote the growth of a materially rich culture and to patronize those individuals, irrespective of religious creed, who could best fulfill the ruler's political ambitions and adorn the reputation of his court.

Arabic literature in Spain reflected the ideal of *arabiyya*, the idea of the perfection of the Arabic language in the Koran and in classical poetry, and its centrality in the consciousness and identity of Islamic peoples. At times it appeared that many Andalusians saw themselves as living within a culture that was defined more by the importance of the Arabic language than by the Islamic religion. Andalusian Jewry adopted the Arabic language as the medium of their oral and literary expression because it defined for them a common cultural ground with the Muslims. They recognized that the very success of prominent Jews living in an Arabic civilization depended on their facility in the Arabic language. Arabic was adopted among the Jews to the extent that much of the Jewish religious literature and biblical commentaries of the period were written in Arabic rather than in Hebrew.

The ideal of *arabiyya* expressed the Muslims' sense of national identity through their language. Arabic poetry was revered by Muslims as the highest form of literary creativity, and the ability to master the art of poetry became the yardstick of cultural literacy. *Arabiyya* stimulated a parallel sense of linguistic nationalism among Jews who turned to the classical Hebrew of the Bible in order to develop a language of poetic expressiveness as refined as Arabic. Although Jews were fully acculturated in all areas of Andalusian society, the expression of the national consciousness of the Jewish people in Spain assumed the form of a renaissance of Hebrew literature, especially poetry. Poetry, secular and religious, was the one genre in which Jews wrote almost exclusively in Hebrew. The ideal of *arabiyya*, therefore, fostered a new growth in Hebrew literacy and cultural identity through the growth of Hebrew poetry.

The Muslim fundamentalist Almohade invasions of Spain in 1145, with their attendant anti-Jewish persecutions, and the disintegration of Muslim rule following the military successes of the Christian reconquest of Spain, brought this "Golden Age" to a tragic conclusion.

Since the eleventh century, Provence had been a center of rabbinic culture, including biblical scholarship, *Talmudic* study, pietistic thought, and liturgical composition. There is no evidence of any influence of the Andalusian secular culture in Provence prior to the second half of the twelfth century.

The beginning of secular Jewish culture in Provence dates from the arrival of Yehudah ibn Tibbon (1120–1190) as a refugee from the Almohade persecution. Ibn Tibbon, who brought with him an extensive library and knowledge of the intellectual tradition of Andalusian Jewry, found a receptive welcome among the Jewish intellectuals of Provence. He was commissioned soon after his arrival by a leading *Talmudist* to translate a number of major Jewish works from Arabic into Hebrew. Beginning with Bahya's work, *Duties of the Heart,* he devoted the next twenty-five years to a series of translations that introduced Hispano-Jewish culture into Provence and Christian Europe. This work was continued by his son, Shmuel (1160–1230), translator of Maimonides' *Guide of the Perplexed*, and other works. Provence emerged as a center of Jewish intellectual and literary life in Europe. Jews served as intermediaries and transmitters of Arabic civilization, and even of classical Greek and Hindu traditions, to Christian Europe in the late twelfth and early thirteenth centuries.

Provence spawned the emergence of Jewish mysticism as well. The movement known as *Kabbalah* began around 1175 among circles associated with one of the great families of Provencal rabbinic leadership.[27] Covert suggestions about mystical revelations from the prophet Elijah began to appear in statements attributed to leading rabbinic figures of the period.

Elijah, a zealous Israelite prophet of the ninth century B.C.E., is described in the Bible as the fierce opponent of all forms of paganism carried out within the boundaries of Israel.[28] The Bible also describes an encounter between Elijah and God that takes place at the same spot where God revealed the Torah to Moses. After a tumultuous array of thunder and fire, God's "still, small voice" addresses the prophet.[29] This account concludes with Elijah's disappearance as he is carried off to heaven in a chariot of fire.[30] According to tradition, Elijah lives on in "concealment." He is also viewed as the messianic harbinger[31] who also appears to men as the revealer of heavenly secrets.[32]

Claims of such revelations by Elijah are attributed to Rabbi Avraham ben Yitzhak of Narbonne (d.1179), the head of the Narbonne rabbinical court; his son-in-law, Rabbi Avraham ben David (*RABaD*) of Posquieres (d.1198), the leading *Talmudist* of his generation; and *RABaD*'s son, Isaac the Blind (d. circa 1236), the first identifiable *Kabbalist* author.[33]

Toward the end of the twelfth century, copies of a manuscript called *Sefer ha-Bahir* (The Book of Clear Light), attributed to Nehunyah ben ha-Kanah, a rabbinic figure of the second century and colleague of Rabbi Akiva, began to circulate among the disciples of Isaac the Blind in Provence. Although the book was still considered part of the *Merkavah* tradition, its authorship was certainly much later than the second century. *Sefer ha-Bahir*, a collection of fragmentary homilies and commentaries on biblical verses, was probably edited in the late twelfth century on the basis of earlier materials that were collected and reworked. The appearance of the book was accompanied by a sharp debate over the authenticity and antiquity of the book.[34]

Sefer ha-Bahir introduced a decidedly new conception of God. No longer was God the transcendent king of *Merkavah* mysticism. In *Sefer ha-Bahir*, God is an amalgam of dynamic divine powers perpetually in a state of ebb and flow. This dynamic being is subject to continuous inner movement and fluidity. At one moment, certain aspects of God may be ascendant while, at other times, those powers may be in decline. In *Sefer ha-Bahir*, God is seen as an ever-changing being whose fluctuations are reverberations and repercussions of human behavior directed at influencing God.[35] The two most prominent powers within this pantheon of divine powers are feminine and masculine dimensions within God. These elements soon became central in the *Kabbalistic* conception of God.

Isaac the Blind, the first identifiable *Kabbalist* in Jewish history, was known as *Yitzhak Sagi-Nahor* (Isaac of the Great Light), hinting euphemistically at his physical handicap. Despite his blindness, he personifies the mystic quest to transcend the limitations of the human intellect as it meditates upon the divine mind in colorful visual images. For Isaac, God is the "incomprehensible," the universal mind that is the source of all thought and being and whose scrutiny is the object of the penetrating mind of the mystic.

The early disciples of Isaac the Blind and followers of the *Sefer ha-Bahir* believed that it was impossible to reach or understand God through rational means. God could only be understood through symbols and traces of His existence that He had planted throughout the universe. Everything becomes a symbol for God—the human soul, the Torah, nature—if one knows how to decipher its meaning. The early *Kabbalists* defined the meaning of the symbols by which God could be understood. They saw themselves as decoders who could reach God if only they could penetrate God's vocabulary, the symbolic code which God embedded in the universe.

The challenge of understanding the symbolism of God was picked up by the disciples of Isaac the Blind in Spain. The center of Jewish mystical activity reverted to Spain around the turn of the thirteenth century. By 1225, the Christian reconquest of Spain from the Muslims was nearly complete. Jewish life then shifted from the provinces of southern Spain to the provinces of Castile in north central Spain, Aragon in the northeast, and Catalonia in the far northeast. The small Catalonian town of Gerona was home to the next generation of *Kabbalists*. The Gerona *Kabbalists* included many important mystics who contributed to early *Kabbalistic* theory and practice.

The acknowledged leader of the Gerona school, Rabbi Moshe ben Nahman (Nahmanides, 1194–1270), was also the most important figure in Hispano-Jewish history of the thirteenth century. His mystical views are expressed in his many writings although he often attempted to conceal these views from non-*Kabbalists*. According to his students, his prodigious Torah commentary was originally intended as a *Kabbalistic* work but, following a premonitory dream, he rewrote it for a more popular readership. Many references to mystical secrets can still be found throughout this work. Many of his transcribed sermons and biblical exegeses contain *Kabbalistic* "secrets" about God, angels, the soul, miracles, and the afterlife. Nahmanides is also distinguished as the first *Kabbalistic* poet.[36]

Nahmanides successfully combined his pursuit of mysticism with traditional religious practice and the mantle of Jewish communal leadership. In 1232, when the rabbis of Northern France and Germany sought to condemn Moses Maimonides' writings as heretical, Nahmanides counseled moderation and compromise despite his own *Kabbalistic* opposition to Maimonides' rationalism. He argued that Maimonides actually made religious ideas attractive for Andalusian and Provencal Jews who had been educated in an atmosphere of secular and philosophic rationalism that was inimical to the teachings of Judaism. In the context of Nahmanides' own culture, however, he regarded Maimonides as too much of a rationalist and too far removed from traditional Jewish teachings.

Not only was this a period of cultural struggle between Jewish traditionalists and philosophic rationalists, but it was also a period in which Jewish fortunes in Christian Spain were in decline. One of Nahmanides' contemporaries, Shem Tov Falaquera, who introduced the Delphic maxim

("Know Thyself") into Hebrew, described his era as "a time of stress and danger when many troubles beset us and every man is poverty stricken by the wrathful rod of fate and must wander through the land in search of sustenance."[37] The restrictions upon Jewish economic activities imposed throughout Europe by the Catholic Church and the intolerance of the urban Christian populace resulted in the decline of Jewish prominence in government service, finance, science, and medicine.

Nahmanides was a physician by profession and the official representative of Catalonian Jewry in dealings with the ruling authorities. With the rise of the Dominican religious order in 1216, Catholic policy towards the Jews changed from criticizing the supposed anti-Christian heresies in the *Talmud* to mounting pressure upon Jews to concede that the Bible prophesies the coming of Jesus Christ. Dominican efforts in Spain to convert the Jews to Christianity grew during this period and gained support through their alliance with King James I of Aragon. With the introduction of the Inquisition to Spain during his rule, the Jews were compelled to debate the Dominicans and listen to sermons that purported to show that the Hebrew Bible confirms the truth of Christianity.

The responsibility for advocacy on behalf of Judaism fell to Nahmanides. In 1263, he was commanded by King James I of Aragon to defend Judaism against the charges of the Dominicans who were led by a converted Jew, Fre Paolo Christiani. Despite Nahmanides' bold and outspoken defense of Jewish beliefs, the conversionist pressure upon the Jews mounted. In 1265, the Dominicans put Nahmanides on trial for supposedly claiming that the Jews actually won the disputation. The king interrupted the trial but Nahmanides was forced to flee Spain for the Land of Israel.[38]

Nahmanides' devotion to *Kabbalah* contributed to the dissemination of Jewish mystical teachings throughout Spain, Italy, and Israel. Although *Kabbalah* remained an esoteric discipline confined to a select but significant few, it continued to grow among learned segments of Jewry throughout the next two centuries.

The most decisive event in the history of Spanish *Kabbalah* was the appearance of a new literary work, *Sefer ha-Zohar* (The Book of Splendor). The dissemination of the *Zohar* around 1290 in Spain ushered in an entirely new era in the history of Jewish mysticism. Although the *Sefer ha-Bahir* continued to serve as the authoritative text of *Kabbalah* for some time afterward, the *Zohar* eventually replaced it as the primary *Kabbalistic* text.

The *Zohar* was introduced to Spanish *Kabbalists* by Moshe de Leon of Guadalajara around 1290.[39] De Leon copied and circulated manuscripts of the purportedly ancient *Midrash* to *Kabbalistic* acquaintances in Spain. Some of his peers regarded his discovery with great excitement because the author was supposedly Rabbi Shimon bar Yohai, the second-century sage and student of Rabbi Akiva. This was indeed a precious find due to its antiquity and the prestige of its assumed author. Other of de Leon's contemporaries viewed his discovery with suspicion. After all, they wondered, how is it possible that such a seminal work should have been hidden and appear suddenly one thousand years later? One contemporary account even quotes the widow of Moses de Leon as saying:

> Let God punish me if my husband alone did not write this entire book! He wrote every word and letter of the *Zohar*. When I saw that he composed every word himself while telling people that Shimon bar Yohai was the real author, I asked him why he did not tell people the truth. He said to me, "If I were to tell people that I composed the words of the *Zohar* and its wonderful mysteries, it would not get the attention it deserves or the price which an ancient book commands. When people hear that Shimon bar Yohai revealed these words under the influence of the Holy Spirit, they will accept it."[40]

Controversy has always surrounded the *Zohar*. The small groups of *Kabbalists* in Spain and the Land of Israel were divided between those who believed that *Zohar* was an ancient *Midrash* and those who believed it was a prodigious literary forgery. What is most surprising is that the tenor of this debate in the thirteenth century was relatively mild. This indicated that while the *Zohar* was regarded as a matter of some contention, even the proponents of its antiquity regarded it as only one among other classic mystical texts.

Because Spanish *Kabbalah* remained the province of a small coterie of devotees, the question of the authenticity, at first, of the *Zohar* excited very few. It was not until several centuries later that the *Zohar* assumed preeminence as the most important classic literary work among *Kabbalists*. The *Zohar* is a comprehensive mystical commentary on many sections of the Torah. It presents a reading of the Torah as a novel of the inner life of God and the dynamics of the divine powers. It was the primary literary vehicle through which the mystical theories and Torah interpretations of the Spanish *Kabbalah* were disseminated.

In the two centuries following the appearance of the *Zohar*, Spanish *Kabbalah* thrived within small circles. There were no academies devoted exclusively to the study of *Kabbalah*, nor were there special associations or congregations. In Spain, *Kabbalah* was the spiritual avocation of a small number of rabbinically literate and religiously conservative Jews. Teachings, theories, and devotions were transmitted from father to son, from teacher to disciple. *Kabbalah* was an elite spiritual movement nurtured by the circulation of mystical manuscripts and private oral teachings.

The *Kabbalists* saw themselves as bastions of religious traditionalism guarding against the incursions of Moses Maimonides' philosophic rationalism that they anathematized as modernism. The term *Kabbalah* itself means "tradition" and was embraced as an emblem of their conservatism. The *Kabbalists* maintained that this tradition originated at Sinai and had been adumbrated, albeit reluctantly, in a series of oral teachings and cryptic writings by ancient sages.

The *Kabbalists* opposed the Maimonidean tendency to see the Torah as an allegory for moral and scientific teachings. They viewed this as an attempt to make the Torah relevant by interpreting it to conform with contemporary mores. In the *Kabbalists'* view, the Torah was a mysterious tapestry woven from hints about the divine world and expressed in language comprehensible to humans. But they warned against understanding the Torah as a book that talks about real earthly and historical events. It may speak in human language, but its meaning is divine. The *Kabbalists* saw themselves engaged in a battle with modernists over the meaning of the Torah. Still, due to the esoteric nature of their teachings and the paucity of their number, they had little general effect on Jewish life in Spain.

Despite the illustrious history of Jewish life in Spain, conditions worsened for the Jews during the fourteenth century. In 1391 anti-Jewish sentiment erupted into popular pogroms throughout Spain. Perhaps as many as one-third of the 750,000 Spanish Jews were slaughtered, and an equal number were forcibly baptized. The forced converts became known as *Marranos*. Over the next twenty-five years, the ranks of the *Marranos* were swelled by the voluntary conversion of many Jews, known as *Conversos*, who sought to escape the stigma and fate of their compatriots by willfully abandoning Judaism.

The presence of a new social and religious phenomenon of converted Christians, some of whom maintained ties to Jews and Judaism, became a matter of great public concern. Debates raged in Spain regarding the fidelity of the new Christians to Catholicism. Despite great differences in the circumstances of conversion and the degree of loyalty to the adopted religion, new Christians were often regarded by native Christians as a homogeneous group. The Church frequently saw the converts as crypto-Jews who continued to practice Judaism in secret. Rabbinic authorities distinguished between the legal status of the forced converts and the voluntary converts, and they sought to define criteria to establish who was and who was not considered to be a Jew in the eyes of Jewish law.

In 1449, the Franciscans moved to extirpate the real and imagined vestiges of Jewishness among the new Christians. The ascent of Ferdinand and Isabella to the throne in 1474 led to efforts to consolidate their political rule over all of Spain. The religious and political forces coalesced in 1481 with the establishment of the Royal Inquisition in Spain. Under the direction of Torquemada, the Inquisition pursued its goals with a legendary blindness to truth and devotion to brutality. Following a two-pronged policy towards the Jews, Ferdinand and Isabella sanctioned inquisitorial measures directed against the new Christians and expelled the remaining Jews from Spain in 1492. Having done so, they were able to establish national rule based on a foundation of ethnic and religious unity.

More than a thousand years of Spanish Jewish history came to an abrupt end in 1492, just as Columbus set sail for the New World. The remnant of Spanish Jewry fled to Portugal, the Ottoman Empire, and the major trading centers of Europe. The exiles saw themselves as the elite of world Jewry. They believed that Spain was the home to which many of the exiles fled after the destruction of the First Temple in 586 B.C.E. They believed that theirs was the oldest surviving continuous Jewish community in the world. They looked back with pride on the prominence of Jews as courtiers, financiers, scientists, philosophers, administrators, and scholars under Arab rule and to a lesser, but significant extent, under Christian rule. They were proud of luminaries such as Maimonides and Nahmanides, and they were proud of the traditions of Hebrew liturgical poetry. Many, too, were proud of *Kabbalah* that had flourished in Spain.

The tradition of Jewish mysticism did not disappear with the destruction of Spanish Jewry. It had already spread to many other communities in Europe and the Mediterranean, but it was soon to undergo a decisive transformation under the weight of the experience of the Expulsion. As the great legacy of Spanish *Kabbalah* was transplanted to the town of Safed in the Galilee region of Israel, one phase of the history of Jewish mysticism came to an end and a new one began.

At this point we shall turn to examine the major elements in the mystic quest in Judaism. Later we shall return to explore the history of Jewish mysticism from 1492 to the present.

3

THE HIDDEN AND
THE REVEALED

The Infinite God of Jewish Mysticism

Gershom Scholem (1897–1982), the leading modern scholar of Jewish mysticism, theorized that mysticism is a definite stage in the historical development of religion and makes its appearance under certain well-defined conditions.[1] He explains that Jewish mysticism is phenomenologically distinct from Jewish religious experiences known through biblical and *Talmudic* records. He further argues that the development of Jewish mysticism was a relatively late development in the history of Judaism.

In the biblical period, which coincides roughly with the period from Abraham to Ezekiel (1500 B.C.E.–586 B.C.E.), man discovers that there is an order and harmony to his world that is not visible. He experiences the hidden hand of a god, gods, or other forces that direct the world and influence his existence. The explanation of the unseen forces in the world covers all contingencies from birth, harvests, and fortune to death, floods, and famines. Often he discovers hidden forces in nature and the presence of god in the wind, the sun, and the rain. The Hebrew genius, however, was the discovery of a god who was outside and beyond nature and who, in fact, ruled over and governed nature for good and for bad, depending upon the moral righteousness or failings of human beings. The God of Abraham and Moses was an awesome, unseen god, all the more powerful for His invisibility. Still, He was very familiar and near.

In the time of Adam, the Hebrew Bible recounts, "The voice of God

43

walked in the Garden."² Man could communicate freely and easily with God. Abraham, too, had an intimate relationship with God throughout his lifetime. When God threatened to destroy Sodom and Gemmorah, Abraham bargains with Him as if He were a familiar merchant in the bazaar. After gaining God's assent to save the cities if fifty righteous men were found, Abraham tries to whittle down the number to ten.³ This is certainly a God with whom one can reason.

When Moses speaks with God in the wilderness several centuries later, God is no longer the intimate stranger walking in the Garden or conversing freely with the patriarchs. Whereas man appears able to initiate dialogue with God in the narratives in *Genesis*, *Exodus* portrays God as initiating dialogue with man. God is somewhat less accessible, but certainly more awesome. When God tells Moses to take off his shoes, for the ground upon which he stands is holy ground,⁴ God has changed the terms of the relationship. God is still present in the world, but His presence now seems to be localized on earth for just a brief moment in which He announces that, "I am what I am."⁵ This is no longer the familiar partner of Abraham but the beginning of the hidden, inscrutable God who soon appears on top of Mount Sinai shrouded in smoke and fog.⁶

The God of Israel, as He is known through the accounts of *Genesis*, is undifferentiated from the world and appears to be in constant dialogue with the patriarchs. The intimate relationship with God is like that between a child and its mother. The God of *Exodus* is still familiar and intimate but becomes increasingly remote, distant, awesome, and fearsome. The emotional tenor of the narrative shifts, and the affective mood is suggestive of what occurs when the child matures. The child may experience less of the all-encompassing nurturing of the mother and more of the power and authority of the father. The impression of God evolves from an almost prosaically familiar being to an increasingly remote, tremendous, and awesome power. The concealed God of Sinai is far more remote than the God of Eden whom Adam heard walking in the heat of the day.

The history of the religion of ancient Israel consists of the discovery of a personal, yet transcendent, God who, in the course of time, becomes increasingly remote and inaccessible to those who seek Him. The primary religious experiences of Abraham give way to the majestic and distant God of Moses. The Bible begins with an account of God's presence and follows His eventual withdrawal and distancing from His people. The earlier, intimate relationship is supplanted by a relationship mediated through a permanent and unchanging account of His wishes, the Torah. Having given His last word, so to speak, He bows out of the picture, leaving man to do the rest. God's voluntary self-withdrawal from the affairs of the people to whom He revealed Himself is not very different from the case of a parent who, having given his child a good upbringing and education, allows the child to mature and make decisions on his own. There is no question about the parent's desires, only about his whereabouts.

The Bible, according to this perspective, chronicles the history of the Jewish religious relationship with God and the subsequent creation of an abyss between man and God that cannot be bridged. By the time of the early rabbinic period (70 C.E.–200 C.E.), the Jewish people have no expectations of having a direct, unmediated relationship with God. Jewish religious experiences become mediated through the Torah in the sense that, in the absence of direct contact, God and man meet when man follows God's will as prescribed in the law. Or, more emphatically, in the absence of God, all man has is His Torah.

Many of the post-biblical, rabbinic or *Talmudic* teachings convey this sense of the unbridgeable abyss between man and God. Rabbinic literature contains many statements that reinforce the notion of God's increasing withdrawal from intimate contact with man over the course of time. Such passages seem to suggest that the history of God and the Jewish people is one of increasing remoteness and widening of an abyss as history progresses beyond the original moments of God's revelation to mankind. This rabbinic conception of history is explicit in the following popular legend which compares the relationship between God and Israel to that between a king and his daughter:

> The case of a king who had a daughter who was a minor: Until she grew up and came of age, he used to speak to her when he saw her in the street; he spoke to her in the alleyways. But, when she grew up and came of age, he said, "It is not in keeping with my daughter's dignity that I should talk to her in public. Make her, therefore, a pavilion and I shall speak with her inside the pavilion." Thus, at first, it is written (in Torah), "When Israel was a child, I loved him."

> God said: "They saw Me in Egypt; they saw Me at the Red Sea; they saw Me at Sinai." But, once they had accepted the Torah and became a complete nation unto Him, He said: "It is not in keeping with the dignity of My children that I should speak with them publicly, but let them make Me a sanctuary and I shall speak with them from the midst of the sanctuary."[7]

This marvelous passage shows how the rabbis of the *Talmudic* era understood the reasons for the end of God's spontaneous revelation to individuals and the subsequent localization of all contact with God in one stationary locale, the portable sanctuary in the desert that later became the foundation of the First and Second Temples. The shift from mobile to stationary places of direct contact with God is portrayed here as a recognition of the increasing maturity of the Jewish people. When the Jewish people were a young nation, individuals were able to have free and easy access to their God. As the nation grew and came of age, they became less dependent upon regular contact with their God and had less need for direct communication. Now that they possess the Torah, direct contact with God is less essential for guidance and direction. Therefore, the frequency of contact is diminished, and the place of meeting is restricted by God. It is even portrayed as a parental gesture of respect for the independence of the child. The passage implies that the Jewish people have less need for immediate revelations of God Himself once they have received His Torah.

The abyss between God and man is also portrayed as a feature of the historical condition of the Jewish people. After the destruction of the Second Temple in 70 C.E., Jewish sources reflect the view that the catastrophe was due to the moral failings of the Jewish people. The liturgy captures the sentiment that the destruction of the Temple and the forced exile from Jerusalem were due to Jewish sin: "Because of our sins, we were exiled from our homeland."[8] Some sources even imply that human sin caused God to withdraw His protection from the Temple and make it vulnerable to attack and destruction. These rabbinic passages forcefully convey the notion that this exile was the direct result of human acts that forced God to remove the immunity against destruction of the Temple that He guaranteed by His presence in the Holy of Holies. This permitted the Romans, who acted as agents of God's dissatisfaction with His people, to attack Jerusalem and send the Jewish people into exile:

> When the Holy One, Blessed be He, wished to destroy the Temple, He said, "So long as I am in it, the gentile nations will not harm it. I shall, therefore, cease to regard it and shall swear not to give it heed until the time of the End." At that moment, the enemy entered the Temple and burned it. When it was burnt, the Holy One, Blessed be He, said "I no longer have a seat upon the earth; I shall remove my presence from there and ascend to my first habitation." At that moment, the Holy One, Blessed be He, wept and said, "Woe unto Me! What have I done? I caused My presence to dwell for

Israel's sake, and now that they have sinned, I have returned to My original place."⁹

Thus, human sin also contributed to the abyss that grew between God and man. This passage describes the abyss in concrete terms as the ascent and return of God to a higher habitation from where He had earlier descended. In fact, other rabbinic passages describe God as having ascended through seven habitations to His permanent dwelling place in "the seventh heaven." Each of these reinforces the notion of God's increasing distance from man, a notion that runs directly counter to the biblical conception of God. There, God is at times described as a transcendent being, hidden in the recesses of his inaccessible habitation, and at other times, immanent within the world, accessible and near.

Some rabbinic authors, such as the second-century Aramaic translator of the Torah, went so far as to suggest that the God of the Bible did not really appear to the forefathers. The translator substituted a new term, *Shekhinah* (Presence), to characterize God's appearance to man.¹⁰ By differentiating between God and His presence, the translator sought to preserve God's invisibility and inaccessibility while maintaining that He could also appear to man. The use of different terms, however, does not suggest two different gods or aspects of God. It merely serves to reinforce the dual nature of God—hidden and revealed—through the use of different proper nouns. Still, the novelty of suggesting that God has two natures was not lost on the readers of the translation. They lived in the period after the destruction of the Temple and consequently felt, in real historical terms, the abyss that separated man from God. By their own account, they recognized that their religious experience differed from that of their ancestors. They were acutely aware of the abyss.

While the abyss prevents man from approaching God, God can still bridge the gap at His will. After all, it is an abyss of His own creation. It does not prevent God from exercising His providential watch over the world:

Rabbi Levi said: To what can the matter be compared? To an architect who built a city and made therein secret places, hideouts, and chambers and, eventually, he became the ruler. He then sought to seize the bandits in the city and they fled and hid themselves in those hiding places. He said to them: "Fools! Are you seeking to hide from me? I, after all, am the craftsman who built the city, and I, therefore, know all the secret places and the entrances and exits of the hideouts better than you." Likewise, the Holy One, Blessed be He, says to the wicked "Fools! Wherefore do you conceal the wickedness in your hearts? It is I who built man and I know all the secret chambers and recesses within him."[11]

The rabbis maintained a respect for the rare individual who possessed the combination of religious and spiritual powers that would allow him to overcome the abyss. They did not deny that it was possible to overcome the abyss. On the contrary, they recorded several instances of individuals who achieved states of mystical contact with God or attained direct communication with Him. The rabbis, however, in deciding points of law, did not give weight to such spontaneous contacts with God because these could lead an individual to claim that his experience gave him greater authority than the legal authority of the Torah or the rabbinic court. Since rabbinic Judaism is predicated upon the foundation of the Torah, the notion of majority rule, and the common consent of the Jewish people to accept rabbinic decisions as legally binding, the mystic posed a potential challenge to the rabbinic system of law.

The rabbis acknowledged the truth and validity of mysticism and other forms of intense personal religious experiences. As a practical matter, however, they deemed such personal experiences irrelevant as a basis for formulating legal decisions. Mysticism simply does not confer any special status upon the mystic. This is clear in the following *Talmudic* legend:

One day, Rabbi Eliezer was in dispute with the other sages on a matter of law. He brought all the proofs in the world in support of his opinion but the other sages would not accept them. He said to them: "If the law is according to me, let this locust tree prove it." And the locust tree moved one hundred cubits. (Some say four hundred cubits.) The sages said to him: "The locust tree cannot prove anything."

Then he said to them: "If the law is according to me, let this stream of water prove it." And the stream of water turned and flowed backward. They said to him: "The stream cannot prove anything."

Then he said to them: "If the law is according to me, let the walls of the House of Study prove it." The walls of the House of Study began to topple. Rabbi Joshua reprimanded the walls: "If scholars are disputing with one another about the law, what business is it of yours?" The walls did not fall down out of respect for Rabbi Joshua and did not straighten up out of respect for Rabbi Eliezer. They are still so inclined!

Then Rabbi Eliezer said to them: "If the law is according to me, let the heavens prove it." A voice then came forth from heaven and said: "Why do you dispute with Rabbi Eliezer? The law is according to him in every case!" Thereupon, Rabbi Joshua rose to his feet and said: " 'It is not in heaven' (*Deuteronomy* 30:12). The Torah has been given once and for all at Mount Sinai. For You have already written in the Torah at Mount Sinai: 'After the majority must one incline' (*Ex.* 23:2)."

Later on, Rabbi Nathan came upon Elijah the Prophet. Nathan said to him: "What was the Holy One, Blessed be He, doing at that moment?" Elijah said to him: "He was smiling and saying: 'My children have defeated me! My children have defeated me!' "[12]

The astounding conclusion reached in this passage is that the disagreements among rabbinic scholars about points of law are no business of God's! God freely transferred the right to interpret his Torah to competent rabbinic jurists. These jurists have established procedures for the resolution of differences in legal matters. No individual has the right to circumvent the process of jurisprudence by claiming special prerogatives or authority. Although the rabbis do not deny that prophets and mystics may converse with God, they do insist that such experiences are legally irrelevant. Among the rabbis of the *Talmudic* period, mysticism is simply regarded as an extracurricular affair.

The rabbis point to another reason for discouraging individuals from attempting to bridge the abyss. In the legend of the four sages who entered the garden, three were afflicted with various unforeseen consequences: death, insanity, and apostasy. The rabbis warn against pursuing the mystic quest not because it is unreachable, but because it is dangerous. Jewish mysticism, they warn, promises great turmoil and unsettling awesomeness rather than calm and serenity. The mystic quest is a path strewn with many dangers and threats even though the road is open to those who wish to tread on it. This is why the rabbis introduced the idea that God makes His presence, not His very being, known to those who study the Torah and who follow a moral code of conduct.

God's presence, called the *Shekhinah*, is the term used to describe the perception of God in the world. Even though God's being is truly inaccessible, there are moments when individuals feel acutely aware of His nearness and involvement with human affairs. Such moments may occur when one witnesses God's activity in the world. In order to distinguish between the transcendent being and the occasional moments of religious intimacy, the rabbis coined the term *Shekhinah* to refer to the latter. This concept domesticates God's being and makes mysticism wholly unnecessary because God is near. Without the yawning abyss, there can be no mysticism.

The rabbis were able to insure the continued belief in the nearness and immediacy of God in the world while preserving the unbridgeable abyss by introducing the concept of the *Shekhinah*. One early rabbinic passage attempts to counter the literal meaning of a biblical text ("After the Lord your God you shall walk") that seems to imply that man can become physically close to God. The rabbinic passage explains that one cannot expect to actually approach God or to have direct encounters with Him. It suggests that to approach God means to emulate His moral attributes.

> "After the Lord your God you shall walk" (*Deut.* 13:5). And is it possible for a man to walk after the *Shekhinah*? Rather, this means that one should emulate the virtues of the Holy One, Blessed be He.[13]

There are few statements in Jewish religious literature that capture more fundamentally the notion that God is believed to be present in the act of study and observance than the following dictum:

> If two sit together and occupy themselves with words of Torah, the *Shekhinah* abides in their midst.[14]

Rabbinic Judaism is, ultimately, a religious system that substitutes rituals of study, communal prayer, and moral goodness for direct religious experience between man and God. In this regard, rabbinic Judaism is antimystical or at least attempts to neutralize the mystical impulse inherent in all religions. Judaism is a religion in which the abyss is filled with the rituals of prayer, study, and morality.

Prayer, in rabbinic Judaism, is one of the most important means of achieving nearness to God and awareness of God's presence in the world. The God who guides history, who judges from heaven, who hears and answers the petitions of His people, and knows the innermost reaches of the heart is the object of these prayers. Prayer is an act of great faith in the transcendent God's concern for the world. Without actually denying the abyss, prayer affirms that it can be traversed by the supplicating human voice.

Mysticism is a form of religious experience that occurs when man is acutely aware of the abyss that separates him from God, knows that his predecessors had a relationship that he cannot have, and attempts to bridge the abyss. Therefore, from the vantage point of Jewish history, mysticism could only have occurred in a post-biblical stage in the history of Judaism. Jewish mysticism is the attempt to bridge the abyss that was formalized in the rabbinic period and to return to the religious experiences common in the biblical period. In religion as in history, however, time can never go backwards. Mysticism is a form of religion that comes to terms with the abyss between man and God.

Rabbinic Judaism established certain norms that shaped the way Jews thought about religious issues. The rabbinic conception of God was, however, based on the paradoxical formulation that God is both transcendent and immanent.[15] He is removed and hidden by nature, yet the performance of his commandments allows us to become aware of His abiding presence; indeed, through our actions we can permit His *Shekhinah* to dwell in our midst. The problem that rabbinic Judaism solved was how to make the experience of God accessible in a period in which we do not hear voices from heaven. They rejected the legal admissibility of the individual religious experience, direct contact with God, or prophecy in favor of the indirect relationship with God that is possible through the fulfillment of the Torah.

The solution of rabbinic Judaism, however, served only to create another, more serious dilemma: How can the individual fulfill God's will without experiencing Him directly as did his ancestors? If all of the force of religion is based on the compelling revelation of God to his predecessors, as it is transmitted by the Torah, why should not the experience of God be available to him as well?

On an even more fundamental level, a religious Jew might ask about the paradox of God's essential remoteness even as his religion promotes nearness. Which shall it be? If God is transcendent, how is it possible for anyone to have a relationship with Him? And if there is no relationship with the hidden God, what is the meaning of the fundamental rituals of Judaism such as prayer? Finally, it is impossible to repeat the accounts of the ancestors' direct encounters with God without, at some point, asking if these experiences are still possible. The desire to experience God as deeply as Abraham or Moses did lies at the heart of the mystical impulse in Judaism as much as does the temptation to bridge the abyss between the hidden God and the God who listens to, cares about, and answers the prayers of man.

Rabbinic Judaism developed a comprehensive theology: a system of teaching about God and His relation to the world. That theology was based on several important principles. Although these principles were never codified, they are implicit in the teachings of all Jewish thinkers from the rabbinic period until the present. They are also important keys to understanding how Jewish mysticism developed out of rabbinic Judaism.

Shortly before the Second Temple was destroyed by the Romans in 70 C.E., the Jewish community in Israel was torn apart by a bitter internal struggle. The issues that divided them involved the tactical question of how best to respond to the Roman presence and pressure and the strategic question of how to define Judaism as a way of life. There were those who promulgated a policy of conciliation and appeasement and believed that it was possible to preserve the institutions of the Jewish people through concessions to the Roman Empire. Many of these were Sadducees, a group from among the priestly class, which was responsible for the Temple administration, tax collection, maintaining the treasury, and insuring the continuation of sacrifices. The Sadducees also believed that the Jewish people had only one central religious institution, the Jerusalem Temple, and that God was localized there in the Holy of Holies. In their view, there was no Judaism without the Temple and no Temple without Roman sanction. Therefore, they pursued a dual policy of submission to Roman rule, accompanied by a degree of assimilation to Roman urban culture, and a staunch defense of the centrality of the Temple and the priesthood within Judaism.[16]

A second segment of the community, the Pharisees, criticized the Sadducees for having assimilated too much of Roman culture and for overemphasizing the centrality of the Temple. They believed that the essence of the Jewish religion was more than sacrifices offered by the priests in the Temple on behalf of the Jewish people who supported the Temple through donations, tithes, and contributions. Moreover, they did not adhere to the Sadducean notion that only priests were able to expiate sin and petition God. They also challenged their claim that only priests were qualified to interpret the Torah, for this led to the impression that only priests could serve God.

The Pharisaic challenge was directed against the Sadducee's fundamental conception of the Torah. The Pharisees believed that the written Torah supported the Sadducean claim to priestly privilege, but the ancient judges and prophets also possessed authority equal to that of the priests. They based this view on the fact that upon Moses' death, leadership passed both to the priests and the elders. The latter were succeeded by the judges and, eventually, the prophets. The Pharisees believed that in addition to the written Torah, which served as the basis of priestly authority, there is another source of authority that goes back to the time of Moses, which they called "the Torah that was (transmitted) orally" (*Torah she-be-al-peh*). This source of authority is enunciated in the opening of one of the earliest Pharisaic manifestos, the Mishnaic tractate *Avot* (Fathers):

> Moses received the Torah at Sinai and transmitted it to Joshua. Joshua (passed it on) to the elders, the elders to the prophets, and the prophets to the men of the Great Assembly.

Since the Pharisees were the successors of the men of the Great Assembly, this tractate supported the Pharisees' opposition to the Sadducean view that only priests have the right to interpret the Torah. The Pharisees asserted the legitimacy of another interpretive tradition, that of orally transmitted guidelines governing the religious rights and responsibilities of nonpriests and the validity of religious rituals performed outside the Temple.

The Pharisaic beliefs were based on an understanding of Judaism that challenged the Sadducean notion of an exclusively Temple-centered religion. The Pharisees taught that every man is a priest, every Jewish home a temple, every table an altar, and every meal a ritual sacrifice.[17] Moreover, any meal that was conducted without words of Torah being spoken was like a sacrifice conducted improperly. The Pharasaic rituals were an attempt to extend the holiness and sanctity of the Temple to the home by expanding upon the notion that the written Torah was accompanied by an orally transmitted interpretation of the Torah that mandated new responsibilities for Jewish householders.

The war between the Jews of Israel and the Romans raged between 66 and 70 C.E. The Roman victory and their destruction of the Temple put an end to the Sadducean or priestly aspirations for a Temple-centered Judaism. The Pharisaic religious outlook made it possible to conceive of the continuation of Judaism without the Temple.[18] The issues of authority and legitimacy that divided the Sadducees and Pharisees became moot, and the groundwork for the continuation of Judaism was guaranteed. The Oral Torah was soon to become as important in determining the future course of the Jewish people as the Written Torah.

The Pharisees made a virtue out of necessity. They developed new institutions and rituals to preserve the religion of Israel. They expanded the "houses of assembly" (Hebrew: *Bet Knesset*; Greek: *synagogue*) where the people assembled on market days and Sabbaths to hear the Torah read publicly as they had done in the Jerusalem Temple. The sacrifices, now extinct, were replaced by prayers of thanksgiving and petition that were offered in the houses of assembly before and after the Torah reading. Soon a regular liturgy developed, and the houses of assembly became central places of prayer and teaching.

The rituals of priestly preparations for sacrifices were now transferred to the home where the head of the house was to assume the holiness of the priests. He was to conduct himself in a ritually and morally pure manner through rituals of washing and reciting blessings. The very act of eating an ordinary meal was transformed into a dramatic reenactment of the priestly sacrifices of wine, grain, fruit, and meat to God and was thereby invested with priestly holiness. Individuals who were trained in the specific require- ments of the priestlike rituals were called rabbis (masters) because of their mastery of the Oral Torah.

Judaism today is the legacy of Pharisaism and the innovations that were based on their understanding of the Oral Torah. All subsequent movements to introduce change in Judaism have attempted to claim that their reforms were part and parcel of the oral tradition in Judaism. In particular, changes in Jewish religious practice are justified by their innovators through citing corroborating biblical verses or statements by *Talmudic* sages.

In the twelfth century, Moses Maimonides (*RaMBaM*) (1135–1204) introduced a sweeping new codification of Jewish law called *Mishneh Torah* (Repetition of the Law). The title boldly suggests both recapitulation of the Oral Torah law code and a book second in importance only to the Torah. This fourteen-volume work was strongly attacked because he did not quote earlier rabbinic authorities. Maimonides was accused of going too far beyond his predecessors and set himself up as a greater authority than the *Talmud*.[19] His *Mishneh Torah*, however, soon gained acceptance and assumed great importance as the basic codification of Jewish law.

Maimonides' *Guide of the Perplexed* presents an interpretation of two of the most important theories contained within the Oral Torah. These teach- ings, "The Account of Creation" and "The Account of the Chariot," are interpretations about the nature of the origins of the world and the nature of the prophet Ezekiel's ecstatic vision of God, respectively.[20] Since the biblical accounts of these two events are rather brief and enigmatic, various specula- tions and theories had been advanced orally, transmitted as unwritten inter- pretations as part of the Oral Torah. Eventually, some of these ideas were recorded in the *Talmud* and other writings.

Maimonides, who was interested in the question of the origin of the world and the problem of whether one can know God, found these biblical accounts perplexing. He did not find the rabbinic explanations of creation and theology wholly satisfactory because they were contradicted by current scientific knowledge and philosophic beliefs. He was drawn to the teachings of ancient Greek and medieval Islamic philosophers as the source of contemporary wisdom. There he found compelling explanations for these problems but, as a rabbi, he was troubled by the fact that he found these interpretations closer to the truth than the ones he knew through the *Talmud*. In order to avoid claiming that Aristotle had more to say on these issues than Judaism, he ingeniously tried to prove that the real meanings of "The Account of Creation" and "The Account of the Chariot" are identical with the teachings of Aristotle. His contemporaries, however, attacked his claim that Aristotle's philosophy was compatible with the Oral Torah as an abuse of the integrity of authentic Jewish oral traditions.

Kabbalah, which originated in Provence and Spain shortly after Maimonides' death, faced a similar challenge. *Kabbalah* sought to introduce a new notion of spirituality without appearing to be new. The very term *Kabbalah* means "that which is received." In fact, the name *Kabbalah* derives from the very same word (*kibbel*) used in the tractate *Avot* to explain the chain of transmission of the Oral Torah—"Moses received (*kibbel*) the Torah . . ." *Kabbalah*, therefore, means "tradition" in the sense that it claims to be another stage in the unbroken transmission of the Oral Torah going back to Sinai.

The early *Kabbalists* used another technique, pseudepigraphy, to identify their new teachings as part of the oral tradition. Pseudepigraphy is the publishing of literature under an assumed name. The *Kabbalists* published many of their most important works under the names of some of the most distinguished figures of the oral tradition. In some cases, forgeries were knowingly introduced as genuine. In other cases, false authorship was ascribed to certain texts over the course of time and circulation. *Sefer ha-Bahir* (The Book of Pure Light), whose real author is unknown, was attributed to Rabbi Nehunya ben ha-Kanah, a sage who lived in the second half of the first century. *Sefer ha-Zohar* (The Book of Splendor), the most important literary work of *Kabbalah*, was written in the late thirteenth century, probably by Moses de Leon of Guadalajuara, who attributed it to Rabbi Shimon bar Yohai, a pupil of Rabbi Akiva. Still, the *Kabbalists* believed that their theories were indeed the true teachings of the Oral Torah, which they had rediscovered.

The belief of the Pharisees and their rabbinic successors, the *Talmudic* sages, in the principle of the authenticity and continuity of the oral tradition made it necessary for every subsequent movement of reform or innovation in Judaism to prove that it was based upon, or part of, the Oral Torah. Jewish mystics could not claim that their experiences entitled them to special knowledge or status within Judaism, nor could they claim to be above the Torah law. There is little encouragement in Judaism for those reformers who openly claim originality; continuity and tradition are held as greater virtues. Jewish mystics were usually rabbis who followed the Torah and tried to assimilate their mystical experiences into traditional Judaism by using prayer and Torah study as the vehicle for the mystic quest. The Torah, written and oral, became the idiom through which Jewish mystics explained their illumination.

The rabbinic conception of God is based on the paradoxical formulation of God's essential closeness to man even as He remains remote and hidden across the unbridgeable abyss. Rabbinic Judaism is based on rituals such as prayer whose purpose is to bridge the abyss with the human voice. The Written Torah contains many accounts of the ancestors who maintained a close relationship with God, whereas the traditions of the Oral Torah emphasize the abyss between man and God and the means of crossing it. Attempts to bridge the abyss found their justification within the oral tradition itself. A Jewish mystic would naturally be guided by the biblical and rabbinic conceptions of God in embarking upon his quest.

Maimonides may not have been thoroughly persuasive in his claim that his interpretation of creation and Ezekiel's vision was based on the Oral Torah. His discussion of God, however, clearly is based upon rabbinic traditions. In fact, Maimonides accepts the rabbinic notion of the abyss and refines the concept in many novel ways.

Maimonides, like the rabbinic sages, teaches that God is unique, transcendent, uncaused, incorporeal, and without limit.[21] He goes further than they did, however, in claiming that God is, therefore, unknowable. All we can know, he asserts, is that God exists. If that is the case, however, how are we to explain all the biblical and rabbinic descriptions that portray God as having physical characteristics such as a face, hand, and arm and emotional attributes such as compassion and anger?

Maimonides explains that these descriptions are the result of events in the world whose cause we attribute to God. In fact, God does not have an "outstretched arm" or a "face," nor does He show anger or compassion. God, however, acts, and the consequences of His actions are described in human terms as being similar to what we know is the result of an action of a hand or an action done with anger or compassion. But, Maimonides warns, we should not confuse human actions with divine actions by attributing to God what are merely human physical or emotional characteristics. God is by nature above that.[22]

Maimonides was troubled by many of the biblical and *Talmudic* expressions that portray God in very human terms. The Bible speaks of God's hand, face, front, back, and eyes as well as his hearing, seeing, and anger. The rabbinic literature even portrays God as crying and wearing a prayer shawl. Were these to be taken literally as suggesting that God has the same characteristics, emotions, and habits as humans? There were, in fact, several popular books in the Middle Ages that asserted that God literally has physical dimensions of awesome proportion. Or were these to be taken as metaphors, symbols, or mere figures of speech? If that were the case, how are they to be interpreted and understood?

Maimonides explained the biblical anthropomorphisms—expressions that attribute human physical characteristics to God—as being necessary to convey to the ancient Israelites a sense of God's existence, actions, and providence. The anthropopathisms—expressions that attribute emotions to God—really mean to convey God's moral attributes and the myriad ways in which He governs the universe. Maimonides was also disturbed by passages in the Oral Torah that describe God as crying and praying. In response to this, Maimonides states: "Anyone who is led to believe that God has a body is a heretic!"[23] Still, in the thirteenth century, his view was criticized by Rabbi Avraham ben David (*RABaD*), Isaac the Blind's father and one of the leading rabbis of France, who defended the belief that God has anthropomorphic and anthropopathic qualities.[24]

Gradually, Maimonides' conception of God gained acceptance and replaced many of the widespread views that God has physical and emotional characteristics. Maimonides' God was the hidden God of the rabbinic tradition taken to the extreme. Maimonides explained that the biblical and *Talmudic* passages that speak of God in human terms are not meant to be taken literally. They are mere figures of speech since "Torah speaks as if in the language of the sons of man."[25]

Maimonides professes that there can be no substantive relationship between God and man since God is unique, incorporeal, and transcendent. There is nothing that God and man share since man is corporeal and rooted in the physical world. There can be no essential relationship between two beings who share nothing in common. Maimonides, in an attempt to refine and purify the rabbinic conception of God, makes God so removed from humanity that there is almost no human contact with Him. Maimonides attempts to resolve the paradox inherent in the rabbinic view that God is both remote and near by concluding that since God cannot be both, He must be one or the other. His philosophic consistency led him to the conclusion that God must be remote and inaccessible.

Maimonides widens the abyss separating God and man. He taught that God is unique and unknowable. From the time of Maimonides, few challenged his notion of God's essential uniqueness and remoteness. The challenge that remained was how to reestablish a relationship between man and the unknowable God. That challenge was met by the *Kabbalists* who sought to restore the relationship between God and man and bridge the abyss between the unreachable God and the human striving for God.

The common term for God among Maimonides' philosophic contemporaries was not the biblical and traditional written name of God: *YHVH* (known as the *Tetragrammaton* or Four-Letter Name; usually pronounced *Adonai* during prayer or *Hashem* in other contexts). They called God *bilti baal takhlit* (One Who Has No Limit, a translation from the Arabic term *la nihaya*, Without Limit), *sibbat kol ha-sibbot* (Cause of All Causes), and *shoresh kol ha-shorashim* (Root of All Roots). The philosophers stressed the impersonal aspect of God in order to emphasize God's uniqueness. For them, there is no personal God; the personal God of the Bible is only a myth, a means by which simple people imagined their God. For those who could live in the rarefied atmosphere of philosophy and had no need for a personal God, it was hard to imagine how one could attribute personality to God without diminishing His greatness.

In most respects, the *Kabbalists* and German *Hasidim* accepted Maimonides' concept of a unique and unknowable God. This is the point at which *Kabbalah* and German *Hasidism* broke with the medieval philosophic tradition and established their own religious movements. Although they agreed with Maimonides up to a point, they found it impossible to dispense with the concept of a personal God. The God of philosophy was hardly one to whom a Jew could pray. Nevertheless, there was little disagreement on the notion of the absolute impersonality of God's essence.

Elazar of Worms, the leader of the German *Hasidim* and a contemporary of Isaac the Blind, composed a poem to God in the late twelfth century in which the difference between the personal yet hidden God of rabbinic Judaism and the impersonal, hidden God of Maimonides is apparent. The passage is from his *Chapters on Mystery, Unity, and Faith*:

> God is One, there is no boundary to His wisdom, no measure to His understanding, no limit to His power, and no end to His unity. He has no begin-

ning and no end. The Shaper of all and the Knower of all has neither front
nor back, height nor depth, for He has neither boundary nor end in all that
He has. The Creator of the world has neither limits nor limbs.[26]

If this impersonal God has none of the attributes given to Him in biblical
and rabbinic literature, how are the traditional attributes to be understood?
The answer of the *Kabbalists* and the *Hasidim* is bold: All the references to
anthropomorphisms and anthropopathisms in Torah and rabbinic literature
do not refer to the hidden God! They refer to something other than the
Infinite God. One of the later *Kabbalistic* writers even asserted that the true,
unknowable, transcendent God is never mentioned once in the Torah,
Prophets, or Writings.[27] To whom, then, are these references made?

The *Kabbalists* introduced a distinction between the hidden and
revealed aspects of God. The hidden, infinite aspect of God is called *Eyn Sof*
(The Infinite). This name came to be understood as the proper name for
the hidden aspect of God: *The Infinite*. The name suggests only that God
exists without implying anything about His character. In fact, according to
the *Kabbalists*, God should be referred to as *It* rather than *He*, although there
is no neuter gender in the Hebrew language. Because of the great sublimity
and transcendence of God, no name at all can be applied to *The Infinite*. The
term *Eyn Sof* only conveys that God is unlike anything we know. According
to these mystics, *The Infinite* is not the object of prayers, since *The Infinite*
has no relationship with His creatures.

The personal aspect of the hidden God is called the ten *Sefirot*, which
literally means the "Ten Numerals." Simply put, the *Kabbalists* believed that
The Infinite possessed ten aspects of His being. There are, therefore, two
natures to God's being—the infinite, unknowable essence and the ten identifiable, noninfinite aspects of His being. The major literary work of *Kabbalah*, *Sefer ha-Zohar*, contains few passages about *The Infinite* but many about
the *Sefirot*. It is possible to examine several of the important passages in *Sefer
ha-Zohar* that convey novel conceptions of *The Infinite*.

The opening passage in *Sefer ha-Zohar* begins with a discussion about
the nature of prayer and sacrifices. It is based on a biblical verse that explains
that a sacrifice is a "burnt offering to the Lord, a pleasing odor."[28] *Sefer ha-
Zohar* asks whether the pleasing odor ascends to God. The underlying problem in this passage is whether sacrifices can actually please God who is
exalted above all finite pleasures:

> Rabbi Elazar asked Rabbi Shimon: The connection between the burnt
> offering and God is made in the Holy of Holies in order to bring illumina-

tion to the world. How high does the union of the priests', Levites', and the Israelites' purposefulness ascend? Rabbi Shimon said: Our masters of Oral Torah taught: The union ascends to *The Infinite*. Every connection, unification, and perfection is hidden in the hiddenness of the One who is not reached nor known and in whom the highest purposefulness is found. *The Infinite* is not knowable and has neither beginning nor end. *The Infinite* has neither purposefulness, nor lights, nor illuminations within its own infinity. All the lights and illuminations depend on it for their existence and are, themselves, imperceptible.[29]

How high does the pleasing odor rise? Does it reach God? Can an individual bridge the abyss and reach God with his sacrifices and prayers? The answer is unambiguously positive: The union ascends to *The Infinite*! Thus, it is indeed possible to bridge the abyss through certain ritual actions and under certain specific circumstances. *The Infinite*, however, is absolutely impersonal and beyond all characterization. All that can be said about this God is that He is above everything and is called *The Infinite*.

The *Kabbalists* understand God as Maimonides describes him, with one crucial difference. The impersonal God of *Kabbalah* is influenced by human action and can, therefore, be said to have a relationship with man. In another passage of this same work, *The Infinite* is described as being impersonal; at the same time, He is characterized as the God of the Bible:

> Rabbi Shimon continued with an explanation of the verse, 'See now that I, even I, am He and there is no God but Me' (*Deut.* 32:39). Shimon said: Friends, hear these ancient words, for it is my intention to reveal a secret after receiving permission from on high. What is the meaning of 'See now that I, even I, am He?' This is the Supreme Cause, the one called The Cause of Causes because He is the cause of all those known causes (i.e., *Sefirot*). None of those known causes can act at all unless they receive permission from a higher cause, as I explained above with reference to 'Let us make man.' I mean, 'Let *us* make,' literally! It refers to two, one of which says to the one above it, 'Let us make,' It did nothing until it had permission and assent from the cause above it which could not act unless it, in turn, had the agreement from the cause above it. But about the One who is called The Cause of Causes, above which there is none and below which it has no equal, it is said, 'To whom shall you liken Me and compare Me,' says the Holy One? (*Is.* 40:25). This is the one who says, 'See now that I, even I, am He and there is no God but Me.'[30]

The hidden God is active and causative of other stages of being, the *Sefirot*. He causes the *Sefirot* to come into existence. They, in turn, are "causes" that produce other stages of being. Each cause has a cause except for *The Infinite*, which is the uncaused cause. It causes but is not caused. The highest cause is identical with God who is unlike, and cannot be compared with, any of the lesser causes. This is also one of the rare instances in which the *Kabbalists* state that *The Infinite* is mentioned in the Bible.

The lesser causes, the *Sefirot*, constitute the personal aspect of God that is manifest in the narratives of the Bible. For example, it is not *The Infinite* but the *Sefirot* who create man. Together, the infinite and the finite, the impersonal and the personal, the higher and the lower aspects of God, constitute the being known as God.

In the century before the appearance of *Sefer ha-Zohar*, a Spanish *Kabbalist*, Azriel of Gerona, composed a catechism of Jewish mystical beliefs. He attempts to convey in direct language the mystical conception of *The Infinite*:

> That which is without limit is called *The Infinite*. It is absolute perfection in complete unity which does not change. If it is without limit, there is nothing beside it. Since it is sublime, it is the root of all things visible and unseen. Since it is hidden, it is the basis of faith and of disbelief. We are unable to grasp it except by saying what it is not.[31]

Azriel represented the school of *Kabbalistic* thought that sought to retrace the stages of being back to the first cause. He concluded that the first cause is unique, infinite, impersonal, and unknowable. Little else can be said about this being.

This understanding of God's nature goes far beyond the notions of divine transcendence found in the Bible. It directly contradicts the more intimate and personal characterizations of God found in biblical and rabbinic literature. This *Kabbalistic* conception was philosophically consistent with the premise of God's uniqueness, but it carried the notion to its extreme. *The Infinite* is certainly not the God with whom one can have a relationship or to whom one might pray for help. It is even hard to imagine that this might be the God who spoke on top of the mountain in Sinai.

The introduction of the concept of *The Infinite* was the common legacy of Maimonides and the early *Kabbalah*. The Jewish mystics followed the basic conception of God introduced by Maimonides, who divested the concept of God of all anthropomorphic and anthropopathic properties. The *Kabbalists*, however, did not follow the philosophers so far as to assert that God was above all relations with man. The *Kabbalists* preserved the imper-

sonality and infinity of God while preserving the essential religious relationship between man and God. The *Kabbalists*, paradoxically, prayed to the
unique, unknowable God of Maimonides. They preserved the notions of
God's transcendence and nearness in a new way. They accepted the widening of the abyss yet, at the same time, made the challenge of reaching *The
Infinite* the central element of their religion. Their mysticism is based on
their pursuit of the unique and unreachable God.

We cannot know the infinite God directly. At the same time, we are
each and all created in the image of God. The image of God—of *The Infinite*—is within each of us. Because we each contain a divine spark, we are
each, in some way, divine. We are each filled with the mysterious presence
of *The Infinite*. In fact, the entire universe is divine. As one Kabbalist said:
"All existence is God: The essence of *The Infinite* is found in every thing."[32]
Another Jewish mystic said: "All the world is divine, even the particles of
earth beneath my feet, as well as the air I breathe within me, and all that
exists is filled with divinity. Master of the World! Draw me close to You,
surround me with all Your blessings, in complete harmony."[33] The presence
of the Infinite cannot be touched, measured, or grasped but it can be experienced. We cannot see God's face but we can experience His presence
within the world. This is what the *Kabbalists* called *The Infinite*.

The essence of divinity is found in every single thing. According to
some *Kabbalists*, nothing but *The Infinite* exists:

> Since *The Infinite* causes every thing to be, no thing can live by anything
> else. It enlivens them; its existence exists in each existent. Do not attribute
> duality to God. Let God be solely God. If you suppose that *The Infinite* ema-
> nates until a certain point, and that from that point on is outside of it, you
> have made two gods. God forbid! Realize, rather, that *The Infinite* exists in
> each existent. Do not say, "This is a stone and not God." God forbid!
> Rather, all existence is God, and the stone is a thing pervaded by divinity.[34]

The Infinite produces something other than itself through a process of emanation, an overflow of the divine essence. Still, because *The Infinite* is itself
in the overflow, the essence of everything is *The Infinite* itself:

> Before anything is emanated, there was only *The Infinite*. *The Infinite* was all
> that existed. Similarly, after it brought into being that which exists, there is
> nothing but *The Infinite*. You cannot find anything that exists apart from it.
> There is nothing that is not pervaded by the power of divinity. If there were,
> *The Infinite* would be limited, subject to duality, God forbid! Rather, God is

everything that exists, though everything that exists is not God. It is present in everything, and everything comes into being from it. Nothing is devoid of its divinity. Everything is within it; it is within everything and outside of everything. There is nothing but it.[35]

The universe is essentially a unity filled with *The Infinite* even though we inhabit a world that appears separate and distinct from God. The *Kabbalists* argue that divine and human existence is indivisible:

God is unified Oneness—one without two, inestimable. Genuine divine existence engenders the existence of all of creation. The sublime, inner essences secretly constitute a chain linking everything from the highest to the lowest, extending from the upper pool to the edge of the universe. There is nothing—not even the tiniest thing—that is not fastened to the links of this chain. Everything is linked in its mystery, caught in its oneness. God is one, God's secret is one, all the worlds below and above are all mysteriously one. Divine existence is indivisible. The entire chain is one. Down to the last link, everything is linked with everything else; so divine essence is below as well as above, in heaven and on earth. There is nothing else.[36]

This mystical outlook is what enables a person to sense *The Infinite* in everything. The mystic quest is the pursuit of oneness through searching for the presence of *The Infinite* in everything we do.

4

THE CALCULUS OF
THE DIVINE WORLD

The Teaching of the *Sefirot*

The primary characteristics of *The Infinite* are impersonal—
incorporeality, absolute immateriality, and unchangeability. The
impersonal description of God is the result of God's absolute dissimilarity to
anything known to humans and our consequent inability to say anything
positive about God. All that can be known about God is that He is not like
anything human. Therefore, the only possible description of God comes
through excluding all those human qualities by which we describe ourselves
such as our corporeality, our composition of body and mind, and our
changeable actions and thoughts. The *Kabbalists* believed that the only statements that we can make about God are what He is not. This did not mean,
however, that we are ignorant of God's existence. On the contrary, it is only
God's nature that is unfathomable.

The *Kabbalists* thought the most likely description of God was as pure
Mind. He is a mind without body, a universal intelligence that is unlike any
other mind, the infinite and inconceivable mind of the universe. This infinite mind is always thinking, never changing, and thinks only infinite
thoughts about itself. Thus *The Infinite* is the perfect mind thinking perfect,
infinite thoughts completely unrelated to anything but itself. God is the one
who is thinking, the very act of thinking, and the object of His own
thought.

This would be an apt and appropriate characterization of a universal intelligence if there were no world. God, the pure mind, does not think about anything but His own essence and has no concern with the world. But Judaism teaches that there is a world which God created, cares for, and with which He has a relationship. The *Kabbalists* teach that this infinite mind neither created a world nor has any relation to it. *The Infinite* is not the God of the Bible nor the object of traditional prayer. The *Kabbalists* agree: "It is inappropriate to say of *The Infinite* 'blessed be He,' 'glorified be He,' 'praised be He,' or similar expressions."[1]

How do these *Kabbalists*, then, solve the problem of preserving God's unity while at the same time preserving the traditional relationship between God and man? Moreover, how is it possible to describe God as unchangeable if at times He has spoken to man and at other times He is silent? Do these *Kabbalists* mean to say that all of the traditional teachings of Judaism about God are wrong? Or do they suggest that the object of our prayers is not the true God but some lower, less infinite manifestation of God?

The *Kabbalists* introduced the idea that *The Infinite* possesses ten aspects of His revealed Being, or instruments of activity, called *Sefirot*. The term *Sefirot* originally meant "numerals" and was taken from the earliest Hebrew text on the nature of numbers and letters, *Sefer Yetzirah* (Book of Formation). It is a generic term that, in itself, just means that the aspects of God's being, or the instruments of God's activity, can be counted—there are ten *Sefirot* just as there are ten cardinal numbers. Some mystics explain that the term *Sefirot* comes from the Hebrew root *sapper*, which means "to tell," suggesting that these aspects "tell" us about God. Others have suggested that it derives from the Hebrew word for the *sapphire* gem since the *Sefirot* illuminate our knowledge of God like a precious and radiant jewel. The term itself tells us little about the meaning and nature of the *Sefirot*.

There have been a variety of attempts to translate the term *Sefirot* into English. They have often been called "spheres," "radiances," and other terms suggesting different occult meanings. The *Sefirot*, however, are symbols of the various aspects of God's being or activities that are identifiable as ten in number. A more faithful English rendition would be *Calculi,* a term that signifies both a means of reckoning and the use of symbols, for the *Sefirot* are numerically identifiable symbols of God's being and activities. Although a good English translation of *Sefirot* would be desirable, the use of the original Hebrew term is still preferable.

The *Sefirot* are the bridge across the abyss, the connective tissue between the infinite God and the finite world. They are the link that makes it possible to preserve God's absolute unity while preserving the relationship between God and man. They, and not *The Infinite*, are the object of human prayers and the subject to which all biblical anthropomorphisms and anthropopathisms refer. The *Sefirot*, not *The Infinite*, are the God of the Bible.

By differentiating between *The Infinite* and the *Sefirot*, it is possible to say that God is incorporeal, immaterial, and unchangeable while still preserving the traditional notion of the God who spoke at Sinai. All the references to the traditional notion of an active, personal God refer to the *Sefirot*, which are the subject of biblical anthropomorphic and anthropopathic references. All the references to God that imply corporeality, composition, and change refer to the *Sefirot*, not to *The Infinite*. Therefore, one Kabbalist can justifiably claim that "*The Infinite* is nowhere mentioned in the Bible." The Bible refers only to the *Sefirot*, not to the hidden God.

The theory of the *Sefirot* is an attempt to explain how the infinite God can have a relationship with any finite thing and how an unknowable God can be known by man. The relationship of *The Infinite* to the *Sefirot* can generally be explained only by drawing an analogy. One of the most common *Kabbalistic* analogies is that of the relation of the soul to the body. The soul, invisible and unknowable, dwells within the body. Although there is only one soul in each body, the soul acts through a variety of physical organs. The soul is, therefore, the essence that uses the "instruments" of the body for its activity. The manner in which the soul is connected to the body is still a mystery. Nonetheless, we claim to know that there is a soul even if it remains inscrutable because of its incorporeal nature.

The *Sefirot* are understood by one school of *Kabbalists* as the vessels or instruments through which God acts.[2] *The Infinite* is like the soul in relation to the *Sefirot*, which are its vessels or organs. In order to avoid suggesting that *The Infinite* itself acts, these *Kabbalists*, who may be called *instrumentalists*, explain that the *Sefirot* are God's vessels. In their view, *The Infinite*, whose infinite nature has nothing in common with the *Sefirot*, remains totally passive and unchangeable. What appear to be changes are only the various modes by which the *Sefirot* channel, reflect, and employ the essence of *The Infinite*. Change, to paraphrase Molly Bawn, is in the eye of the beholder.

Other *Kabbalists*, who might be called *essentialists*, believe that the *Sefirot* are God's essence, and that there is a common nature to *The Infinite* and the *Sefirot*. They adopted this position in order to avoid suggesting that we pray to some being other than God. If prayer is directed to the *Sefirot*, the worshipper might, in their view, be praying to a false god or, worse yet, to different gods, unless the *Sefirot* were indistinguishable from *The Infinite*.

These two views, the theory of "vessels" and the theory of "essence," were one of the few major points of difference among the *Kabbalists*. Although there was only one *Kabbalah*, these two schools of thought represented two fundamentally different approaches to the problem of how God could be both hidden and revealed.

The instrumentalist doctrine of the *Sefirot* as vessels seeks to avoid attributing change or composition to God's essence by relating them to His vessels, not His essence. The only essence of God is His infinite, unchangeable essence. The *Sefirot* are mere instruments of His activity. None of the changes attributed to God through the anthropomorphic or anthropopathic descriptions in the Bible refer to the hidden God; they refer to the *Sefirot*, which are distinct from the hidden God. Each *Sefirah* is separate and distinct from the hidden God because each one is an instrument through which *The Infinite* acts. Each instrument is another dimension of divine activity. When the Bible speaks of God's compassion or judgment, it does not refer to *The Infinite* that is above all definition, but to the *Sefirot*, instruments such as "compassion" or "judgment." When the Bible speaks of God's hand, eye, front, or back and the like, it refers symbolically to the *Sefirot*. Therefore, all the attributes of God refer to the *Sefirot*, the vessels through which God acts that are distinguished from God's essence.

The *Sefirot* can be seen as containing the divine essence like the body contains the soul. They share, in some way, the infinite nature of the essence that acts through them. The *Sefirot* are not the hidden God, but neither are they *not* the hidden God. They are both infinite and finite because they are the bridge that links God's infinity to everything else. They are infinite because they are the vessels of *The Infinite*; they are finite because they are not *The Infinite*. God acts through the *Sefirot* in bringing all other things into existence and in governing the world. Prayers, praises, and descriptions of God are directed at the *Sefirot*, not to the infinite God who remains recondite and inscrutable, infinite and impersonal, unrelated and indifferent to the world. The doctrine of the *Sefirot* as vessels succeeds in avoiding attributing change or activity to the hidden God at the expense of the concept of a personal God.

The portion of the *Zohar* known as *Ra'aya Mehemna* (Faithful Shepherd) contains many selections that reflect the instrumentalist theory. In one such section, God is described as acting without being known because He acts through the instrumentality of the *Sefirot*. Like an overflowing ocean, *The Infinite*, called here the first *Sefirah*, emanates the next two *Sefirot*, described as a channel and a basin, to contain the vast ocean waters:

Woe to one who compares *The Infinite* to any of the human characteristics or even to one of His own attributes, all the more so to one who compares Him to humans who are born and die. God may be characterized according to His governance upon a particular attribute (i.e., one of the *Sefirot*) or even upon all the created beings. When He disappears above and beyond that attribute, He cannot be said to have that attribute, characteristic or form. God is like the ocean for the waters of the ocean cannot be grasped and have no shape except when they are channeled into a vessel, such as the land, and take on a shape; then we are able to measure them: the source—the waters of the ocean—are one. Then, a tributary comes forth and is channeled into a round basin. The source is one and the channel which comes from it is two. Next, a large vessel is formed, as if one dug a large basin which becomes filled by the waters of the channel; this becomes three. Now, if the artificer would break these vessels which he created, the waters would return to the source and only broken vessels would remain, dry and without water. Likewise, the Cause of Causes made ten *Sefirot*, calling the Crown—*Source*. There is no end to the fullness of the source's light and, therefore, He called himself *The Infinite*. Everything is within His power, to withhold from the vessels or to replenish them with fullness and withhold according to His will. There is no other God above Him who can add to Him or diminish Him.[3]

Moshe Cordovero, a leading *Kabbalist*, proposed that one can even visualize the *Sefirot* as vessels in several ways. First, the divine essence flows through the *Sefirot* as water flows through vessels of different colors. Second, the infinite essence is like the sun when it shines through a prism or stained-glass window. Neither the water nor the sunlight changes except in the eyes of the beholder:

To help you conceive this, imagine water flowing through vessels of different colors: white, red, green, and so forth. As the water spreads through those vessels, it appears to change into the colors of the vessels, although the water is devoid of all color. The change in color does not affect the water itself, just our perception of the water. So it is with the *Sefirot*. They are vessels, known, for example, as *Hesed, Gevurah,* and *Tiferet,* each colored according to its function, white, red, and green, respectively, while the light of the Emanator—their essence—is the water, having no color at all. This essence does not change; it only appears to change as it flows through the vessels. Better yet, imagine a ray of sunlight shining through a stained-glass window of ten different colors. The sunlight possesses no color at all but appears to change hue as it passes through the different colors of glass. Colored light radiates through the window. The light has not essentially changed, though so it seems to the viewer. Just so with the *Sefirot*. The light that clothes itself in the vessels of the *Sefirot* is the essence, like the ray of sunlight. That essence does not change color at all, neither judgment nor compassion, neither right nor left. Yet by emanating through the *Sefirot*—the variegated stained glass—judgment or compassion prevails.[4]

The first three *Sefirot* are described as follows: *The Infinite* is described as being indistinguishable from the first vessel. This first *Sefirah*, an infinite and undifferentiated expanse, is the source of everything else. Then the essence of *The Infinite* is channeled into a tributary that gives the first definition to the boundless expanse. This tributary is the second *Sefirah*. Next the channel empties into a basin that is defined by the contours of the land around it. The basin is the third *Sefirah*, and the land around it constitutes the other *Sefirot*. This analogy suggests that the *Sefirot* are vessels or channels that limit *The Infinite* and give finite definition to everything else. The description is also reminiscent of the creation narrative in *Genesis* and suggests a parallel between the creation of the *Sefirot* and the creation of the world.

The instrumentalist conception of *The Infinite* is profoundly impersonal. *The Infinite* is thoroughly removed from everything and never reveals itself. All the descriptions that are usually associated with the personal concept of God as the being who reveals Himself, cares about man, and answers his prayers are relegated to the *Sefirot*. In order to consider *The Infinite* as God, the mystic must be willing to engage in an unusual degree of remoteness and abstraction.

The doctrine of the *Sefirot* as the essence of God is an attempt to preserve the concept of a personal God. It does, however, imply that God's essence changes according to the differences among each of the *Sefirot*. *Kabbalists* of this persuasion believed that it was more important to preserve the notion of a personal God than it was to preserve the unity of God. These *Kabbalists* describe the relation of *The Infinite* to the *Sefirot* by an analogy to a candle. Many candles can be lit from one candle without ever changing the nature of the first candle. Therefore, one unique essence can be the source of many other essences without undergoing any essential change.

The essentialists also believed that the descriptions and attributes that appear in the Bible refer to the *Sefirot* and not to *The Infinite*. Unlike the instrumentalists, however, they claim that God is portrayed in the Bible since the *Sefirot* are God's essence. Thus, they are able to preserve the personal concept of God while referring all of the anthropomorphisms and anthropopathisms to the *Sefirot*, not *The Infinite*.

The difference between *The Infinite* and the *Sefirot* is one of degree.

The Infinite emanates the *Sefirot* like a powerful transmitter that broadcasts signals through space. They call this process *Atzilut* (emanation). The *Sefirot* are the broadcast signals, which do not differ essentially from the original transmission no matter how far they travel. The *Sefirot* are the same as *The Infinite*, but their distance from the source produces a slightly different impression depending upon the reception. Therefore, the only difference between *The Infinite* and the *Sefirot* is according to the reception, that is, according to which particular *Sefirah* receives the emanation. God is *The Infinite*, but sometimes He is perceived through one *Sefirah*, whereas, at other times He is perceived through another. God never changes; only our perception changes. The changes in our perception, or reception, correspond to the different *Sefirot*.

In the essentialist scheme, each *Sefirah* differs from the other according to its distance from *The Infinite*. There are altogether ten *Sefirot*, and each one emanates from *The Infinite*. The first is more sublime and more pure than the tenth, but each one contains the essence of *The Infinite*. Each one reflects another aspect of God's nature, or essence. When it appears that God acts in different ways, it is really a different *Sefirah* acting.

If, as the essentialists maintain, the *Sefirot* are just different aspects of one infinite essence, the personal aspect of God is preserved although the unity of God is somewhat compromised. On the other hand, the instrumentalists preserve the integrity of the divine unity while sacrificing the personal aspect of God. While neither theory is able to preserve both divine personality and unity, the two schools of thought flourished side by side according to the predilections and theological inclinations of the Kabbatists.

The term *Sefirot* first appears in one ancient text—*Sefer Yetzirah*—and later in a medieval text—*Sefer ha-Bahir*. These texts, however, do not employ the term in the same sense that it came to mean in *Kabbalah*. The earliest *Kabbalistic* treatises in Gerona, particularly the writings of Azriel, describe the *Sefirot* in ways that came to be accepted among all subsequent *Kabbalistic* writers. The Gerona *Kabbalists* also codified the names of the individual *Sefirot* although some variations in the exact names persisted.

The *Kabbalists*, following the definition found in *Sefer Yetzirah*, taught that there are ten *Sefirot*. It was left to the Gerona *Kabbalists*, the disciples of Isaac the Blind, to identify the *Sefirot* by name. Six of the names were derived from the biblical verse:

> Yours, Lord, are greatness (*Gedulah*), might (*Gevurah*), splendor (*Tiferet*), triumph (*Netzah*), and majesty (*Hod*) . . . to you, Lord, belong kingship (*Mamlakhah*) . . .[5]

Each of these terms was understood as an attribute of God that the *Kabbalists* included in their list of ten *Sefirot*. To these six they added three others to represent the idea that God is pure Mind. These three, *Keter* (crown), *Hokhmah* (wisdom), and *Binah* (understanding), were placed at the top of the list. A ninth, *Yesod* (foundation), was inserted, and the decad was complete.

Keter (crown), is the first *Sefirah* emanated from *The Infinite*. It is the highest and most glorious of the *Sefirot* and crowns them all. It stands as the barrier between *The Infinite* and the other *Sefirot* and, so, encircles and crowns *The Infinite*. Because each *Sefirah* is emanated from another, the highest one, *Keter*, stands hierarchically above them all. *Keter* is the archetype of God as king. It is *Keter* who calls Himself "I Am That I Am" in Torah.

Sometimes *Keter* is identified with *The Infinite*. Most often, however, *Keter* is the first *Sefirah* radiated, or emanated, by *The Infinite*, which stands above it. Those who identify *Keter* with *The Infinite* lean toward the essentialist view and believe that the *Sefirot* are only different stages in the unfolding of God's infinite essence. Those who believe that *Keter* is the first *Sefirah* and is not identical with *The Infinite*, generally follow the view that *The Infinite* acts through vessels, the *Sefirot*, and that God and His vessels are not similar. Therefore, the essentialists favor the personalist notion of God and theorize that *Keter* is the same as *The Infinite*. The instrumentalists believe that God is impersonal, and *The Infinite* is above *Keter*.

There are many other names for *Keter* in *Kabbalah*. It is often called *Ayin* (nothingness) because it is beyond all existence yet is the cause of all existing things. In the *Prayer of Nehunyah ben ha-Kanah*, written in the thirteenth century, a hymn to *Keter* appears:

> Everything is in it, for the internal powers of the *Sefirot* are in it. The vitality and existence of everything stem from it. It is analogous to the soul that gives life to the body and constitutes it. The constitution of everything is in *Keter*. There is no front or back, right or left, in this *Sefirah*. It is called Indifferent Unity.[6]

It is also called *Hokhmah Penimit* (internal wisdom) because it is the hidden potentiality of divine wisdom before it is revealed. It is sometimes called *Mahshavah Elohit* (divine thought) because it is produced by *The Infinite*, Pure Mind. *Keter* is similar to *The Infinite* in many of these respects but different in others. It differs in that it is the highest aspect of God that moves into activity out of the repose of *The Infinite*. Both *The Infinite* and *Keter* are unknowable and imperceptible. *Keter* is the more active representation of God's will which cannot be known except during the rare moment when God chose to reveal Himself as *Ehyeh Asher Ehyeh* (I Am What I Am). The *Kabbalists* display a certain ambivalence about whether *Keter* can be known.

In the following passage, *The Infinite* and *Keter* are described paradoxically as the hidden and revealed will of God, respectively. *Keter*, however, cannot be known except through the unique intuition that comes about through mystical revelation.

> Rabbi Shimon said: I raise my hands upward in prayer. When the Divine Will up above (i.e., *The Infinite*) shines upon the Will which is eternally unknown and imperceptible, the first hidden Upper Will (i.e., *Keter*) produces its unknowable creation and radiates what it does secretly. Then, the Will of Divine Thought pursues the first Will in order to be illuminated by it. A curtain is then opened and, from inside, with the Divine Will pursuing (the Upper Will), it reaches and yet does not reach (up) and the curtain begins to radiate. Then, the Divine Thought is illuminated secretly and remains unknown, hidden. The illumination coming from the hidden unknown Upper Will strikes the light of the curtain which is lit up by the Will which is unknown, unknowable and concealed. The light of the Concealed Thought strikes the light of the curtain and they both radiate, creating nine palaces.[7]

This passage illustrates how, in moments of deep revelation, Rabbi Shimon bar Yohai, the voice of the *Zohar*, reveals his mystical knowledge. *The Infinite* emanates its essence upon *Keter* and activates it. Then *Keter* turns back to *The Infinite* to draw down further essence linking them together. As *Keter* turns back to reflect its light towards *The Infinite*, its source, it strikes a barrier that stands between it and *The Infinite*. The barrier reflects the light of *Keter* back to it and creates the third *Sefirah*. A similar process of emanation and reflection continues with the creation of each of the ten *Sefirot*.

The *Kabbalists* placed great importance on the inner workings of God, especially on the relationship between *The Infinite* and *Keter*. They attempted to explain how the infinite God can bridge the abyss between Himself and the world. In the passage above, there is very little difference between *The Infinite* and *Keter* except the slight gradations of difference between the Divine Will and the Upper Will. Still, there is a curtain that separates them. When they sweep aside that separation, they radiate against each other and create the other *Sefirot*.

Some *Kabbalists* were disturbed by the idea that there is little difference between *The Infinite* and *Keter*. They believed that there were a series of three imperceptible luminous beings that interposed between *The Infinite* and *Keter*. They radiate out from *The Infinite* and become embedded in *Keter*. *Keter* then becomes God's Pure Thought. This is described in the following passage quoted from the pseudepigraphic *Responsum of Hai Gaon*:

> The three supernal lights have no beginning for they are the name and essence and Root of All Roots. Thought cannot apprehend them because apprehension is impossible and the knowledge of all creatures is too weak to comprehend the Holy Name. We have learned their names: Primordial Internal Light which radiates in the hidden root and shines, from its radiant power, the likeness of the two great luminaries; Polished Light and Clear Light, all of which are one light, one essence, and one root hidden infinitely.[8]

Keter cannot be known because it is either identical with, or only slightly different from, *The Infinite*. Like a king who is hidden from most of his subjects, he can be known by his venerable crown, which is filled with precious gems and diamonds. *Keter* is, however, identified as Divine Thought and the source of all the other *Sefirot*. The thirteenth-century *Tradition of Wisdom from the Sages of Mata Mehasya* describes *Keter*:

> Supernal *Keter* is a world hidden unto itself. All the *Sefirot* receive from its emanation even though it is separate, recondite and bound up with the Root of All Roots which cannot be apprehended by thought. *Keter* receives from the root without any interruption in a subtle whisper. It emanates and pours forth from its reservoir upon the other crowns which are always close to its emanation.[9]

The unknowability of *Keter* is due to its identity with, or proximity to, *The Infinite*. Yet it is also the root of all the other phenomena of the world, especially the other *Sefirot*. It is the cause of the *Sefirot* and produces them through emanation. Emanation, according to most *Kabbalists*, is a process of hypertrophy, or overflow, from *The Infinite*. *The Infinite* is, by nature, effulgent and tends to spread its essence outward. The *Sefirot* are there to receive this essence.

Emanation, according to other *Kabbalists*, most notably Nahmanides, is a process in which *The Infinite* limits its own infinity through contracting or constricting itself. God cannot create anything directly from His own boundless and infinite essence unless He voluntarily limits Himself.[10] The

Kabbalists use the analogy of the sun to explain this process. The radiant light of the sun shines endlessly due to its great power and brilliance. Nothing could be seen, however, unless the unbridled light of the sun is restricted, allowing for the emergence of shapes, contours, and details. In the same manner the radiance of *The Infinite* must be contracted and limited through the emanation of *Keter*, a channeling of the infinite Mind and Will into the more defined Thought and Will. *Keter* is the means by which the infinite God makes all other creations possible. It is the transition between God's infinity and the finite world.

It is ironic that the *Kabbalists* should have so much to say about an unknowable God. They speculated endlessly on the nature of God and on the *Sefirot*. Although much consideration was given to *The Infinite* and *Keter*, the *Kabbalists* recognized that human knowledge could never adequately penetrate the secrets of the infinite God. Much more analysis was devoted to the *Sefirot* below *Keter*, beginning with *Hokhmah*.

In the biblical Book of *Proverbs*, several passages speak of God's Wisdom, which existed alongside Him before He created the world:

> The Lord created me at the beginning of His course as the first of His works of old.[11]

Later, the rabbinic sages developed this notion with the suggestion that God employed His Wisdom (*Hokhmah*) in the creation of the world.[12] The *Kabbalists* elevated His Wisdom, gave it individual existence, and made it the second *Sefirah*. They called it *Hokhmah*, *Reshit* (Beginning), *Yesh* (Being), and *Abba* (Father), because it is the first being to have existence outside of *The Infinite*. *Hokhmah* is the first aspect of God that is knowable. It is knowable through the Torah that existed in God's mind as His thought before it was given to Moses. *Hokhmah* is the totality of divine thought before any single thought occurs. All archetypes, ideas, things, principles exist within *Hokhmah* in potentiality. *Hokhmah* is the active power of God that emanates all the archetypes, ideas, things, and principles. *Hokhmah* is the archetype of God as father. *Hokhmah* is called *Yah* in the Hebrew Bible.

Hokhmah contains within itself the archetypes, the ideal prefiguration of all things. It is the divine realm of the perfect model and blueprint of everything that might come into existence at some later stage of God's unfolding of His being. Since *The Infinite* and *Keter* are the divine will, *Hokhmah* is the sum total of all the possibilities of existence. Everything that might conceivably come into being anywhere and at any time exists within

Hokhmah as sheer possibility. In *Hokhmah*, things exist in a general way as concepts, ideas, or principles, not as individual phenomena. The archetypes are static and undifferentiated and *Hokhmah* is the blueprint and ultimate model upon which the universe is created. *Hokhmah* is God's idea of what the world should be.

Hokhmah is the ideal pattern for the world and exists deep within the recesses of the divine Mind. Because *Hokhmah* is associated both with the essence of God and the blueprint of the universe, the *Kabbalists* imply that the universe must first exist within *Hokhmah* before it can stand on its own. The universe is ultimately indistinguishable from God's essence. Everything that is later to be found in the universe is first found in *Hokhmah*.

The very tendency to emanate the archetypes of existence is also associated with *Hokhmah*. *Hokhmah* is the generative and active power within God that emanates the archetypes into reality. Because *Hokhmah* is understood to be active and even procreative, it is often described in masculine terms as the Father of the other *Sefirot*. *Hokhmah* is, therefore, the archetype of masculinity and activity.

The sexual overtones and the association of masculinity with activity lead to a differentiation between so called masculine and feminine *Sefirot*. If *Hokhmah* is masculine, *Binah* (understanding), which is emanated from it, is feminine. *Kabbalistic* treatises describe how *Hokhmah* emanates the third *Sefirah*, *Binah*, also called *Imma* (mother). *Binah* is impregnated with the archetypes found within *Hokhmah*. Within *Binah*, the embryonic archetypes become more distinct and differentiated into specific phenomena. *Binah* is the second aspect of God that is knowable. *Hokhmah* impregnates *Binah* with the archetypes, ideas, and principles of all things. They grow within *Binah* as within a womb. *Binah* is the receptive power in God that allows all the archetypes, ideas, and principles to develop. *Binah* is the totality of divine ideas. *Binah* is the archetype of God as mother. It is *Binah* who is called *El* in the Torah.

Hokhmah becomes associated with masculinity and the trait of activity. *Binah* becomes associated with femininity and receptivity. While these notions reflect the way the *Kabbalists* understood the process of emanation, they also reflect medieval ideas about sex-role differentiation. With these two *Sefirot*, the *Kabbalists* set the stage for the establishment of opposing, or contrary, powers that would carry out the process of emanation. From this point on, the *Sefirot* are divided into masculine and feminine vessels or essences.

The fourth and fifth *Sefirot*, called *Hesed* (mercy) and *Din* (judgment), are emanated from *Hokhmah* and *Binah*. They, too, represent archetypes of contrary powers that act in the world. *Hokhmah* emanates *Hesed*, which symbolizes the power of unmitigated love and mercy. Surprisingly, *Hesed* is associated with the masculine domain. *Binah* emanates *Din*, which signifies the power of severity and absolute justice. *Hesed* and *Din*, like the two *Sefirot* before them, are seen as opposites because they represent extremes.

Hesed illustrates the divine inclination to emanate and fill the universe. It is associated with the tendency to radiate the essence of *The Infinite* without end. If this were to occur, the divine essence would permeate all corners of the universe leaving no room for anything but God. Therefore, God had to constrain Himself from acting this way by limiting Himself. This necessitated that His *Hesed* be tempered by His *Din*. *Din* represents the ability of God to limit His goodness by halting its emanation. This attribute is associated with the archetype of femininity, which the *Kabbalists* understood in terms of severity and limitation. *Hesed* is the tendency to emanation; *Din* is the tendency to withhold the emanation. Since too much emanation would not allow room for the universe to exist, both are necessary.

Hesed is also called *Gedulah* (Greatness). *Hesed* is the excess, abundance, and overflow of divine love without end. It is an active power, the impulse to fill the world with divinity. It appears as the merciful God who has compassion upon the world even when it does not deserve compassion. It is exemplified in the biblical patriarch Abraham.

Din is also called *Gevurah* (Power). *Din* is the withholding of divine love that appears to us as divine judgment. It is dormant by itself but, like a volcano, it can erupt and spew evil and punishment into the world. It appears as the God who judges the world severely. It is also considered to be the sinister "left hand" of God. Primitive notions that associated femininity and sinister forces also entered *Kabbalah*. The *Kabbalists* linked together the *Sefirah Din* with femininity, left-sidedness, and the demonic. As the feminine, *Din* curtails the activity of *Hesed*. *Din* itself is said to be capable of issuing its own emanation, which takes shape outside of the world of the *Sefirot* as the realm of demonic forces. The "left emanation" from *Din* creates a universe of evil that stands locked in permanent and mortal combat with the power of the *Sefirot*. The mythology of *Din* is meant to convey that there is not a great essential difference between good and evil, and that one God has created them both.

The archetypes of *Hokhmah*, *Binah*, *Hesed*, and *Din*, respectively, also represent the ideal types of intellectual and moral qualities that are found in man. The archetypes are the blueprint upon which God lays out the plan of the world. But ideal archetypes rarely exist in nature because they are rarely found except in combination with other qualities. Also, these ideal types are extremes that tend to stand in conflict with their opposites. Therefore, the *Kabbalists* introduced the sixth *Sefirah, Tiferet* (splendor), in order to harmonize the intellectual and moral opposites within the *Sefirot.*

The *Kabbalists* taught that the world is a place of conflict between opposing forces: good and evil, life and death, holiness and impurity, obedience and sin, reward and punishment, masculinity and femininity, knowledge and ignorance. They further believed that these polarities were rooted in the *Sefirot,* particularly in the polar *Sefirot* of *Hesed* and *Din.* On the other hand, they believed that no one power is able to act by itself. The masculine *Sefirot* need the feminine in order to act. Without its opposite, each of the *Sefirot* could only act in a monolithic and extreme fashion. *Hokhmah* could not be truly creative unless *Binah* gave definition to the archetypes within it. *Hesed* could not bring about a universe unless *Din* gave the world definition and limit. Alone, the polarities of the *Sefirot*—right and left, active and passive, male and female, good and evil—are inadequate. A universe of extremes cannot endure. All opposites need to be moderated by another element in order to be brought into a state of harmony and balance.

If the two pairs of *Sefirot* (*Hokhmah* and *Binah, Hesed* and *Din*) are the polarities of Father-Mother, Love-Judgment, *Tiferet* is the state of harmony between these opposing forces, the moderation of opposites. While God may act in absolute ways through these four *Sefirot, Tiferet* balances these opposite qualities. *Tiferet* is the axis and stable center of God. *Tiferet* is the traditional God who is the subject of religion and the object of prayers: "The Holy One, Blessed Be He." It is also signified in the biblical name of God—*YHVH.*

The moderation of opposites among the *Sefirot* of *Hesed* and *Din* occurs with the emanation of *Tiferet.* This *Sefirah* harmonizes the boundless love of *Hesed* and the strict judgment of *Din.* It is often portrayed as the masculine offspring of the *Sefirot Hesed* and *Din.* It is the point of harmony between the upper *Sefirot* and the ones that come after it. Because of its pivotal role as harmonizer of the various opposing tendencies, *Tiferet* is regarded as the axis and stable center of the *Sefirot.* Because *Tiferet* symbolizes the state of harmony among the *Sefirot,* it came to be associated with the traditional name for God in rabbinic literature—*Ha-Kadosh Barukh Hu* (The Holy One Blessed Be He). *Tiferet* was understood to be the subject to which many traditional prayers were directed. Prayers that emphasized God as father and king were usually prayers referring to *Tiferet* in particular or, through it, to the *Sefirot* in general. In this way *Tiferet* was often portrayed as the representative of the other *Sefirot*. *Tiferet* came to symbolize the aspect of God that was known as the traditional God of Judaism, the God of the Hebrew Bible. *Tiferet* was the *Sefirah* that most closely symbolized the transcendent deity. It was the *Sefirah* that spoke at Sinai as the representative of the other *Sefirot*.

The *Sefirot Netzah* (triumph) and *Hod* (majesty) are often described as the instruments through which God governs the world. They correspond respectively to *Hesed* and *Din* and represent a lower manifestation of these upper *Sefirot*. Divine providence, or governance, was understood as the result of God's emanation of His essence upon the world. The further away this emanation flows from God to the world, the more diluted it becomes. In fact, if God would withhold his favor from the world, the emanation would temporarily cease and leave the world vulnerable to demonic forces or chaos. The *Sefirot* serve as the conduits for the transmission of divine grace upon the world. The *Sefirot Netzah* and *Hod* were understood as filters that pass along the emanation from *Hesed* and *Din* to the *Sefirot* below. These two *Sefirot* are the conduits by which the divine essence is transmitted from the upper *Sefirot* to *Tiferet* and, from there, to the lower *Sefirot*, especially *Malkhut*. They are the means by which divine preservation of the world is assured.

Netzah is the conduit that inspires prophecy in gifted individuals. It is divine inspiration and authority that is represented in the earthly person of Moses. *Hod* is the conduit through which God exercises his watchfulness and providence over the world. It is divine holiness that comes to be represented in the biblical figure of Aaron, the first priest.

Yesod serves as the conduit that transmits all archetypes, ideas, and the principles of all things to the last *Sefirah*. *Yesod* impregnates the tenth *Sefirah* with all that is has received from the *Sefirot* above it. Therefore, it is considered to be the phallic expression of God's masculine traits. It is also God's capacity to exercise limit, control, and restraint so as not to overwhelm the world with the power of God. Therefore, it is represented in the biblical name of God—*Shaddai* (The One Who Says: Enough!).

The tenth and last *Sefirah*, *Malkhut* (kingship), is also called the *Shekhinah* (divine presence), *Atarah* (diadem), and *Kavod* (glory). It is the last vessel of God's activity and the vehicle through which the rest of the *Sefirot* act. It is the boundary of the divine realm and the outermost vessel through which God acts. When the *Kabbalists* describe the *Sefirot* in a hierarchical scheme, this is the last of the *Sefirot*. Below this is the beginning of the nondivine realm, the end of God. *Malkhut* is also the least infinite of all God's aspects and the most accessible dimension of his personality. Thus, this *Sefirah* is the one that is most frequently known to man and the object of many prayers. *Malkhut* is the funnel through which the divine essence, carried along through the vessels of the *Sefirot*, overflows upon man and the world.

Although *Malkhut* has a masculine name, this *Sefirah* is wholly feminine. It is the intimate God of Judaism, the God who consoles, comforts, and addresses us. As the wholly feminine aspect of God, it is called the *Shekhinah* (Divine Presence). As the God who communicates with us, it is called the "Oral Torah" and the "Voice of God." *Malkhut* is the funnel through which God's essence overflows into the world. It is represented in the biblical name of God—*Adonai*.

This overflow creates the worlds below God and gives substance and sustenance to humanity. By means of this emanation, which is channeled across the abyss from God to man through this *Sefirah*, individuals are able to retrace the path to God and bridge the abyss. Knowledge of how God conveys His essence to the world through this *Sefirah* provides the key to unraveling the mystery of how one can bridge the abyss. To paraphrase the neo-Platonist Plotinus: "Everything comes from the One, and everything returns to the One." The secret of the *Sefirot* is the secret of reaching oneness with God.

Kabbalah teaches that we must imitate and emulate the *Sefirot* in order to sharpen the divine image in which we were created. *Keter* is the undifferentiated, overflowing, and selfless source of all being. We can emulate *Keter*, for example, through altruism by desiring the well-being of other people and letting another person's honor be as precious to us as our own. We can also emulate *Keter* through forgiveness by reconciling with someone who had once angered us. Just as *Keter* implants the divine presence in the *Sefirot*, we must recognize the presence of God in other people. Just as *Keter* descends into the *Sefirot* below it, so we must lower ourselves and be humble. *Keter* also leads us to other qualities, including the ability to listen positively and speak positively to others rather than listening to or engaging in gossip, anger, and provocations. A person emulating *Keter* should also be compassionate and nonjudgmental.

Hokhmah is the ultimate source of wisdom. In order to imitate *Hokhmah*, a person should foster and disseminate wisdom to others through teaching, mentoring, and communicating in measured ways that others can absorb. Just as *Hokhmah* distributes wisdom through the other *Sefirot* by drawing on its source, *Keter*, we must draw on our own source of wisdom, *Hokhmah*. Therefore, the imitation of *Hokhmah* involves the solitary turning to God in our private moments as well as reaching out as social beings to educate other people.

Binah is the source of understanding, insight, and comprehension. How do we emulate *Binah*? We turn inward, apply wisdom to the circumstances of our own lives, and gain insight into our own selves. This leads us to authenticity and self-fulfillment. When we turn towards *Binah*, we set our sights on understanding and correcting our own human flaws. Just as *Binah* seeks to return to *Keter*, we concentrate on returning to the source of our own being. *Binah* is the eternal path to our own authentic selves. But this is not an easy path and involves going deep into the recesses of our own soul. It is perhaps characterized by the awe and trembling that Kierkegaard described: "There is nothing of which every man is so afraid as getting to know how enormously much he is capable of doing and becoming."

The human quality of *Hesed* is achieved by cultivating the capacity to express an overabundance of love towards other people. Maimonides defined *Hesed* as "excess in goodness."[13] Therefore, we imitate *Hesed* by acting to nullify hostility, jealousy, and anger by responding with selfless, excessive love. We should express love to thus who attack us and act without regard for our own selves. This quality is also the ability to give fully, without limit, in order to satisfy, please, and help another person. It allows us to put the needs of another person before our own and to be generous without any ulterior motive or expectation. We may also emulate *Hesed* by religious passion that is expressed by loving God without restraint.

Din is the divine quality of judgment, severity, and stringency. If carried to excess, it can lead to harshness, cruelty, and anger. That is why the *Kabbalists* believe that *Din* must be regulated. Sometimes God must act with *Din* to establish limits. For example, if God were to act only with *Hesed*, He would never be able to limit his unbridled generosity and give birth to a finite universe. In order to establish the existence of something other than Himself, God needed to invoke limits, definitions, and boundaries. We emulate this virtue by recognizing that there are situations that call for us to act with discipline rather than excessive love. There are times when we must challenge, discipline, and, set limits or be uncompromising and firm. It is necessary, however, to be extremely careful in being measured and proportional in how far we take this quality. If we take *Din* too far, or internalize it, we may become unnecessarily harsh, cruel, or hateful. Therefore, *Din* must be invoked, when it is summoned at all, in proportion to the requirements of each particular situation rather than incorporated as a personal characteristic. We do not become *Din*; rather we utilize *Din* rather than letting *Din* use us or become us.

When we find the proper balance between excess and discipline, we have achieved harmonious balance. The *Kabbalists* view this as attaining the characteristic of *Tiferet*. Tiferet is balance, proportion, and equilibrium within the divine realm. When an individual achieves the proper balance between passion and control in their own life, he has achieved the state of *Tiferet*. The *Kabbalists* see equilibrium and self-control between the extremes of *Hesed* and *Din*—excess and constraint—as the ideal of masculinity. To emulate *Tiferet* is to have power over the conflicting forces that exist within us and to find balance between the tendency to love freely and the need to exercise emotional discipline. We can imitate *Tiferet* by achieving balance, harmony, and by responding in a tempered way to the situations that we face in life. Since *Tiferet* represents the masculine aspect of God, a man may also emulate *Tiferet* through entering into harmonious relationship with a woman. To imitate *Tiferet* is to enter into a loving and mutual relationship with a woman. Because *Tiferet* is also associated with the heavenly Torah, an individual may further emulate *Tiferet* by devoting himself to Torah study, by entering into a loving relationship with the text.

The *Kabbalists* often describe *Yesod* as the sexual dimension of divine masculinity. A man may imitate *Yesod* through sexuality directed towards his female partner within the context of a loving, monogamous relationship. Male sexuality as emulation of *Yesod* is regarded as holy to the extent that the female partner is regarded as a surrogate for the female aspect of God, *Malkhut* or *Shekhinah*. Therefore, a woman may emulate *Malkhut* or *Shekhinah* by engaging in a loving and sexual relationship with her spouse who is regarded as a surrogate for *Tiferet*, the masculine aspect of God.

The *Zohar* contains many passages that describe the emanation of the *Sefirot* in rich symbolic detail. Rarely does it present the *Sefirot* in a vocabulary that a modern reader can comprehend. It uses symbols for these divine processes that are taken from the language of the Bible. The *Kabbalists* had an unusual approach to the Bible and read it differently than a modern reader would. They believed that the *Sefirot*, and not *The Infinite* itself, are described in the Bible and that biblical descriptions of God refer to the *Sefirot*.

This approach can be illustrated by their interpretation of the different Hebrew names used to describe God in the Bible. For example, *Elohim* (Lord) refers to the *Sefirah Binah* and *Adonai* (*YHVH*, God) refers to *Tiferet*. In addition, biblical narratives were not taken at face value. They refer to the *Sefirot* that are portrayed symbolically in all of the biblical stories. Stories about the patriarchs in *Genesis* are read as symbolic accounts of the various *Sefirot*. For example, Abraham represents *Hesed*, Isaac symbolizes *Din*, Jacob refers to *Tiferet*, and Joseph points to *Yesod*. This meant that the biblical narratives were not only about real people but were also about cosmic dramas involving the *Sefirot*. Even the story of creation in *Genesis* depicts the creation, or emanation, of the *Sefirot*, not just the physical creation of the world.

The *Zohar*'s commentary on the creation narrative from *Genesis* vividly exemplifies the mystical interpretations of *Kabbalah*:

"In the Beginning . . ."

When the King conceived ordaining
He engraved engravings in the luster on high.
A blinding spark flashed
within the Concealed of the Concealed
from the mystery of *The Infinite*,
a cluster of vapor in formlessness,
set in a ring,
not white, not black, not red, not green,
no color at all.
When a band spanned, it yielded radiant colors.
Deep within the spark gushed a flow
imbuing colors below,
concealed within the concealed of the mystery of *The Infinite*.
The flow broke through and did not break through its aura.
It was not known at all
until, under the impact of breaking through,
one high and hidden point shone.
Beyond that point, nothing is known.
So it is called Beginning,
the first command of all.

"The enlightened will shine like the splendor of the sky, and those who make the masses righteous will shine like the stars forever and ever" (*Dan.* 12:3).

Zohar, Concealed of the Concealed, struck its aura.
The aura touched and did not touch this point.
Then this Beginning emanated
and made itself a palace for its glory and its praise.

There it sowed the seed of holiness to give birth for the benefit of the universe.
The secret is: "Her stock is a holy seed" (*Isa.* 6:13).

Zohar, sowing a seed for its glory
like the seed of fine purple silk.

The silkworm wraps itself within and makes itself a palace.
The palace is its praise and a benefit to all.

With the Beginning
the Concealed One who is not known created the palace.
The palace is called *Elohim*.
The secret is: "With Beginning, (the Concealed One) created *Elohim*" (*Gen.* 1:1)[14]

This passage poetically describes how the impulse to emanate its fullness upon the universe welled up within *The Infinite* and finally burst through in a dazzling display of radiance. The flow of divine essence congealed into the *Sefirah Hokhmah*, the first point in the new universe. This mystical world remained paradoxically concealed within itself and yet revealed in the point called *Hokhmah*. This point was then enveloped in *Binah*, also called by the divine name *Elohim* (Lord), a garment for *Hokhmah*. The *Zohar* concludes the passage with an intentionally playful misreading of the first verse in *Genesis*. Instead of reading the verse as "In the beginning, God created . . . ," it offers the verse as follows: "By means of the (*Sefirah* called) Beginning (i.e., *Hokhmah*), (*The Infinite*) created *Binah* (which is *Elohim*)." Thus, the creation story is transformed from an account about the birth of the world into a narrative about the origins of the *Sefirot*.

The *Sefirot* may be either God's essence or His instruments of activity, but they are, nevertheless, divine. The incorporeal world of divinity, the realm of the *Sefirot*, is the first stage in the unfolding of God's relationship to the world. This realm was explained by the *Kabbalists* as the aspect of God that was unknown to those philosophers who believed only in the hidden God. This is the revealed dimension of God, the personal aspect, the God to whom we pray, the object of the mystic quest. It is the essence that fills the vacuum of the abyss and allows man to establish a relationship with God.

It is not surprising, therefore, to find that the *Kabbalists* composed their own prayers to God that were directed at *The Infinite* and the *Sefirot*. The introduction to *Tikkunei Zohar*, a book written in the style of the *Zohar*, begins with the following prayer to be recited before embarking upon the mystic quest for God:

> Master of the worlds, You are one but not according to number. You are elevated above all heights, more hidden than all hidden things. No thought apprehends You at all. You are He who brought forth ten perfections that we call the ten *Sefirot* through which You govern the worlds, hidden, concealed, and revealed. Because there are ten *Sefirot*, You are also hidden from man. You join the *Sefirot* together and cause them to be one. Since You are present in them, one who considers one in isolation from the rest is regarded as one who thinks of You as having separate parts.

> Master of the worlds, You are the cause of causes, the first cause who waters the tree from your spring. This spring is like the soul to the body, the life of the body. Nothing can be compared to You, within or without. You created the heavens and the earth, the sun and the moon, the stars and the constellations. There is no one who knows You at all, and there is nothing as unique or unified as You, above or below. You are called the Lord of all. You have no proper name since You are the very essence of the divine names, the perfection of the names. When You withdraw from your names, they are left like a body without a soul.[15]

The *Sefirot,* through which *The Infinite* reveals itself and establishes a relationship with the world, span the abyss between man and God. The emanation of the ten *Sefirot* from God unfolds in a sequential process in which the hidden God reveals Himself through His attributes, thereby weaving the strands of His own personality. The *Sefirot* are not as infinite as the hidden God but, together with Him, constitute God. God is primarily *The Infinite,* but He is also the *Sefirot.* Together they are divinity and constitute the God who, according to the religious tradition, is the object of prayer. The *Kabbalist* acknowledges thereby that God is both transcendent and immanent.

The *Sefirot* form triads or groupings that represent aspects of God's creativity and goodness. *Keter, Hokhmah,* and *Binah,* respectively, symbolize the triad of God's pure Mind, His act of thinking, and the object of His thought, which is His own infinity. A perfect being must only contemplate itself, but, consequently, His thought takes on a life of its own. Thus God's thought, the idea or archetype of perfection, becomes a *Sefirah* and takes on an independent life of its own. This archetype is the perfect representation of God's wisdom, the highest of His qualities, and the symbol of divine perfection.

The second configuration of *Hesed, Din,* and *Tiferet* is the triad of archetypes of God's ethical perfection. These *Sefirot* are, respectively, the symbols of God's moral attributes of unqualified love, strict and unforgiving justice, and tempered judgment. The first two characteristics are extremes that are mitigated by the third attribute. The third triad, *Netzah, Hod,* and *Yesod,* represents the agents of God's governance and providential guidance of the world.

The first nine *Sefirot* form three triads of archetypes—intellectual, moral, and providential—that God employs in creating a blueprint for all of existence. God then employs these archetypes as would an architect who refers to the symbols or blueprint that he has drawn up before actually creating his edifice.

The *Kabbalists* frequently chart the *Sefirot* in a drawing that depicts them in the form of a human body. This chart (figure 4.1) suggests that the *Sefirot* correspond to the human constitution: the first three intellectual archetypes within God are the blueprint for the human intellect and are depicted by the head; the second triad of moral virtues corresponds to human moral actions associated with the hands and regulated by the heart; the triad of providential or governing archetypes is symbolized by the human thighs and sexual organs, the seat of power.

The *Kabbalists* explain the relation of the world of the *Sefirot* to the other realms in terms of this triadic principle. The world of the *Sefirot* gives birth to the world of spiritual forms, the realm of "pure forms" in which all of the archetypes of God's attributes assume independent existence outside of God. This realm of forms contains the ideal model and prefiguration of all of the forms of the world. In this realm, however, they are only the forms or ideas of all things and not the things themselves. For example, this realm of forms is the storehouse of the souls, the abode of the heavenly Torah and heavenly Jerusalem, and the world of forms of such human attributes as greatness, might, and splendor.

These forms take on matter and become real things in the natural world, which is below the spiritual world. In this realm, the spiritual forms are combined with matter and become sensible and perceptible objects. Souls enter into bodies, the earthly Torah and the earthly Jerusalem are built according to their heavenly model, and the divine attributes become the moral qualities that the Jewish tradition enjoins man to adopt and exhibit in daily conduct.

Emanation from *The Infinite* is a substantive process in which God's being is distributed and conveyed through the *Sefirot*. *Keter*, coeternal with *The Infinite*, contains within itself the roots of all subsequent being in an

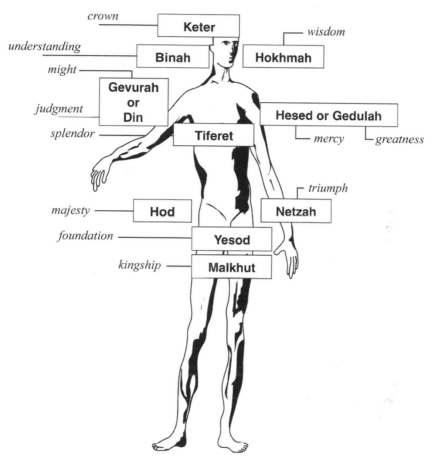

Figure 4.1   The Sefirot of Being

undifferentiated state. Through the process of emanation these roots of existence change from a state of no-thing-ness to the potentiality of everything. *Keter*, however, is identical with *The Infinite* in respect to its infinity and, on the other hand, it is related to the other *Sefirot* in respect to its being the source of emanation.

The first moment of emanation is an act of self-contraction, or constriction (*Tzimtzum*), of the infinity of *The Infinite*. *The Infinite*, because it is infinite, remains inaccessible to anything else. It must become limited and diluted in order for the divine essence to become accessible. God cannot be made known to the world unless He presents Himself in a worldly form. The role of the *Sefirot* is to serve as the intermediate link that translates infinity into more limited essences. God's being is then communicated to humanity in a worldly form through the revelation of the Torah. The beginning of this process of translating God's being into comprehensible forms is an act whereby God brings Himself down to a less infinite level.

Some mystics describe the phenomenon of God limiting Himself in order to make Himself more available to the world by an analogy. The father of an infant often needs to act in childish ways in order to communicate with his young child. Talking to the infant in "baby talk" can be a necessary strategy of self-limitation that must be employed in order to establish communication. The father remains an adult even though he must temporarily speak the language of the infant. So it is, they explain, with God who limits Himself for the sake of humanity.

This self-limitation of God creates *Keter*, the unbounded, infinite potentiality for existence. *Keter*, also called *Ayin* (nothing), is not a nonbeing; it is the undifferentiated unity of all being. It is the indeterminate nothing from which all being unfolds and it exists only through an act of self-limitation by *Eyn Sof*.

The conception of emanation as "self-contraction" is based on the idea that God can only bring things into existence from that which already exists. God, therefore, cannot create anything directly from His own infinite essence. Thus he constricts his own infinity into *Keter*, the fullness of all, the undifferentiated source of all being. The infinity of God is described as the radiant light of the sun that shines endlessly due to its overwhelming magnitude. But this unbridled light must be directed and channeled in order for details, shadows, contours, and shapes to emerge. In the same manner the radiance of *The Infinite* must be restricted in order to allow for the emergence of the *Sefirot*. It is not, however, a change in *The Infinite*, only within the vessels that receive the light. "Contraction" is not an essential change within *The Infinite* as much as it is the creation of possibility and differentiation through *Keter*. The subsequent process of emanation is a dynamic process in which *Keter* radiates the light of *The Infinite* through the other *Sefirot*.

The first act of divine expression consists of *Keter*'s emanation of *Hokhmah*, God's sublime wisdom, which is hidden deep within *Keter*. This manifestation of the hidden essence of *Keter* produces the *Sefirah Hokhmah*.

Whereas *Keter* is hidden and indistinct from *The Infinite*, *Hokhmah* is distinct from *Keter*. *Hokhmah* is the first essence, or vessel, to exist separately from *The Infinite* even though it contains the infinity of *The Infinite*. The emanation of *Hokhmah* is the first self-expression of *The Infinite* in which the infinite deity represents itself in a more limited form. This phenomenon of autorepresentation—God expressing Himself, occurs through an act of self-limitation. The mystics call this *Tzimtzum* (contraction), an act of divine expression in which God limits His own infinite intelligence and causes it to be contained in a vessel.[16]

The *Sefirot* are also God's linguistic expression. All beings reveal their essence through thought that eventually assumes the form of speech, and the *Sefirot* are the divine language. Even the term *Sefirah* conveys the notion of the *Sefirot* as God's language in the verse, "The heavens tell (*mesapprim*, from the same root as *Sefirah*) the glory (*Kavod*) of God.[17] The common Hebrew root of the terms *Sefirah* and *sapper*, the Hebrew letters *spr*, which mean "to tell," suggests that God's means of expression, the *Sefirot*, are also His language.

Each *Sefirah*, beginning with *Hokhmah*, constitutes a distinct stage in the process of the unfolding of the divine language. The sequence of divine self-expression begins with the manifestation of God's essential *Hokhmah*. The *Kabbalists* characterize this as the creation of a primordial "text," a vessel in which the author's wisdom is inscribed. Like any text, the implicit wisdom needs to be revealed by one who also interprets it and draws it out for all to see. Therefore, *Hokhmah* is followed by the emanation of *Binah*, the interpreter or commentator, that draws out the hidden thoughts and gives them meaning. This *Sefirah* is the intellect that understands the infinite wisdom of God concealed in the text of *Hokhmah* and reveals it. *Binah* is the third stage in the process of divine autorepresentation. It differentiates the undifferentiated wisdom of God hidden in *Hokhmah*.

The emanation of the first three *Sefirot* is an intellectual process in which God's thought achieves existence distinct from His hidden essence. As this process continues beyond *Binah*, God's wisdom becomes increasingly particularized and differentiated and culminates in the linguistic expression of this wisdom through divine language. Divine language is both the particularization of God's own thought and the extension of His own intellectual essence. Divine language eventually becomes concretized as the language of the Torah. The Torah is the ultimate repository, or vessel, of God's essence and wisdom and is the final stage in the process of divine autorepresentation.

Hokhmah is the repository of divine wisdom and a treasury in which the potentiality of divine linguistic expression is inscribed. In this *Sefirah*, wisdom is inscribed as the ideal prefiguration of the letters of the Hebrew alphabet. The Jewish mystics understood letters as the outward means of expressing inner thoughts. *Hokhmah* is a repository, a matrix upon which God's thoughts are inscribed as Hebrew letters. These letters remain hidden deep within *Hokhmah* throughout the process of the emanation of the *Sefirot*. The process of differentiation in which these ideal letters become real letters occurs only after the process of divine autorepresentation concludes with the emanation of *Malkhut*.

The *Sefirot* are the principles of all existent things, the ideal prefiguration of all being, vessels, or instruments of divine activity and expressions of divine wisdom. With the conclusion of the emanation of the last *Sefirah*, the divine world comes to an end. The next lower world, the spiritual world, begins below *Malkhut* and consists of the distinct and differentiated forms that were hidden in an undifferentiated form within the *Sefirot*. This spiritual realm of forms, separate from matter, exists in an intermediate state between the world of divinity above it and the natural world below it and contains corporeal objects of form and matter together. The letters that were hidden in *Hokhmah* and that were brought out by *Binah* come into their own in this spiritual world of pure forms.

The radical innovation introduced by *Kabbalah* is the idea that all of creation, the corporeal world below the spiritual realm, is made up of the letters of the Hebrew alphabet which contain God's own essence. In other words, God's essence is His thought and the expression of His essence is the emanation of the Hebrew letters. The letters assume concrete form in a series of stages that culminate in the Hebrew language.

The linguistic process of emanation is the process of creation. The *Kabbalists* explain that the etymology of the Hebrew word for "letter" (*ot*) is the root "to come from" (*ata*). They suggest that the letters of the Hebrew alphabet come from the spiritual forms of the Hebrew letters which, in turn, come from the hidden letters or thoughts of God within the *Sefirot*. Although the letters have a mysterious and unknowable character in the upper worlds, they are still the building blocks of creation because they are the instruments of God's self-expression.

Creation is portrayed as the unfolding of divine language from the *Sefirot* into ideal letters of the spiritual realm which were then impressed upon the physical world. Seven of the Hebrew letters correspond to and create the seven known celestial planets; twelve other letters correspond to and create the twelve constellations of the Zodiac; three Hebrew letters create the material elements—air, water, and fire—out of which the world itself was thought to be created.[18]

Hokhmah is the repository of divine wisdom and contains within it the undifferentiated potentiality of the letters. In the *Midrash*, the Torah is identified as the outward manifestation of divine wisdom. The *Midrash* explains that the Torah is one of six things that existed prior to the creation of the world.[19] The *Kabbalists* point out that the Hebrew word for "things" (*devarim*) and the term for "words" (*dibburim*) share a common root. Therefore, the *Midrash* supports the *Kabbalistic* idea that the world was created by the preexistent divine language. To support this view, the rabbis cite the biblical verse that describes God's wisdom: "The Lord created me at the beginning of his course."[20] Wisdom was created before anything else. The *Kabbalists* also based their belief on another *Midrash* that described the preexistent Torah as "the vessel of God's craftsmanship" (*keli omanuto*).[21] They concluded that the *Sefirah Hokhmah* is the ultimate source and cause of existence.

The appearance of the written Torah is the final expression of this linguistic process and is the very instrument by which God created the world. The process that began with the emanation of *Hokhmah*, the unfolding of the letters, their differentiation in the spiritual realm, and their inscription in the preexistent Torah culminated in their final appearance as the letters of the written Torah. The Torah is, therefore, the final stage in the process of divine autorepresentation.

The gradual and sequential process of divine emanation through linguistic expression brings the world into existence. The spiritual forms of the letters create the constellations, the planets, and the earthly elements. The preexistent Torah is the blueprint that God employed to create the world out of the elements that came from God's essence. The world is ultimately the final expression of divine language.

The act of revelation is the transformation of thought into word. The word itself is, reciprocally, the means towards understanding the original thought. The text of the Torah is not remote from God's original wisdom since it is nothing more than another stage in the manifestation of God's thought. The Torah is called *Hokhmah* because it is the last stage in the elaboration of God's wisdom. The *Kabbalists* explain this notion through the metaphor of human speech. God's wisdom is His internal speech, the product of His eternal activity, His thought. The Torah is the direct manifestation of this internal speech just as language is itself the extension of thought.

The process of emanation infuses the individual letters of the earthly Torah with meaning; the vessel of the Torah contains the essence of the *Sefirot*. The difference between the internal and the external speech, the Torah, is one of degree.

Another way of understanding the unfolding of divine language is to see emanation as the process of creating names. Names are vessels that contain essences or refer to subjects that exist. The *Kabbalists* describe the emanation of the vessel *Hokhmah* as God giving Himself His first and most important name, *YHVH*, traditionally pronounced as *Adonai* and called the four-letter name (*Tetragrammaton*). The combination forming this name is the first emanation of the divine letters through *Hokhmah*. All other divine names are elaborations of the *Tetragrammaton*.[22]

The *Sefirot* are now seen as a series of elaborations of the first divine name, as linguistic vessels that contain the divine essence. Since the first name is *Hokhmah—YHVH*, God's name is identical with the preexistent Torah. Since the Written Torah is the elaboration of the preexistent Torah, the Written Torah is also the elaboration, or manifestation, of God's name through other words and names. Nahmanides had this in mind when he declares that "the entire Torah is composed of the names of God."[23] This means that the Torah is the earthly manifestation of the *Sefirot*, which are God's own names and the means by which He created the world.

The Torah has two natures. It is the medium of divine expression and the vehicle through which the mystic can retrace the steps of the process leading back to God. The words of the Torah are not merely combinations of letters that constitute narratives; they are vessels that point to hidden essences, the *Sefirot*. The relation of the *Sefirot* to the words of the Torah is analogous to the relation of the soul to the body. The words of the Torah are "bodies" that contain the "soul" of God's *Hokhmah*. The names, or words, of the Torah are ultimately expressions of divine power not just words referring to earthly things. One who knows how the divine power is infused in the words of the Torah is able to harness and utilize the power contained in them. In other words, the mystic who understands the proper connection between the language of the Torah and the *Sefirot* is able to manipulate the power in the names and establish a connection between himself and God.

Jewish mysticism, therefore, is a system of creating relationships with God across the abyss through the medium of the Torah. One who can perceive the divine names in the Torah is able to cleave directly to God's *Sefirot* and transcend the world in which he lives. The study of the Torah is, therefore, the highest form of knowledge.

The *Kabbalistic* theory of language is based on the notion that there is a real connection between a name and the object that it represents. The name is the concept of the thing to which the name applies. As an example, they point to passages in the Torah where God gives names to the forefathers that hint at their destiny, such as Jacob who is renamed "Israel" because he "struggled" (*sarita* from the same root as *yisrael*, Israel) with God. Many biblical figures are so named such that their names convey something significant about who they are. This indicates that names are not arbitrary but are correct or incorrect according to the degree to which they express the nature of their bearers.

The *Kabbalists* opposed the theory of names that was common among many rationalist biblical commentators in the Middle Ages, including Maimonides.[24] Maimonides believed that there is no essential connection between a name and the object to which it refers, thus all names are conventional or arbitrary.[25] Most names are merely sounds that people mutually agree to assign to objects. The same objects could just as well be called by different names. Some names, however, are definitions such as when man is called a "rational animal." Generally, however, there is no real connection between a name and an object, there are no specifically "correct" names, and names do not express the nature of a thing. Moreover, there is no knowledge of the essence of something in knowing its name. According to Maimonides, even divine names found in the Torah are conventional designations, not essential names.

According to the *Kabbalists*, however, names express the nature of things. Language is fundamentally divine because all names have a connection with the *Sefirot* and unfold from *Hokhmah* in the process of emanation. Actually, all names are elaborations of the name of God—*YHVH*—the origin of existence and the genesis of language. The *Kabbalistic* theory of language maintains that all names are symbols that refer to the *Sefirot*. Names do not really have meanings as much as they point to their correct referent, a *Sefirah*.[26] The Torah is a "code book" of divine names that refer to *Sefirot*. A *Kabbalist* is one who decodes the Torah and traces the meaning of terms back to their source. *Kabbalah* is also a theory that sees the world as a series of names, or vessels, that contain and even conceal God. The Torah, therefore, is full of symbols that hint at the divine essence, not a collection of words that can be read like any other story.

The doctrine of the *Sefirot* is a complex and comprehensive attempt to explain all of reality. It teaches that what we see of this world is only the visible tip of the iceberg, outward manifestations of divine attributes and spiritual forms that come from God. All of existence pulsates and vibrates with an inner life of form and attributes. Like matter composed of atomic particles, nothing is static, and everything reverberates with inner spiritual forms and an essence that flows from God. Everything in the world is an essence that comes from God and is clothed in vessels. Some vessels are more spiritual, like the Torah, and others are more material, like the human body. But every object contains divinity in one form or another, and, therefore, it is possible to retrace the steps of existence back to God, the source.

5

THE *SHEKHINAH*

The Feminine Aspect of God

*M*alkhut, the tenth *Sefirah*, elicits a special fascination for *Kabbalists*. It is the vessel that gathers the essence that has been transmitted through the other *Sefirot* and channels it outward. It is, for the *Kabbalists*, the symbol of God's presence in the world and the aspect that is most readily accessible to mankind. This function of the tenth *Sefirah* is called the *Shekhinah* (divine presence).

In the *Talmud*, the term *Shekhinah* refers to the personification of God's presence in a particular location. It is the noun used to describe the human perception of God's presence on earth. It is a synonym for God that is used by the sages to describe God's nearness and presence, to be distinguished from the term *Ha-Kadosh Barukh Hu* (The Holy One, Blessed Be He), which they used to describe God's hidden persona. They are both the same God except that the former term describes His immanence and the latter, His transcendence.

The term *Shekhinah* itself was coined by the rabbis from the verb root "to dwell" (*shakhan*) since it was associated primarily with God's localized presence in the *Mishkan*—the portable tabernacle in the desert that later became the central element in the Temple. God commands Moses on Sinai to build a tabernacle that will house the divine covenant. The term *shakhan* appears here: "And let them make Me a sanctuary that I may dwell (*shakhanti*) among them."[1]

The term is used interchangeably with other names for God especially when He is said to be present in the world. For example, the rabbis offer the following explanation of the biblical verse, "After the Lord, your God, you shall walk" (*Deut.* 13:5): "And is it possible for a man to walk after the *Shekhinah*? Rather, it means that one should emulate the virtues of the Holy One, Blessed be He."[2]

Thus, in order to avoid suggesting that God "walks" or that man can "walk after God," the rabbis suggest that "walking" means emulation. It was more acceptable to suggest that one can emulate the moral actions of the immanent presence of God rather than His transcendence. Thus, it is the *Shekhinah*, not The Holy One, Blessed be He, that is mentioned.

The sages of the rabbinic period introduced new concepts to explain the reality that they experienced. In doing so, they institutionalized the concept of the abyss between God and the universe and required that it be taken into account as a religious fact. The remedy for this abyss, in the rabbinic period, was the concept of the *Shekhinah*, which helped explain how God could be remote and near at the same time. After Maimonides further widened the abyss, undermined the concept of immanence, and made God wholly transcendent, the concept of the *Sefirot* served to restore God's immanence.

The *Shekhinah* became a synonym for God's nearness and the personification of God's presence among practitioners of Jewish rituals of study, worship, and eating in a state of purity. With the destruction of the Temple and the transference of priestly purity to Jewish homes, the presence of God that had been in the Temple was now extended to those same homes and to the academies in which the Torah was studied. The new role of the home and Torah academy as replacement for the Temple is indicated in the following rabbinic aphorism: "If two sit together and occupy themselves with words of Torah, the *Shekhinah* abides in their midst."[3]

God's immanence was not destroyed with the destruction of the Temple. Generally, rabbinic sources promote the belief that God's immanence is permanently attached to the Jewish people, guarding over them wherever they may be. Rather than arguing that the destruction of the Temple suggests God's abandonment, most sources reassure the people of God's abiding interest in and concern for their fate:

> Wherever Israel went into exile, the *Shekhinah*, as it were, was exiled with them. They were exiled to Egypt, the *Shekhinah* was with them. They were exiled to Babylon, the *Shekhinah* was with them.[4]

The rabbis believed that the destruction of the Temple was due to human sinfulness. The reassuring position that God had not abandoned the Jewish people hardly softened this self-critical accusation. Jewish immorality, responsible for the loss of the Sanctuary, could still cause the banishment of God's nearness from the world. Individual morality can also influence God's nearness or remoteness:

> Whoever is humble will ultimately cause the *Shekhinah* to dwell with men on earth. But whoever is haughty will bring about the defilement of the earth and the departure of the *Shekhinah*.[5]

The rabbis attempted to conceptualize the notion of God's nearness in such a way that allowed it to be localized in a particular place without being restricted to one address. The *Shekhinah* could be in any place: "Why did the Holy One, Blessed be He, reveal Himself to Moses in a lowly thorn bush? This teaches us that there is no place on earth void of the *Shekhinah*."[6]

The nearness of God does not imply that there are different *Shekhinot* (plural of *Shekhinah*) for each localized presence of God:

> The Roman Emperor said to Rabban Gamliel: You say that wherever there is a company of ten Jews, the *Shekhinah* abides in their midst. How many *Shekhinot* are there then? Rabban Gamliel replied: The sun shines upon each individual and, at the same time, upon the world as a whole. Now, the sun is just one of the thousand myriad attendants of the Holy One, Blessed be He. How much more so the *Shekhinah* of the Holy One, Blessed be He.[7]

The rabbinic conception of the *Shekhinah* did not entail a being separate or distinct from God. Any time the name *Shekhinah* appears, the term "God" could just as easily be substituted. The rabbinic *Shekhinah* has no character of its own and serves only to refer to God in His nearness to man.

The concept of *Shekhinah* undergoes a major transformation in *Kabbalah*. It is no longer synonymous with God but appears as a separate and distinct being with a character all its own. The character is feminine, and the *Kabbalistic* descriptions of the *Shekhinah* accentuate her separateness from the hidden God and her own femininity.

The earliest *Kabbalistic* portrayal of the *Shekhinah* describes her as God's daughter whom he gives to the world as *its* wife. He longs to hold on to her but recognizes that she now belongs to a different realm. Therefore, God creates the *Sefirot* as a window between himself and the *Shekhinah* who dwells in the world. The *Sefirot* are now the link between God and his daughter. God can relate to the world by means of the *Sefirot*, and his *Shekhinah* can approach him by the same avenue:

> A certain king had a good, beautiful and perfect daughter. He married her to a prince and dressed her, crowned her and adorned her. The king also provided a large dowry for her. Now, can the king dwell apart from his daughter? Of course not. But can the king dwell with her all day long? Of course not. So what does he do? He places a window between himself and her, and whenever the daughter needs her father or the father needs his daughter, they meet together at the window.[8]

This resembles the earlier passage that describes God as making a meeting place for his daughter. There the meeting place is the Temple, not the *Sefirot*. Here, the meeting place is the world. More significantly, however, the daughter in the former passage is the Jewish people, and here it is God's daughter, the *Shekhinah*.

In Jewish mysticism, *The Infinite* is inaccessible, and so are many of the *Sefirot*. The last *Sefirah*, the *Shekhinah*, is accessible through the mystic quest and offers some insight into the other *Sefirot*. Because the *Shekhinah* is the vessel in which all of the other *Sefirot* are gathered, it reveals the higher aspects of God to those who know it. The *Kabbalistic* sources caution against attempting to penetrate directly through the divine realm to *The Infinite* and instead direct the mystic towards the *Shekhinah*, the gateway to the other *Sefirot*. God is not accessible except through the *Shekhinah*:

> A certain king dwelt within the inner chamber of his palace. There were thirty-two chambers in all and each chamber had its own path. Now, is it proper for everyone to come to the king's chamber by simply following all the paths? Of course not. And is it proper for the king to openly reveal his pearls, brocades and hidden, precious treasures? Of course not. So what did the king do? He appointed his daughter and set in her and in her garments all the different pathways. Anyone who wishes to enter the palace should look to her.[9]

The term "thirty-two chambers" has symbolic significance in Jewish mysticism. It is an ideal number that signifies the totality of all possible phenomena that might exist in the world. The mystics believed that the ten *Sefirot* and the twenty-two Hebrew letters were the building blocks of the universe. "Thirty-two" thus represents the infinite possibilities that can emerge from the combination of divine essences and human language.

The *Shekhinah* is referred to as "she" or "her" in *Kabbalistic* literature. This represents both a linguistic and substantive innovation. The word itself is classified among the Hebrew terms that are governed by noun endings of the feminine gender. The term also has substantive connotations as the feminine aspect of God, the divine mother and protector of the world.

The abyss between God and the world cannot easily be bridged. The *Shekhinah*, however, is that aspect of God that can serve to link the two realms. The *Shekhinah* is the lowest of the *Sefirot* and the boundary between the divine and nondivine world. Thus, the *Shekhinah* has a certain ability to link the two realms.

The *Shekhinah* is God's delegate from the realm of the *Sefirot* to the world. Although the *Shekhinah* is never described as an emissary that literally descends into the world in an earthly form, it is still more imaginable than any other aspect of God. The *Shekhinah* is the caring part of God, which can be experienced as God's immanence in the world. The *Shekhinah* dwells in the midst of her people without ever leaving the abode of the *Sefirot*.

The *Shekhinah* can stand apart from the other *Sefirot*. It acts at times as the delegate of the *Sefirot* to the world and at other times as the intercessor on behalf of the world to the *Sefirot*. The *Shekhinah* thus serves as the link between the realms of God and the world.

Only this *Sefirah* can enter directly into contact with humanity. According to *Kabbalah*, God's presence can be felt in the world when one observes the ritual requirements of Judaism. Through observance, the world is reminded of the origin of the *Shekhinah* in the realm of the *Sefirot*. She is called God's *Kavod* (glory) and comes from a far more remote origin than did the rabbinic *Shekhinah*:

> Why is it written "Blessed be God's Glory from its place?" (*Ezek.* 3:12). Because no one knows its exact place. A parable. The daughter of a king came from far away and people did not know from where she had come. After a while, they saw that she was strong, beautiful, and perfect in all that she did. They said, "She must surely have been taken from the Realm of Light because through her deeds, the world shines." They asked "Where are you from?" She answered "From my place." They said, "Then, the inhabitants of your place must be noble. May you and your place be blessed."[10]

Sometimes the *Shekhinah* is inaccessible and remote to all but the other *Sefirot*. But her eventual presence in the world is always insured. In the following passage, the *Shekhinah* is now the queen, not the daughter, and is hidden in the king's chambers. The *Sefirot*, and not the king, mate with her and produce offspring—angels—for the king. The *Shekhinah* is the mother of all life even when she is not present in the world or fulfilling her role as God's emissary and presence:

> What is meant by "God's Glory?" A parable: To what can this be compared? To a king who had a queen in his chamber. All the king's soldiers took delight in the queen. She had children and they would come every day to see the king and bless him. The children asked, "Where is our mother now?" The king answered, "You cannot see her now." They responded, "May she be blessed wherever she is."[11]

If the *Shekhinah* is portrayed as God's daughter, other *Sefirot* are understood as having given birth to her. The second and third *Sefirot*, *Hokhmah* and *Binah*, are often described as having male and female properties, respectively. Every *Sefirah* is seen as standing in a tense or even contrary relationship with another, and the opposites are resolved through the production of a third and mediating power. Thus the opposites *Hokhmah* and *Binah* are resolved by the emergence of *Tiferet*. The *Kabbalists* often resort to explicitly sexual metaphors to portray the emanation of the *Sefirot*. The emanation of *Tiferet* is described as a son to *Hokhmah* and *Binah* and a balance to their opposing natures. The *Shekhinah*, their daughter, completes this ideal "family":

> *Hokhmah* spread out and brought forth *Binah*. They were found to be male and female: *Hokhmah*, the father, and *Binah*, the mother. Then, these two united and lighted up each other. The mother conceived and gave birth to a son. Through the birth of a son, the mother and father found perfection. This led to the completion of everything and the inclusion of all—father, mother, son and daughter.[12]

The perfection and unification of the divine world depends on the harmonious balance between individual *Sefirot* as well as harmonious interrelationships between all the *Sefirot*. God depends upon the actions of Jewish mystics who unite the *Sefirot* and restore the balance within the divine realm. God is dependent, therefore, on the mystical activity of the Jewish people. As the *Zohar* says: "As long as Israel is found with the Holy One, Blessed be He, He, so to speak, is in a state of completion."[13] A *Kabbalist* is one who attempts to perform the necessary steps that will preserve or restore the unity of the divine realm and make God whole. His work begins with the *Shekhinah* but affects the rest of the *Sefirot*.

The process of preserving God in a state of completion places a heavy burden of moral and mystical responsibility upon the individual. The task of completion or restoration of unity within the *Sefirot* focuses on the unity of *Tiferet* and *Malkhut*. The *Sefirot Hokhmah* and *Binah* are always united. They are, like an idealized father and mother, united in enduring harmony:

> Since the father and the mother are found in union all the time and are never hidden from each other or separated, they are called companions. They find satisfaction in perfect union.[14]

The *Kabbalists* make a daring equation of *Tiferet* with the Holy One, Blessed be He, the traditional rabbinic name of God. This suggests that God, as He is known in the Jewish tradition, is actually the *Sefirah Tiferet* and not *The Infinite*. Moreover, the *Shekhinah*, God's presence, is His spouse, *Malkhut*. The union of *Tiferet* and *Malkhut* signifies the state of unity among the upper and lower, or masculine and feminine, *Sefirot*. It also represents the state of divine harmony necessary in order for peace to prevail in the world.

These two *Sefirot* can be, but are not always necessarily in, a state of harmony. The union of the Holy One, Blessed be He and His *Shekhinah* is the desirable state of affairs in the divine realm and in the world. This union is brought about by human efforts and is disrupted by sin. Whatever occurs below determines what occurs above; whatever occurs above is a reflection of what occurs below. When there is an absence of harmony above, it is a reflection of disharmony in the world, and the tension above, in turn, exacerbates the situation in the world.

The notion of the feminine aspect of the deity may be the boldest conceptual innovation in Jewish mysticism. The fascination with the feminine aspect of God has its origin in human sexual consciousness. The Jewish mystics believed that everything in the terrestrial world has its roots in the divine realm. Since femininity must have its roots in God, there must indeed be a feminine aspect of God. This doctrine elevates human sexuality to a divine principle and thereby legitimates human sexuality. At the same time it humanizes God by attributing the source of the vicissitudes of human sexuality to divinity. Most important, the concept of the feminine aspect of God paves the way for understanding human sexuality as a metaphor for the mystic quest in Judaism.

The mystics were fascinated by the relationship between *Tiferet* and *Malkhut*. They portray the union of these two *Sefirot*, also called "the son and the daughter," as being in constant jeopardy whereas the union of "the father and mother" (*Hokhmah* and *Binah*) was intractable. This notion does not have any incestuous implication and the mystics alternate freely between the son-daughter and the husband-wife metaphors. Whereas the "parents" are in perpetual union, human sinfulness prevents the permanent union of *Tiferet* with *Malkhut*.

The holy marriage of *Tiferet* and *Malkhut* is the most important task that the mystic assumes in his quest. The Jewish mystic does not always seek his own union with God but rather attempts to influence the last *Sefirah* to cause her to mate with *Tiferet*. Sexuality within marriage between a man and a woman is considered one of the mystic techniques for influencing the holy marriage above. The proper and dedicated fulfillment of the marriage is a means for uniting the masculine and feminine *Sefirot*. The *Zohar* emphasizes the parallel between earthly and heavenly oneness as a form of sexual arousal within a marital relationship which, in the Jewish tradition, is called *kiddushin* (sanctification):

> When is "union" said of man? When he is male together with female and is highly sanctified and zealous for sanctification. Then, and only then, is he designated "one," without any flaw of any kind. Hence, a man and his wife should have a single inclination at the hour of their union. The man should rejoice with his wife, attaching himself to her with affection. So joined, they make one soul and one body: A single soul—through their affection; and a single body—for only when male and female are joined do they form a single body. When male and female are joined, God abides upon them as "one" and endows them with a holy spirit.[15]

Kabbalah teaches that humans are able to manipulate God through the performance of Jewish rituals. The most important effect that one's actions can have is the unification of *Tiferet* and *Malkhut*. The *Zohar* contains many extensive passages that detail this thesis. For example, the simple declaration of monotheistic faith, *Shema Yisrael Adonai Eloheinu Adonai Ehad* (Hear, O Israel, The Lord Our God, The Lord Is One),[16] becomes the occasion for elaborating a dramatic myth of the divine marriage between *Tiferet* and *Malkhut*.

In order for a modern reader to follow the intricate symbolism of the mythology, it is necessary to provide a list of *Kabbalistic* terms that appear in the following passage:

- *Illumination*: the overflow from *The Infinite*, which is often portrayed as a radiant light.

- *The Flame of Darkness*: This symbol is an oxymoron, an inherently contradictory expression. It refers to *Keter*, the only *Sefirah* to contain within itself contradictory powers.
- *Lights*: emanations
- *The Tree of Life*: a symbol for *Tiferet*
- *Odors and fragrances*: emanations and overflow of the divine essence upon the world
- *The Garden (of Eden)*: a symbol for *Malkhut*, the garden in which *Tiferet* is planted
- *The Bride*: a symbol for *Malkhut*
- *Husband*: a symbol for *Tiferet*
- *Israel*: another name for *Tiferet*
- *The Heavenly Limbs*: the six *Sefirot*: *Hesed, Din, Tiferet, Netzah, Hod,* and *Yesod*
- *The Lord (Adonai)*: a symbol for *Tiferet*. This *Sefirah* also refers to the divine name, The Holy One, Blessed be He
- *Limbs, Directions*: another term for *Sefirot*
- *The Hebrew letter Vav*: This letter corresponds to the letter V in the word *YHVH*. In Hebrew, *Vav* has the numerical value of six and is related to the *Sefirah Tiferet*.
- *Attendants*: the ministering angels
- *Name*: a symbol for *Malkhut*

This glossary should be used in deciphering the following passage from the *Zohar*:

At the hour when Israel brings about the unity of the mystery of "Hear, Israel," with complete devotion, an illumination deep within the sublime supernal world issues forth immediately. This illumination collides with the flame of darkness and divides into seventy lights. These seventy become the seventy branches of the Tree of Life. At that moment, this tree emits odors and fragrances as all the trees of the Garden (of Eden) do toward their master. At that moment, the bride is adorned in order to enter beneath the canopy with her husband. All the heavenly limbs bind together in one desire, one devotion, in order to be one, with no division at all. Then, her husband turns his attention to her in order to bring her under the canopy in one union, to unite with his bride. Therefore, awaken to her and say: "Hear, O, Bride, Israel is coming! Prepare yourself! Your husband is approaching in his adornments. He is ready for you." Then: "The Lord our God, The Lord is One—" In one union, one devotion, with no division. All the limbs are united and enter into one devotion. When Israel says, "The Lord is One—" through the arousal of the six directions, they unite in one devotion. This is the mystery of the Hebrew letter *Vav*: one extension alone with nothing else adhering to it, only it alone, apart from the rest, complete. At the same moment, the bride is being prepared and adorned. Her attendants present her to her husband in a thin whisper, saying: "Blessed be the Name of the Glory of His Kingship (*Malkhut*) forever." This is said in a whisper for this is how she must be presented to her husband. Happy are the people who know this and prepare an exalted service of faith.[17]

The *Kabbalist* presents a new reading of the prayer "Hear, O Israel." It is no longer the fundamental credo of Jewish monotheistic belief but a dramatic enactment of a holy marriage between the two *Sefirot* of *Tiferet* and *Malkhut*. "Hear, O Israel," is not an invocation to the Jewish people to enunciate their belief in one God. It becomes the call to perform a mystical ritual of uniting *Tiferet* and *Malkhut* in a holy wedding ceremony:

Hear, *Tiferet-Israel!* You who are united with the other *Sefirot!* Through this call, *Tiferet* and *Malkhut* become one in holy marriage, so "The Lord—*Tiferet*—is One." Thereupon, the wedding party announces, "Blessed be *Malkhut,* the name of Glory, united, forever, with *Tiferet.*

The *Kabbalists* were acutely aware, however, that this holy marriage was far from guaranteed. If it were, the world would always be governed by harmony, and God's everlasting abundance would illuminate the world. On the contrary, the *Kabbalists* saw the world in which they lived as hostile and threatening. *Kabbalah* flourished in medieval Spain at the time of increasing Christian persecution of Jews. The *Seven Part Codes*, which prohibited Jews from conducting their affairs like their Christian neighbors, and the restrictions of the Lateran Council in Rome curtailed Jewish civil, economic, and religious rights. In Spain, home to *Kabbalah*, the anti-Jewish attacks of 1391, the forced conversions of the Marranos, and the inquisitions finally led to the expulsion in 1492. This was hardly a period in which *Tiferet* and *Malkhut* appeared to be in union.

The mystics were more conscious of their failure to "unite" God than of their success. The mystic quest centered upon a mission to rise above the vicissitudes of this world and address the problem at its source—the world of the *Sefirot*. Only if *Malkhut* were banished from her mate, only if she indeed were in exile, could the world be in such a condition as it appeared to be. The *Kabbalists* knew, believed, experienced, and felt that "the *Shekhi-*

nah is in the dust," separated and exiled from her realm. The elevation of *Malkhut* becomes a precondition for bringing her under the nuptial canopy. On page after page, the *Zohar* portrays this sense of anguish and exile in vivid imagery:

> Think of a king who in anger against his queen banished her from his palace for a stated time. That time elapsed and she returned to the king. Thus it came to pass several times. Then came a time when she was banished from the palace of the king for a long time. The King said: "Now is not like before when she returned to me. This time, I shall go with all my followers to seek her out." When he found her, she was in the dust. Seeing her thus trampled, and yearning anew for her, he took her by the hand, raised her up, led her back to the palace, and promised on his oath that He would never send her away.[18]

This *Kabbalistic* reading of history suggested that the period of slavery in Egypt and the destruction of the First Temple were temporary exiles of the *Shekhinah* that ended with her voluntary return. The *Kabbalists* viewed the era in which they lived as qualitatively worse than previous epochs. Since the time of the destruction of the Second Temple in 70 C.E., the Temple had not been rebuilt and the sense of exile persisted. The redemption from this exile, which had already lasted more than a millennium, required stronger measures. God, according to the *Zohar*, was not content to wait for the *Shekhinah* to return. It was now the task of God and the Jewish people to actively pursue the return of the exiled *Shekhinah*. The *Zohar* sanctioned utopian activism and, perhaps, even active messianism.

To the *Kabbalists*, the palpable sense of exile was the result of the exile of the *Shekhinah*. With the divine presence "in the dust," the mystic assumed the burden of lifting her up out of the ashes of despair, cleansing and purifying her once again, and dressing her in preparation for her long postponed wedding with her groom. If only this could be accomplished, the world would be a better place.

This feeling of anguish was familiar to the *Kabbalists* throughout Jewish history. The prophet Isaiah portrayed the destruction of the First Temple through the image of the fallen Jerusalem. The prophet anticipated the rebuilding of Jerusalem through a descendant of King David, the Bethlehemite, the descendant of Peretz. The imagery and hope of Isaiah consoled generations, evolved into the belief in a Messiah, and nourished Jewish hopes even in the period after the Expulsion of 1492.

There was, however, one significant difference. The *Kabbalists* knew that it was only through human efforts that the bride would enter the bridal chamber; the Messiah would not arrive until humans fulfilled their responsibility. The *Kabbalists* saw this duty as preparing the bride—*Malkhut*—and ushering her into the wedding ceremony with *Tiferet*. In actual terms, Jewish mystics developed the belief that once a week, at the sundown that marks the beginning of Sabbath, they could actually reunite the bride and the groom, at least for the next 25 hours. The Sabbath, for the *Kabbalist*, is an auspicious moment, an anticipation of a better age.

The *Kabbalists* were well-versed in Isaiah's prophecies about the rebuilding of Jerusalem, which he portrayed as an aggrieved mother, the symbol of Jewish hope. The prophetic characterization of Zion's desolation captured the feeling and personal experience of the Spanish exiles, many of whom were *Kabbalists*. In the generation after the Expulsion, Isaiah's prophecies appeared to speak directly to the condition of the *Shekhinah* "in the dust." Therefore, it is not surprising that Isaiah should have provided these mystics with the vocabulary of redemption.

These *Kabbalists* created new rituals of redemption whose purpose was to bring about the resurrection of the *Shekhinah* and her reunion with *Tiferet*. The most significant and enduring contribution of this period was the introduction of special hymns to the *Shekhinah* that were incorporated into the Sabbath liturgy. The most outstanding hymn of this genre is the famous *Lekhah Dodi* (Come, My Beloved) composed by the *Kabbalist* Shlomo ha-Levi Alkabetz in the Galilean town of Safed around 1560.

This hymn, which ushers in the Sabbath, transformed the Friday sundown liturgy into a drama of the highest order. The congregation, dressed in white as if attending a wedding, would literally go out into the fields around Safed to greet the *Shekhinah*. This ritual is based on the *Talmudic* invocation for the Sabbath: "Let us come and go out to welcome the Sabbath bride."[19] The rabbinic metaphor of the Sabbath as a bride is linked with the *Kabbalistic* notion of the Sabbath bride as the *Shekhinah*. The *Shekhinah* arrives from the west with the setting sun, greeted by *Tiferet* who arrives from the east. The congregation is the wedding party that ushers the groom toward the bride by saying to *Tiferet*: "Come, my beloved, to meet the bride. Let us greet the Sabbath." The congregation rises for the final stanza and faces the rear of the sanctuary, the west, to greet the arriving Sabbath bride.

The Sabbath is transformed into a cosmic wedding ceremony between the masculine *Tiferet* and the feminine *Shekhinah*. The role of the congregation is to bring the lovers together, for this cannot be accomplished without their assistance. This ritual was adopted into the Friday evening service, which became known as *Kabbalat Shabbat*. This service became prominent throughout the Jewish world under the growing influence of *Kabbalah*. *Lekhah Dodi*, as a majestic ritual of redemption, became the centerpiece of this service. The *Kabbalistic* contribution to the creation of this ritual is indisputable and *Lekhah Dodi* even became known as "the Jewish Marseillaise."

In most congregations today, however, this hymn is repeated without any real awareness of its *Kabbalistic* significance. A vestige of the medieval custom is preserved when the congregation rises and faces the rear of the sanctuary for the final stanza. The symbol of the Sabbath bride, however, has entered popular Jewish culture stripped of its peculiar *Kabbalistic* nuances.

In order to understand *Lekhah Dodi*, we must first explain some of its internal references and symbolism. The language is drawn from the biblical books—*Isaiah*, *Psalms*, and the *Song of Songs*. The *Song of Songs* is a Hebrew love poem between the male "beloved" (*Dod*) and the female "lover" (*Ra'aya*). Here, the two lovers are equated with *Tiferet* and *Malkhut*, respectively. The Sabbath itself is associated with the *Sefirah Malkhut*, which rains down blessings upon the world when the union between the two lovers is consummated. *Malkhut* is also identified with the heavenly Jerusalem, the voice of God at Sinai, God's name, and the divine crown.

The opening line, "'Keep' (*shamor*) and 'remember' (*zakhor*) in one divine word," requires special explanation. The original Sabbath injunction in Torah appears in the list of the Ten Commandments. The list of commandments, however, appears twice in the Bible, in *Deuteronomy* 5:12 and *Exodus* 20:8. In the first version, the commandment regarding the Sabbath reads "Keep (*shamor*) the Sabbath day," and in the latter, "Remember (*zakhor*) the Sabbath day." The sages explain the variation by saying that God issued one commandment, but it was heard by the Israelites at Sinai in these two different ways. The *Kabbalists* associate *shamor* with *Malkhut* because *Malkhut* "keeps" and protects the world. *Zakhor*, which can mean "remember" or "to be masculine" (*zakhar*), is associated with *Yesod*, the phallic symbol within the *Sefirot*.

Many of the other phrases in this hymn are cryptic references to other names of the *Sefirot*. For example, "beauty" (*Tiferet*), "king," "glory" (*Kavod*), and "God" (*YHVH*) are synonyms for the *Sefirah Tiferet*. "Praise" (*Tehillah*) refers to *Binah*.

With this glossary in mind, the hymn takes on a new level of meaning. The *Lekhah Dodi* can easily be decoded and its *Kabbalistic* significance uncovered with these keys. We will now turn to a translation of *Lekhah Dodi* followed by an explanation of its hidden meaning. In the first section, the literal translation of the hymn appears with annotated references to the primary biblical allusions. Then, in the second section, we provide a rendition of *Lekhah Dodi* that explains its true *Kabbalistic* meaning.

Lekhah Dodi

Come, my Beloved (*Song of Songs* 7:12), to meet the Bride.
Let us welcome the Sabbath.

"Keep" and "Remember" (*Deut.* 5:12; *Ex.* 20:8) in one divine word.
Thus, the unified God to us made heard.
God is one, His name is one (*Zekh.* 14:9);
As is His name, His splendor, and His praise.

Toward the Sabbath, let us now go.
For she is the source of blessing,
Appointed since the earliest time, the beginning,
Last in creation but first in thought (*Ber. Rabba*).

Shrine of the king, royal city—
Rise up from your ruins,
Too long have you dwelled in the valley of tears (*Ps.* 84:7).
To you, He will show merciful compassion.

Arise and shake off the dust (*Isa.* 52:2).
Dress yourself with your clothes of splendor, My people,
With the help of Jesse's son (i.e., David), the Bethlehemite king.
Come near to my soul, redeem it!

Awake, Awake! (*Isa.* 51:17).
For your light has come, Arise, my light (*Isa.* 60:1).
Wake, wake (*Isa.* 52:1)—sing out with song.
The glory of God upon you is displayed.

Be not ashamed, be not distressed (*Isa.* 45:15; *Jer.* 22:22).
Why are you bowed, and why do you yearn (*Ps.* 42:12)?
In you shall the poor children of my people be comforted (*Isa.* 14:32).
The city upon its ashes will be rebuilt (*Jer.* 30:18).

They who destroyed you will themselves be destroyed (*Jer.* 30:16).
Your foes will be routed (*Isa.* 49:19).
Your God will then rejoice in you
As a bridegroom rejoices in his bride (*Isa.* 62:5).

Spread out to the right and the left (*Isa.* 54:3),
Revering God
With the help of a descendant of Peretz (i.e., David) (*Ruth* 4:18),
We will rejoice and celebrate (*Ps.* 118:24).

Come in peace the crown of her spouse (*Prov.* 12:4).
Come in joy and radiance.
To the faithful of the chosen people.
Come, O bride! Come, O bride!

Come, my Beloved, to meet the Bride.
Let us welcome the Sabbath.

The following is a faithful rendition of *Lekhah Dodi* that presents the underlying *Kabbalistic* meaning:

Lekhah Dodi

Come, my beloved *Tiferet*! Unite with the bride, *Shekhinah-Malkhut*.
Let us welcome the *Shekhinah* into our midst.

Malkhut and *Yesod* were emanated as one by *Tiferet,* God's voice, at Sinai.
On the Sabbath, *Tiferet* and *Malkhut* are one.
And, then, *Malkhut,* God's name,
Ascends to *Tiferet*, and, then, to *Binah*.

To greet *Malkhut*, let us now go.
Malkhut is the spring which draws from *Binah*.
Malkhut, anointed by *Hokhmah*, is the last *Sefirah* to be emanated
But the first to be conceived in God's *Hokhmah*.

Malkhut is heavenly Jerusalem, the sanctuary,
The vessel for *Tiferet*, the king.
Rise up from disunity!
Too long have you been separate from *Tiferet*.
Tiferet will draw *Hesed* upon you
And reunite with you.

Awake! End your exile from *Tiferet*!
Adorn yourself with the garments of *Tiferet*
With the aid of the Messiah, from the house of David,
He is nourished by *Malkhut*.
Shekhinah, come close to my soul,
Redeem it!

Awake, Awake!
For the light of *Tiferet*, your mate, has come.
Wake, wake—sing out with song.
Tiferet, God's glory, will join with you.

Be not ashamed, be not distressed!
Why are you bowed, and why do you yearn?
Through you, *Shekhinah*, the Jewish people will be restored
And the earthly Jerusalem will be rebuilt.

Those who destroyed you will themselves be destroyed.
Your foes will be routed.
Tiferet will then rejoice in you
As a bridegroom rejoices in his bride.

You will spread out to *Hesed* and *Din*,
The right and the left.
And *Tiferet* you will revere.

The Sabbath will foreshadow the messianic age
Brought by a descendant of Peretz (i.e., the messiah from the house of David)
In this we shall rejoice and celebrate.

Come, now, *Malkhut*, The lower crown of *Tiferet*,
Come in joy and radiance!
Come to the *Kabbalists* among the chosen people!
Come, O bride! Come, O bride!

Come, my beloved *Tiferet*! Unite with the bride, *Shekhinah-Malkhut*.
Let us welcome the *Shekhinah* into our midst.

The bold conceptualization of *Kabbalah* is the notion that God's masculine and feminine aspects can be reunited by religious actions. The traditional notion of God as father and king has been dramatically transformed into God as the sum total of all the possibilities and polarities in the world. God is a dynamic whose strongest polarities are the masculine and feminine *Sefirot*. Jewish mysticism is predicated, therefore, on a series of abysses. The abyss between God and the world mirrors an abyss deep within God between two aspects of his being. The mystic quest in Judaism is the effort to bridge the abyss between God and the world by healing the rift within God.

6

ENTERING THE GARDEN

The Meaning of Torah

Divine revelation did not end at Sinai when Moses received the Torah.
Continuing revelation of the divine mysteries could be uncovered
through individual mystical inspiration and through finding new depths of
meaning in the Torah text itself. Torah is, after all, the record of Moses'
unbounded consciousness and connection with God. The depths of what
could be discovered within Torah are nearly limitless. As one Kabbalist
wrote: "All the words of Torah hint at the divine mystery: If all the oceans
were ink, all people were scribes, and the heavens and earth were parchment, we would still be incapable of writing even one iota of what could be
said about each and every verse of Torah."[1] Torah, in addition to individual
mystical experience, leads the Kabbalist directly to God. By plumbing the
depths of meaning hidden within Torah, the mystic can follow in Moses'
footsteps and trace each word back to God.

Each verse of Torah speaks of worldly things, but hints at the divine.
For example, the *Kabbalists* believe that *Genesis* speaks about earthly creation
but hints at the deeper level of creation of the spiritual universe. According
to this view, *Genesis* describes both the creation of the universe and the creation of the *Sefirot*. They reinterpreted the creation narrative as an account
of how God created the world deep within Himself rather than outside
Himself. Each day of Creation represents another stage in the process of the
emanation of the *Sefirot*. Thus *Genesis* is not about the physical creation of
the world but about a spiritual meaning and order to the human universe.

113

Other *Kabbalists*, however, believed that this creation occurs within God and that we are, ultimately, in God and we ourselves are filled with divinity. One *Kabbalist* wrote: "Before the creation of the world, *The Infinite* withdrew itself into its essence, from itself to itself within itself. It left an empty space within its essence, in which it could emanate and create."[2] Another *Kabbalist* wrote: "How did God create the world? Like a person taking a deep breath and holding it, so that the small contains the large. Similarly God contracted his light to a divine handbreath, and the world was left in darkness. In the darkness God carved cliffs and hewed rocks to clear wondrous paths of wisdom."[3]

We should not read the Torah literally as stories about human events but as mysterious and veiled hints about the inner workings of God and the relationship of the divine to the world. The Torah is the vehicle by which the mystic knows God. This notion of the Torah is different from the contemporary idea that the Torah is a book to be read like other books. One does not, according to *Kabbalah*, "read" the Torah; one searches out the hidden or secret meanings. These meanings are the *Sefirot*, their dynamics, and the secrets of how the realm of God is related to our world. The *Kabbalists* believe that "the Torah speaks in the language of the sons of man, speaking of lowly matters that hint at higher matters."

The study of the Torah is the loftiest purpose of human life because it is the self-revelation of God and the means by which God created the world. To the *Kabbalist*, the entire world is Torah because all of existence is a garment for the Torah, which is itself a garment for the *Sefirot*. The *Sefirot* are garments, or vessels, for God's essence. Everything is essence within garment and garment within garment. The mystic quest is described as the act of unpeeling the layers of the garment in order to reach the essence at the very core. This is the basis of Jewish mysticism and the path to God. The Torah is the roadmap to God.

The following passage from the *Zohar* illustrates this idea:

> Rabbi Shimon said:
> Woe to the human being who says
> that Torah presents mere stories and ordinary words!
>
> If so, we could compose a Torah right now with ordinary words
> And better than all of them!
> To present matters of the world?

Even rulers of the world possess words more sublime.
If so, let us follow them and make a Torah out of them!
Ah, but all the words of Torah are sublime words, sublime secrets!

Come and see:
The world above and the world below are perfectly balanced:
Israel below, the angels above.
Of the angels, it is written:
"He makes His angels spirits" (*Ps.* 104:4).
But when they descend, they put on the garment of this world.
If they did not put on a garment befitting this world
They could not endure in this world
And the world could not endure them.

If this is so with the angels, how much more so with Torah
who created them and all the worlds
and for whose sake they all exist!
In descending to this world,
If she did not put on the garments of this world
The world could not endure.

So this story of Torah is the garment of Torah.
Whoever thinks that the garment is the real Torah
And not something else—
May his spirit deflate!
He will have no portion in the world that is coming.

That is why David said
"Open my eyes
So I can see the wonders out of Your Torah!" (*Ps.* 119:18).
What is under the garment of Torah?

Come and see:
There is a garment visible to all.
When those fools see someone in a good looking garment
They look no further.
But the essence of the garment is the body;
The essence of the body is the soul!

So it is with Torah.
She has a body:
The commandments of Torah.
Called 'the embodiment of Torah.'

This body is clothed in garments:
The stories of this world.
Fools of the world look only at that garment,
The story of Torah;
They know nothing more.
They do not look at what is under the garment.
Those who know more do not look at the garment
but rather at the body under that garment.
The wise ones, servants of the King on high,
Those who stood at Mt. Sinai,
look only at the soul, root of all,
Real Torah!
In the time to come
They are destined to look at the soul of the soul of Torah![4]

So what are the sublime mysteries of Torah? According to Daniel Matt, one of the leading scholars of *Kabbalah*, the *Zohar* is a Torah commentary that explains that the ideal human state of affairs is intimacy with the divine, cultivation of unbounded mystical awareness, and strengthening of the primordial connection between the human soul and God. In Matt's view, the Torah depicts a state of humanity that has fallen from grace having lost our oceanic, unbounded mystical consciousness. This fall from grace occurred in the Garden of Eden when Adam and Eve, apparently, chose to eat from the tree of rational, worldly knowledge rather than maintain their mystical, otherworldly innocence.

Just as Adam realized after eating from the Tree of Knowledge that he was naked, *Kabbalah* teaches that the Torah exists in an "unveiled" form before Adam's sin and a "veiled" form afterward. The "unveiled" Torah is pure and free; the "veiled" Torah is restricted and closed. If Adam had not disobeyed God, the universe would have been governed by the "Torah of the Tree of Life." "The Torah of the Tree of Life" would be the source of wisdom about human freedom and harmony with God rather than a guide to permitted and prohibited human behavior. Instead, we are governed by the "Torah of the Tree of Knowledge," a series of prohibitions and restrictions. The *Kabbalists* even suggested that, in the Messianic era, the "Torah of the Tree of Life" will be restored and we will be freed of the burden of the *mitzvot*.

Kabbalah, according to this view, is a discipline that allows us to live in the world while preserving mystical consciousness. The Torah is the prime vehicle for lifting the individual beyond mundane knowledge to higher, mystical consciousness. As Matt says, "The original sin lies in losing intimacy with the divine, thereby constricting unbounded awareness. This loss follows inevitably from tasting the fruit of discursive knowledge; it is the price we pay for maturity and culture. The spiritual challenge is to search for that lost treasure—without renouncing the self or the world."[5]

Ultimately, the reason why *Kabbalists* read Torah not for its narrative meaning but its reference to the *Sefirot* is that this leads them to shift their consciousness from the mundane to the divine. This shift in consciousness is intended to lead the Kabbalist towards "intimacy with the divine, unbounded awareness." It is an attempt to overcome the barriers of time and place that separate us from the immediacy of Sinai. It is an effort to reach across time and fathom the timeless.

Kabbalists do not read the Torah for its narrative meaning but, rather, they read it in search of the *Sefirot*—the essence that is symbolized in the words of the Torah. The words of Torah might tell stories, but that is only incidental. The Torah is more a texture than a text. The *Kabbalist* is not concerned with the historical figure of Abraham; he is interested in understanding the proper, divine referent that is symbolized by the name. Even the names of the forefathers, such as Abraham, do not refer only to earthly humans. Abraham is an essential name, according to *Kabbalah*, whose referent is the *Sefirah Hesed*. This association is suggested by the verse: "Deal graciously (*Hesed*) with my master Abraham."[6] The *Kabbalists* identify countless names in the Torah and specify the *Sefirot* to which the names refer. Each of the various names of God, for example, refers to a different *Sefirah*.

The following is a brief glossary of some of the important names of God and the *Sefirot* they symbolize:

Y (first letter of *YHVH*)	*Hokhmah* (wisdom)
H (second letter of *YHVH*)	*Binah* (understanding)
V (third letter of *YHVH*)	*Tiferet* (splendor)
H (fourth letter of *YHVH*)	*Malkhut* (majesty)
YHVH	*Tiferet* (splendor)
Elohim	*Binah* (understanding)
Ha-Kadosh Barukh	*Hu* (The Holy One, Blessed be He)
	Tiferet (splendor)
Adonai	*Malkhut* (majesty)

The letters of the Hebrew alphabet are hidden in *Hokhmah*, which is the beginning of the name of God. The linguistic process of the unfolding of divine language through the particularization of these letters corresponds to the unfolding of the divine name. The stages in the process of the emergence of these letters correspond to the stages in the process of emanation.

The first letter of the divine name, *Y (yod)*, is symbolic of this process. The Hebrew letter begins with a "point," indicating that *Hokhmah* is the beginning of the process of linguistic expression and the start of emanation. The flourish on the tip of the Hebrew letter signifies and points to *Keter* and *The Infinite* that are above it. The second letter, *H (hei)*, is associated with the *Sefirah Binah*. This *Sefirah* gives form to the letters that are hidden and undifferentiated in *Hokhmah*. The third letter, *V (vav)*, is written as a straight line and has a numerical value of six, symbolizing the emanation of the six *Sefirot* from *Hokhmah* to *Yesod*. The final *H* brings all the potencies and forms of the *Sefirot* into actuality below this realm just as *Binah* did in relation to *Hokhmah*.

Kabbalah teaches that Torah can be understood according to four different interpretive methods: literally (*Peshat*), allegorically (*Remez*), morally (*Derash*), or mystically (*Sod*). The *Zohar* coined the acronym *PaRDeS* (Garden or Paradise) as a mnemonic device referring to the four methods of approaching Torah. *PaRDeS* refers to (1) *peshat*, the plain or literal meaning of the text, (2) *remez*, the veiled meaning which the text hints at but does not make explicit, (3) *derash*, the *Midrashic* or homiletic interpretation which is derived from reading between the lines of Torah, and (4) *sod*, the esoteric or mystical meaning.

The approach of *peshat* is to define the plain sense or literal meaning of the text. The *peshat* meaning is the goal of the Jewish interpretive tradition and its major contributors including Rashi, Nahmanides, and others. Today, *peshat* includes the techniques of biblical linguistics that help us to develop a clear analysis of each passage. It utilizes the findings of archeology that provide data from the ancient Near Eastern cultures, which corroborate and refute some of the common assumptions of biblical interpretations. For example, the comparative studies of ancient Near Eastern creation myths showed that several of the *Genesis* narratives are retellings of common myths from a monotheistic perspective. These studies highlighted the uniqueness of Israelite religion, its borrowings, and differences from contemporaneous civilizations.

Derash, which means to "search out," was the product of Jewish literary analysis of textual passages. This technique employed rules of interpretation called hermeneutics, which paid close attention to comparison of similar expressions in different passages and drew on other logical techniques including inference, induction, deduction, and contradiction. *Derash* sought to develop extended meanings of individual words or phrases based on these rules of interpretation in order to derive moral teachings or *halakhic* rulings. *Derash* also employed literary analysis in order to supply meaning to cryptic biblical passages. When a biblical passage would puzzle the reader or raise questions without apparent answers, the reader could employ the technique of *derash* to find an answer.

Frequently, *derash* or *Midrash* became the basis for elaborate and fanciful excursions into folklore, legend, and anecdote. For example, the biblical account of the patriarch Abraham leaving his father's house did not supply any detail about the conditions of his upbringing. Therefore, the *Midrash* filled in the missing pieces by supplying a fanciful story about how Abraham was the son of an idol-maker. One day, he was moved to destroy the idols in his father's workshop but panicked when he realized that his father was about to catch him in the act. He placed the hammer in the hand of the one remaining idol as his father walked in. He told his father that the surviving idol destroyed the others. When his father scoffed at this absurd notion, Abraham pointed out that the very absurdity of the answer proves the folly of idolatry. This legend is typical of the attempt on the part of *Midrash* to fill in the missing holes in the Torah text.

Remez employs "hints" and allegory to derive new and extended meanings from unlikely Torah passages. This technique was especially useful to those biblical interpreters who wanted to reconcile secular knowledge with Jewish tradition. For example, Jewish philosophers who favored this technique interpreted the narratives of the biblical patriarchs allegorically as representing the destiny of the soul in this world and in the afterlife. This made it possible for them to preserve the Torah as a source of higher truth while introducing new theories beyond the plain meaning of the text.

Another technique employed by practitioners of *remez* is the use of *gematria*, an analogy between two words based on the numerical equivalence of the Hebrew letters of each word. If two words have equal numerical significance, practitioners of *remez* can attribute a deeper significance and analogy between the words. For example, the rules for the Sabbath that appear in Exodus are introduced by the phrase, "These are the things (*elleh ha-devarim*) that the Lord has commanded you to do." The practitioners of *gematria* noted that the numerical equivalence of "these are" (*elleh*) is thirty-six. They add to this the following values: "the" (*ha*) counts as one word and "things" (*devarim*) as two since it is plural. Together, the sum equals thirty-nine. In their view, the verse hints at the thirty-nine classes of labor that are prohibited on the Sabbath.

Sod is the technique employed primarily by the *Kabbalists* who believed that each word or combination of words of Torah corresponded to the *Sefirot* or to processes within the world of the *Sefirot*. *Sod* is the symbolic technique of uncovering the hidden allusions in the words of Torah through mystical insight. The *Kabbalists* studied Torah, or decoded Torah, because it was a window to divinity. They were not concerned with the plain meaning of the text but with the meta-text of the Torah. This meta-text was the version that existed within God and represented a higher reality than the apparently mundane events recorded in Torah. Still, the *Kabbalists* adopted the normative practices and rituals derived from Torah.

It is against the background of a mystical understanding of Torah that the *Kabbalists* present their ideas in the form of biblical commentaries and homilies. After all, this is no ordinary book. *Kabbalah*, and *Zohar* in particular, utilize the methods of classical rabbinic *Midrash* to present the type of interpretation called *Sod*. The method employed by *Zohar* usually works as follows: A biblical verse is introduced. Sometimes, it is difficult for a novice reader to understand the significance of the verse because a *Midrash* might only cite the first part of the verse and assume that the reader remembers the rest of the verse. Often, the part of the verse not cited is the very basis for the interpretation that follows. Next, a question or problem raised by the verse is identified as the subject of the *Midrash*. At other times, the question or problem is left unstated and the reader must supply it as the key to what follows. Then, a second verse may be introduced. When that occurs, the reader must ask: what is the relationship between the two verses? Is there a contradiction, a term that appears in both but with different meanings, or some other interpretive challenge or question raised by the apposition of the two verses? The reader must identify the question or problem because this is the key to understanding the *Midrash* that follows. Then, an explanation of the first or second verse might follow and additional views may be introduced. Then, there is a conclusion that refers back to the original verse and ties the *Midrash* together.

For example, one *Midrash* that appears in *Zohar* opens with the verse from *Genesis*: "And God said: Let the earth bring forth a living soul after its kind." Then, a second verse is introduced: "Not like these is the portion of Jacob, for the creator of all is He." The apposition of these two verses set up an implied problem. The implicit *Midrashic* question is: if God is the creator of all, how can the text say that it is the earth itself that brings forth the soul? The key to the *Kabbalistic sod* interpretation, the solution to the *Midrashic* problem, is that Torah speaks of worldly things, but hints at the divine. Therefore, the interpretive key is that "earth" refers to a *Sefirah* not to the created ground. The *Zohar* goes on to explain that "Jacob" refers to *Tiferet*, which is actually the *Sefirah* that creates souls. *Tiferet* then transmits souls to *Malkhut*, the *Sefirah* called "Earth," which brings souls into the world. Thus Jacob, or *Tiferet*, the Creator of all, creates souls, while the Earth, or *Malkhut*, brings forth the living souls into the world. The contradiction between these two verses is resolved through the *Midrashic* method and the *sod* interpretation neatly wraps it up.

Sometimes, *Zohar* uses *remez*, allegory, to promote a *sod* interpretation. For example, *Zohar* takes the following biblical verse in which God says to Abraham: "Go forth from your native land and from your father's house to the land that I will show you."[7] *Zohar* then suggests the following as the *remez* interpretation of the verse: *Tiferet* (God) said to the soul (Abraham): "Go forth from the realm of the *Sefirot* and from *Tiferet*, your source, to a specific human body below."

At other times, *Kabbalah* elaborates on core concepts from earlier periods in the history of Jewish thought and expands their mystical significance. For example, the *Midrash* from the rabbinic period introduced the idea of a primordial Torah, a blueprint of the Torah that existed within God's mind before the creation of the world. If the primordial Torah is the blueprint, then God's wisdom is the hidden code built into the architecture of the universe. The architecture of the universe—the patterns of nature, human life, the soul—is not merely created by God; it is God's own creative self-expression. If we uncover the hidden architecture of the universe, we can know the wisdom of the architect. Torah is the operating system of the universe, the software that operates the world and our own souls.

Indeed, this concept advanced the idea that God created the world so that He could give the Torah when people were ready to receive it. The *Midrashic* concept of primordial Torah was expanded in *Kabbalah* and *Hasidism*. Based on a *Midrash* on verses from *Proverbs*, the rabbis declared that the primordial divine wisdom, the hidden vitality within Torah, is called *Reshit* (source or beginning). Because this primordial wisdom is the blueprint from which God created the world, the *Midrash* states: "By means of this wisdom, God created the world." The *Midrash* further explains:

> The Torah itself declares: "I am the vessel of God's artistry." It is an accepted practice that when a mortal king builds a palace, he doesn't start to build

from his own thoughts but, rather, does so based on the concept of an architect. And the architect doesn't start to build from his own thoughts but,
rather, does so from drawings and sketches so that he knows how to construct the rooms and doorways. Similarly, God gazes into the Torah and thus
creates the world.[8]

Then, twenty-six generations after Creation, the primordial Torah was
given to the Jewish people as the Written Torah and the hidden wisdom of
God becomes revealed. The *Midrash* sees the Written Torah as just a more
explicit expression of God's wisdom than the primordial Torah that preceded creation. Prior to Sinai, it would have been possible to discover God's
wisdom in the architecture of the universe but it still remained hidden.
Now, since Sinai, God's wisdom is revealed in the text of Torah and,
through it, in the universe. With the giving of the Torah, God's hidden
wisdom is revealed. From Sinai on, it is possible to uncover the divinity
revealed in the universe and in the text of Torah.

The holiday of *Shavuot*, the anniversary of the giving of the Torah, is
also the holiday that celebrates the spring harvest ("the day of first fruits").
One nineteenth-century Jewish mystic connected these two themes of *Shavuot* as follows:

> By means of the Torah, God created the world. The inner vitality of all cre-
> ated things is the power of "the Source" that comes from the Torah, as the
> Sages taught: "The world was created by the Torah which is called the
> Source." The Torah is the power behind Creation. But at the time of Cre-
> ation, the inner vitality is hidden. Then, on the day of "the Giving of
> Torah," the inner vitality is revealed and every created thing cleaves to its
> divine source. At that moment, the inner vitality of Torah is revealed and
> overflows into every created thing. The whole world is filled with God's
> glory. Until then, God was hidden. Therefore, this day is called "the day of
> first fruits" because, from now on, every created thing cleaves to the Source
> and, through it, is reborn.[9]

Zohar takes this *Midrashic* concept to a new level. Since each verse of Torah
speaks of worldly things, but hints at the divine, the ultimate meaning of
Torah is the significance of the *sod* interpretation. That means that the *Kabbalist* needs to trace backwards from the words of the Written Torah to the
source of each word in the realm of the *Sefirot* and as a reference to the inner
workings of the *Sefirot*.

On a deeper level, a *Kabbalist* is also charged with the responsibility of uniting the *Sefirot*, of restoring harmony within the realm of the *Sefirot*, through Torah study and ritual action. For example, the holiday of *Shavuot* celebrates the anniversary of the giving of the Torah on Mount Sinai. Each year, on *Shavuot*, a *Kabbalist* is faced with the awesome challenge of recreating the auspicious conditions under which God revealed the Torah—the alignment of *Tiferet* and *Malkhut* in perfect balance and harmony with each other. The *Zohar* describes this in near orgasmic terms as a consummation of a holy wedding ceremony joining together the masculine and feminine aspects of God.

The significance of the night of *Shavuot* generated the creation of a ritual night vigil, called *Tikkun* (restoration), in order to restore the unity of *Tiferet* and *Malkhut* as it once was when Moses received the Torah on Mount Sinai following his own night vigil. According to a guide to *Kabbalistic* ritual, one should stay awake all night on the eve of *Shavuot*, studying Torah, *Midrash*, and other related texts in a state of mystical devotion as if preparing for a wedding:

> It is a great *mitzvah* and a high rung to engage in Torah study on the night of *Shavuot*. As the *Zohar* says: "He who arrives in a pure state on that day is not without divine consideration that night. He should enter the study of Torah, unite with her, and maintain his sacred purity when he approaches her on that night and is purified by her. And what Torah should he study on that night? The Oral Torah—so that he should be purified as one channel from a deep stream. Later on the same day, he should study the Written Torah and unite with it. Then they will be found in one harmonious divine coupling. On that night, *Knesset Yisrael* (*Malkhut*) rests like a crown upon him and unites him with the King (*Tiferet*). Then, they both rest like a crown upon his head for they are worthy of this."[10]

In the following passage, the hero of the *Zohar*, Rabbi Shimon bar Yohai, a student of Rabbi Akiva, describes the preparation for a night vigil on *Shavuot* that ritually prepares *Malkhut*—the divine bride for her wedding with the Holy One, Blessed be He—*Tiferet*. The Jewish people, the *Shavuot* celebrants—the companions, are the attendants at the wedding of the male and female aspects of God:

> Rabbi Shimon would sit and study Torah all night when the bride was about to be united with her husband. And we have learned that the companions of the household in the bride's palace are needed on that night when the bride is prepared for her meeting on the morrow with her husband under

the bridal canopy. They need to be with her all that night and rejoice with her in the preparations with which she is adorned, studying Torah—from the Torah to the Prophets, and from the Prophets to the Writings, and then to the *Midrash* and mystical interpretations of the verses, for these are her adornments and her finery. And she enters with her maidens and stands above their heads, and she is made ready by them, and rejoices with them throughout the night. And on the morrow she does not enter the bridal canopy without them, and they are the ones called "the sons of the bridal canopy." When she enters the bridal canopy the Holy One, blessed be He, inquires after them, and blesses them, and crowns them with the bridal crowns. Blessed is their portion. And Rabbi Shimon with all his companions would sing the song of the Torah, and they would produce, every one of them, new interpretations of Torah, and Rabbi Shimon and all his companions would rejoice. Rabbi Shimon said to them: My children, blessed is your portion, because tomorrow the bride will not enter the bridal canopy without you, for all those who concern themselves with her adornments on this night and rejoice with her will be listed and inscribed in the Book of Memorial, and the Holy One, blessed be He, will bless them with the seventy blessings and crowns of the supernal world. . . . But at this time, when the bride is aroused so that she may enter the bridal canopy on the morrow, she is prepared and made to shine with her finery, together with the companions who rejoice with her all that night, while she too rejoices with them. On the morrow, they there are assembled together with her large entourage and many companies, and she waits with them for each one of those who had helped to prepare her on that night. They are together and she sees her husband—this is the bridegroom who enters the bridal canopy and illumines her with the radiance of the sapphire which shines from one end of the world to the other. Now that she has entered the canopy, she is called "the glory of God—glory upon glory, light upon light, power upon power." At the moment when "heaven" (i.e., *Tiferet*) enters the bridal canopy and comes to illumine her, all the companions who have helped to prepare her are designated there by name.[11]

The purpose of the giving of the Torah is not only to uncover the inner workings of the *Sefirot* but, ultimately, to lead the mystic back to oneness with God. Even the word "Torah," which is usually translated as "teaching," can be linked with the word for "illumination" (*or*). Torah is a source of illumination that reveals God's presence to us. Torah is called "God's Name" because to uncover the hidden meaning of Torah is to know God's name, the wisdom of God. Torah is a mystical source of illumination that reveals God's presence to us. The following passage by an early *Hasidic* author draws together these various approaches to Torah:

> God gave us His Torah to meditate upon for its own sake and so that we should achieve mystical union with God. God conceals Himself within His Torah just as the *Zohar* says: 'It is called Torah because it illuminates (*orei*) and reveals the One who is hidden.' God is both hidden and revealed—hidden from the sight of all but revealed in the hearts of those who desire Him, focus on Him constantly, seek Him constantly in their hearts and minds, and cleave to Him by means of Torah and *mitzvot*. In this way, God, who is hidden within His Torah—which is His Name—is revealed in the hearts of His people. The heart is where we feel the love and awe of God most deeply. This is the meaning of *Torah l'shmah* ("Torah for its name," meaning "Torah learning for its own sake"): Torah is like its name in that it points to (*toreh*) and reveals to us that which is hidden, namely God.[12]

Another example of how *Kabbalah* elaborates on earlier rabbinic concepts is the belief in the primordial light. The *Midrash* describes the presence of a hidden light within creation, the light created on the first day that preceded the creation of the sun, moon, and stars on the third day. The *Midrash* describes this as the light with which the righteous could see from one end of the universe to the other. But the *Zohar* offers the following elaboration:

> Rabbi Isaac said, "The light created by God in the act of creation flared from one end of the universe to the other and was hidden away, reserved for the righteous in the world to come. Then, the worlds will be fragrant and all will be one. But until the world to come arrives, it is stored and hidden away." Rabbi Judah responded, "If the light were completely hidden, the world could not exist for even a moment! Rather, it is hidden and sown like a seed that gives birth to seeds and fruit. Thereby the world is sustained. Every single day, a ray of (divine) light shines into the world, keeping everything alive. With that ray God feeds the world. And everywhere that Torah is studied at night, one thread-thin ray appears from that hidden light and flows down upon those absorbed in her. Since the first day, the light has never been fully revealed, but it is vital to the world, renewing each day the act of Creation."[13]

The founder of eighteenth-century *Hasidism* taught that this light can be found in Torah:

> With the light of the six days of creation, one could see from one end of the universe to the other. Where did God hide it? In the Torah. Whoever

attains the light hidden in the Torah can see from end of the universe to the other.[14]

Kabbalah is incompatible with a fundamentalist approach to Torah. The *Midrash* explains that each individual must understand Torah according to his own capacity just as our ancestors did at Sinai. As our capacity increases, so does our understanding of Torah. Meaning shifts, increases, and changes as our capacity grows:

> Come and see how the divine voice went forth to Israel (at Sinai), each one according to his capacity. The elders heard the divine voice according to their capacity, the young men according to their capacity, the adolescents according to their capacity, the children according to their capacity, the infants according to their capacity, and the women according to their capacity. Even Moses heard the divine voice according to his capacity, as it says, "Moses spoke and God answered him by a voice"—by a voice that Moses was able to withstand. Likewise, it is said: "The voice of the Lord is in strength" (*Ps.* 29:4). It does not say "in His strength" but "in strength," according to the capacity of each of them to withstand. Even the pregnant women heard the divine voice according to their capacity. Thus, I would say that each one hears the divine voice according to one's own capacity.[15]

The *Kabbalists* take the notion of multiple meanings even further. Some mystics say that there are at least seventy valid interpretations of Torah. They cite, for instance, the absence of vowels and punctuation in Torah that allows for creativity in interpreting the text.

> It is a fundamental principle that the Torah was given without vowels or punctuation so that it could be interpreted in seventy ways and vocalized in order to fit the interpretation. For the same reason, it was given without punctuation.[16]

Others say that there are 600,000 faces to Torah, one for each adult male who stood at Sinai, each of whom heard the voice of God in a slightly different way. The *Midrash* teaches that, before we are born, the primordial light that shines from one end of the universe to the other infuses our souls with divine wisdom, saturates our soul with Torah, and illuminates the entire Torah within us. We are not born as a blank slate but as vessels filled to capacity with wisdom. But when we are born into the world, an angel, as it were, taps us on the *philtrum*—the indentation on the upper lip, and causes us to forget the Torah. Life then becomes a process not of learning but of relearning Torah. This same light of divine wisdom within each one of us leads us to our personal relationship with Torah.

One astounding passage in rabbinic literature goes so far as to assert that there is no such phenomenon as objective meaning, only the meaning that we attribute to that which we experience. The *Midrash* turns the following biblical verse on its head: "Says the Lord: Who created you, O Jacob? Who formed you, O Israel?" (*Isaiah* 43:1). By reading this as a declarative statement rather than as a question and by shifting the punctuation, the *Midrash* creatively misreads the verse as stating that it is we, not God, who assign meaning to Torah and all of human experience. The *Midrash* reformulates the verse as follows: "God said to His world, 'My world, My world, I shall tell you who created you, who formed you—Jacob created you, Jacob formed you!'"[17]

The Kotsker Rebbe points to the fact that the holiday of *Shavuot* is called "the Season of the Giving of Torah" and not "the Season of the Receiving of Torah" as proof that Torah depends upon us, not God, to give it meaning:

> Why is *Shavuot* called "the Season of the Giving of Torah" and not "the Season of the Receiving of Torah?" Although the Torah was given in equal measure to all, it was not received in the same way. Each person received it according to his own level and understanding.[18]

My own teacher, Gershom Scholem, once wrote that, even today, we need to find the voice of our own soul in Torah if it is to have contemporary significance:

> Each Jewish soul has its own unique mystical path by which to read the Torah, in the sense of it being a living body and a true manifestation of the divine word; a path connected with the root of each person's soul in the upper worlds, which he, and he alone, is able to reveal.[19]

This is perhaps what one *Hasidic* author meant when he wrote:

> Why is Torah called "the ancient parable" (I *Sam.* 24:13)? Sometimes a parable depicts an event that never actually occurred in order to elevate those who cling to simplicity and falsehood and bring them closer to wisdom. . . . The Torah that God gave to Israel contains everything from top to bottom because it itself is without limit or end. Rather, each one of us understands

Torah according to the degree of our own openness to it and according to the root of our own soul. The degree to which Torah reveals its secret to us is according to the extent of our passion and love for it. Certainly, a wise person will find illumination and divinity in it. Therefore, Torah is called "the ancient parable" because just as a parable helps us to understand startling and sublime wisdom—the primordial wisdom of the divine mind is clothed within the Torah. This is how it is with Torah. The enlightened will understand this.[20]

Torah is not a text like other texts and cannot be reduced to objective interpretation. The sublime mysteries of Torah are the faces of Torah that each person must uncover. Torah is a parable in which God's primordial wisdom is clothed in human language. The *Kabbalist* must trace that wisdom back to its source. *Kabbalah* is a spiritual discipline that teaches its adherents to hear the voice of God in the received text. *Kabbalah* also tries to uncover the original experience behind the recorded text and helps us place ourselves at Sinai alongside the 600,000 and more Israelites who stood there. It is an attempt to overcome the barriers of time and place that separate us from the immediacy of Sinai. It is an effort to reach across time and fathom the timeless. Torah is not just the biblical text, but the inner meaning, the voice within the text. The *Kabbalist* seeks to become, like Moses, an ear that hears what the Torah is constantly saying to us.

7

THE ONENESS OF BEING

The Destiny of the Soul

The mystical dimension of *Kabbalah* is also evident in its teachings about human life. The Jewish mystical conception of human psychology is based on a spiritual theory of the origin and destiny of the human soul. Unlike modern psychology, Jewish mysticism posits the existence of a spiritual realm beyond the individual that animates and energizes the life of the soul. The mystic believes that the boundaries between the outer world in which he lives and the spiritual realm of divinity can be traversed easily. The Jewish mystic believes that the soul is the vehicle that links heaven and earth. He is especially conscious of the power of actions that can elevate the soul from its bodily residence to its heavenly origins. For the Jewish mystic, this is the very meaning of Judaism.

In the Bible there is no concept of a body-soul dualism as there is in later Western philosophy.[1] The body and soul are integral, harmonious, and inseparable as one living being. Biblical Judaism has no concept of a soul that is separable from the body and, therefore, has no term that can actually be translated as "soul." Although post-biblical Judaism introduced the notion of a separate soul, it took three biblical terms—*nefesh*, *ruah*, and *neshamah*—and gave them new meanings in order to describe the soul as separate from the body. We will begin by exploring how these three biblical terms took on new meanings in post-biblical Judaism and, especially, in *Kabbalah*.

A man or a woman is seen as a unified organic being described, in the

Hebrew Bible, as a *nefesh*. *Nefesh,* probably best translated as "living being," refers both to human life, in general, and to human character, in particular. In the following biblical verse describing creation of the first human being, *nefesh* is synonymous with a living being: "The Lord God formed man from the dust of the earth. He blew into his nostrils the breath of life (*nishmat hayyim*), and man became a living being (*nefesh hayyah*)."[2] In a later passage, *nefesh* simply refers to life: "And they seek my life (*nafshi*), to take it away."[3] But *nefesh* also refers to human feelings, the essence of being human, not only to physical existence. In the following passage, the Hebrew Bible admonishes the Israelites who have left Israel to have regard for the dignity and worth of non-Israelites because they understand what it means to be mistreated by the Egyptians: "You shall not oppress a stranger, for you know the feelings (*nefesh*) of the stranger."[4]

In the Hebrew Bible, *ruah* refers to human aspiration, the breath that brings about life, life's visible manifestation. The Hebrew Bible describes God as the source of life who sustains life by preserving human breath within us: "In whose hand is the life (*nefesh*) of every living thing, and the breath (*ruah*) of all mankind."[5]

By the second century of the Common Era, the rabbinic sages had accepted the view that the human being is composed of two distinct natures—body and soul. This dualism not only reflected the view that man had two natures, but also that each nature derived from a different source— the body from the earth and the soul from heaven. One rabbinic passage describes the angels, the animals, and human beings as God's creations, each of which has a body and a soul. The difference is that angels have ethereal bodies and souls, animals have earthly bodies and souls, while humans a combination of two natures. They have earthly bodies like the animals and heavenly souls like the angels:

> All created beings (i.e., angels) that were created from heaven, their soul and body are from heaven; all creatures that were created from the earth (i.e., animals), their soul and body are from the earth, except man, whose soul is from heaven and whose body is from the earth.[6]

In this view, man is a being with two distinct natures and is intermediate between the heavenly angels and the earthly animals. Consequently, man is capable of achieving great transcendence through the exercise of his soul or degradation through the actions of his physical body. Dualism replaced biblical monism as an expression of the strong spiritual bias of the rabbinic sages. In rabbinic theology, the purification of the human soul through study, worship, and good deeds is the path to transcending our earthly nature and becoming like the angels. This view does not lead, however, to a negative estimation of the physical aspects of human life. It merely serves to promote the view that the soul must regulate the activities of human beings.

Greek philosophy exerted a powerful influence upon rabbinic thinking about the soul as the result of two decisive encounters between Judaism and Hellenistic civilization. First, Hellenism spread Greek philosophic ideas throughout the Middle East between the fourth century B.C.E. and the second century C.E. Rabbinic Judaism, which emerged in the period when Israel was under Roman domination, was acquainted with Hellenism although it often opposed it. Second, the revival of ancient Greek philosophy in the Muslim world during the Islamic Abbasid period between the ninth and twelfth centuries, led to the dissemination of Greco-Arabic philosophy from Baghdad to Cordova. It was during this latter encounter that Jews, integrated culturally and intellectually into the Islamic world, were particularly receptive to Greco-Arabic philosophy and to the harmonization of rabbinic and philosophic teachings.

The Greek conception of the soul penetrated Jewish thinking during both of these encounters and was incorporated into rabbinic theology and medieval Jewish thought. Plato defined the soul as an essence that penetrates the body from without and gives it power. The soul comes from the realm of pure forms—independent of matter and individuality—that exist as universal, ideal prototypes of worldly phenomena. Subsequently, Aristotle defined the soul as the "capacity" (*entelechy*) or "principle" (*logos*) of the body that gives it actuality. For Aristotle, the soul is not, itself, identical with the body. The soul, however, as the actuality of the body, cannot exist independently from it.[7]

The human soul, according to Aristotle, has three faculties. The first, the appetitive faculty, is found among vegetable, animal, and human life. It is the natural, inherent impulse responsible for the self-preservation of the individual through nutrition and growth. The second, the cupiditive faculty, common to all forms of animal life, is the instinct that seeks attainment of pleasure and the avoidance of harm and operates through the five physical senses. The third faculty, conscious reason, found only in man, is the power of judgment, memory, and thinking. This faculty can govern the cupiditive faculty or, if not actualized, can succumb to it and reduce us to mere animals. The exercise of the intellect, according to Aristotle, is what makes us truly human.

In the first encounter between Hellenism and Judaism, the rabbinic sages generally accepted the Platonic premise that the soul and the body are opposites and that the soul penetrates the body "from without," but which the sages understood to mean "from God." In the second encounter, medieval Jewish intellectuals accepted a version of Aristotle's philosophy refracted through many interpretations. The human soul was understood as a hierarchically ordered capacity of the human body of which only the intellect comes from God. Still, they adopted the nomenclature from Aristotle of the vegetative, animal, and rational soul. Most important, however, both the concepts and the nomenclature were aligned with the rabbinic theories of *nefesh*, *ruah*, and *neshamah*. *Nefesh* became the vegetative soul; *ruah* the animal soul; and *neshamah* became the rational soul.

The Jewish mystical conception of the soul was influenced by these traditions. The human soul, according to the Jewish mystics, consists of *nefesh*, *ruah*, and *neshamah*. *Nefesh* is the physical force in all living beings, the soul that gives life. This faculty is common to all living beings. Following the rabbinic view, the *Zohar Hadash* says: "This is the power given to animals, beasts and fish which are created from the earth."[8] But *Zohar* explains the functions of the different souls in a sense different from the Aristotelian scheme. Since the *Kabbalists* believed that observance of the Jewish religious commandments leads to self-preservation, *nefesh* is regarded as the impulse to observe the *mitzvot*. *Ruah* is a higher faculty that enables humans to rise above their limited physical existence and to achieve religious transcendence. *Ruah* is the religious faculty in human beings that leads a person to study Torah and to delve into the meaning of the commandments. Once a person has attained *nefesh* through religious observance and *ruah* through contemplative Torah study and religious experience, God may confer *neshamah* upon him. The following passage describes the sequential progress that may lead to attaining *nefesh* as the capstone of human spiritual achievement:

> The purpose of the *nefesh* is sustenance of the body by means of religious observance which it arouses. The purpose of *ruah* is to arouse the body to Torah and to guide it in this world. And if one is deserving—the *nefesh* through religious observance and the *ruah* through involvement in Torah—an exceptional benefit (*neshamah*) immediately descends upon it from above according to his actions.[9]

The three souls are arranged hierarchically in man, beginning with *nefesh*, and the higher soul is attainable only after the lower soul has been acquired.

In *Kabbalah, nefesh* serves the nutritive and preservative function for the body as in Aristotelian psychology. The *Zohar*, however, defines the performance of Jewish ritual observances as the real cause of human survival. The religious actions of man are motivated by the *nefesh*, and they in turn preserve his physical existence. *Ruah* is the faculty that motivates man to understand the deeper, spiritual meaning of the Torah beyond the merely physical observance of the commandments. If one perfects his understanding of the Torah on this deeper level, he achieves a greater spiritual station, the *neshamah*. The *neshamah* is attainable only by those who follow the Torah and who lead exemplary lives. This is the soul that enables man to achieve mystical insight into the Torah and that leads to religious communion with the *Sefirot* and, ultimately, to achieve immortality. It is the mystic faculty in humans:

> *Nefesh* is the lowest awakening. It is attendant to the body which it nourishes. The body clings to it as it clings to the body. If it reaches its fulfillment, it becomes a throne upon which the *ruah* is installed as a result of the awakening of the *nefesh*, which clings to the body. After these two are arranged, they are disposed toward acquiring *neshamah*, and the *ruah* becomes a throne for the *neshamah*, which is installed upon it.[10]

Neshamah is the mystic aspect of the human soul that links a person to the divine world of the *Sefirot*. The description of the *neshamah* in relation to the other faculties of man is indistinguishable from descriptions of the relationship of *The Infinite* to the other *Sefirot*: According to the *Zohar*, "This *neshamah* is hidden, above all else, and the most sublime."[11] Man is, therefore, conceived as a structure parallel to and analogous with the *Sefirot*. The soul in man is what the essence of *The Infinite* is to the *Sefirot*. The connection between man and the *Sefirot* is believed to be even deeper, because the soul originates within the *Sefirot* and creates an essential connecting link between the divine realm and man. The important element in this notion is that one who has the correct insight into this relationship is able to direct the activities of his *neshamah* towards mystical union with the *Sefirot*.

Nefesh is associated with God's *Hesed*, a freely given gift of life, a pristine state of animal existence. *Ruah*, identified with *Din*, severity, is the human power and ability to choose good or evil. *Neshamah*, linked with *Tiferet*, not only provides a balance between *Hesed* and *Din*, but also the reconciliation of the animal and spiritual tendencies in man. When man acquires the *neshamah*, he has reached an inner state of equilibrium that represents the state of harmony within the divine realm.

Man has complete autonomy to direct his spiritual life towards mystical union. On the other hand, this freedom also entails the choice to accentuate the lower human faculties—body and *nefesh*—and the possibility of failure to achieve transcendence. The *Kabbalists* also believe that human mystical achievement may advance only up to a point. Beyond that point, a limit that is never specified, God reaches out and carries the mystic the rest of the way. The *Kabbalists* were fond of quoting the rabbinic aphorism, "He who comes to purify himself, receives divine assistance." *Neshamah* is that divine gift which allows the spiritually accomplished individual to become a mystical virtuoso:

> *Nefesh* and *ruah* are inextricably joined together while *neshamah* dwells in the character of man, which place is a sublime and unknown abode. If a man seeks fulfillment, he is granted the assistance of the holy *neshamah*, through which he is fulfilled and made holy and called a 'saint.' And if he does not strive to reach fulfillment, he acquires only the two levels of *nefesh* and *ruah*. He will not achieve the holy *neshamah*.[12]

The *nefesh*, closely related to the body, is similar in substance and existence to the material world, whereas the nature of the *neshamah* is related to the divine world. The *Kabbalists* who accept the medieval concept of the dualism of body and soul also accept a dualism of *nefesh* and *neshamah*. This analogy between body and soul, earth and heaven can be seen in the following mythological passage that recasts the creation story in a new narrative form. It retells the creation of the earth from the primordial water, earth, and heaven described in *Genesis*. God turns to these elements to assist Him in creation. The water receded to produce the solid earth. The earth produced the various species of animals. The so-called upper water above the earth receded and, in that space, the heavens were created as a great expanse. Then, God called upon the water, earth, and heaven to produce the human body. But, finally, God alone created the human soul from His own being and placed it in the first human body. The term *neshamah* is used here in a general sense rather than the specific meaning of the highest soul. Man has two natures—earthly and divine, body and soul. By virtue of the soul, man will be able to transcend his earthly nature and achieve oneness with God:

> When the Holy One, Blessed be He, created the world, the basis of all was water and from water everything was sown. The Holy One, Blessed be He, made three craftsmen who would carry out His plan in this world. They were: heaven, earth and water. By means of these three, everything in the

world was created. God called upon each of these three to fashion the beings necessary for this world. To the water, He said: "Bring forth the earth which is below you; go and gather into one spot." This was done, as it is written: "Let the water be gathered" (*Gen.* 1:9). To the earth, He called and said: "Bring forth the creatures from within you, animals, beasts and the like." It was done immediately, as it is written: "God said, 'Let the earth bring forth every kind of living (*nefesh*) creature'"(*Gen.* 1:24). To the heavens, He called and said: Place yourselves between the upper and lower water. And they did, as it is written: "God made the expanse" (*Gen.* 1:7). By means of these three, the entire work of creation was completed, each one according to its kind. When the sixth day arrived, they were ready to create as on the previous days. The Holy One, Blessed be He, said to them: "None of you alone is capable of creating this creature (i.e., man) as with the other creatures which came to life so far. All of you, join together with Me, and let us make man! You cannot make him by yourselves. The body will belong to the three of you, but the *neshamah* belongs to Me!" Thus, He called to them and said: "'Let us make man' (*Gen.* 1:26), you and Me, I will make the *neshamah* and you will make the body." And so it is, that the body is from these three elements, craftsmen in the work of creation, while the *neshamah* was given by the Holy One, Blessed be He, who joined with the others in this. "'In our image, after our likeness' (*Gen.* 1:26), means that man should be worthy of us. Through the body which is from you, he will know you and resemble you. And with that which is taken from Me, the *neshamah*, he will separate himself from mundane affairs and his cleaving and desire will be for holy and divine matters. Moreover, the body which is taken from you three will not have permanent existence just like you. How is he like you? He is like the other creatures which you brought forth, since he is dust like all the other creatures. But the holy *neshamah*, which I gave him, not the body, will grant him eternal existence and through it he will resemble Me!"[13]

Earlier rabbinic writings explained that "in our image, after our likeness" means that Adam was created in the image of the dignity of God. The rabbis concluded that the creation of human beings is the very purpose of the creation. There is no one other than a human being who can perfect or destroy the world. Humanity must live with the consequences of their dominion over the earth, for there is no one else to clean up after them. According to one *Midrash*:

When the Holy One created the first man, He took him and led him around all the trees of the Garden of Eden, and said to him: Behold My works, how beautiful, how splendid they are. All that I have created, I created for your sake. Take care that you do not become corrupt and thus destroy My world. For once you become corrupt, there is no one after you to repair it.[14]

The *Midrash* explains that there were several explanations as to why the Bible refers to "our" image and "our" likeness in the plural. After all, was not God the sole creator? One rabbi said that it referred to God's own heart with which he took counsel. Another view suggested that God was assisted in the creation of man by his ministering angels in heaven. A third offered the opinion that God, who saw the future havoc which men would wreak, invoked the aid of his own attribute of mercy in His decision to create the world.

According to rabbis of the *Talmudic* era, there were differences of opinion as to why only one Adam was created. Some argued that this was to accentuate the importance of each individual. Others argued that it was to establish a measure of human equality by attributing common ancestry to all human beings. Another suggested that the creation of a solitary man points to one solitary God as creator. Yet another maintains that human worth and distinctiveness are insured when so many different individuals can be traced back to the father of all humanity:

> Man was created alone in order to teach you that if anyone causes a single soul to perish from Israel, Scripture imputes to him the destruction of the entire world; and if anyone saves alive a single soul in Israel, Scripture imputes to him the saving alive of the entire world. Again, (man was created alone) for the sake of peace among men, that one might not say to his fellow, "My father was greater than yours;" and that heretics might not say, "There are many ruling powers in heaven." Another reason: To proclaim the greatness of the Holy One. For if a man strikes many coins from one die, they all resemble one another; in fact, they are all exactly alike. But though the King of kings of kings, the Holy One, blessed be He, fashioned every man from the die of the first man, not a single one of them is exactly like his fellow. Hence, each and every person should say, "The world was created for my sake."[15]

Other rabbis explained that man was originally created as an androgynous being, one which has male and female gender characteristics. This interpretation, which does not imply that the rabbis accepted homosexuality or bisexuality, explains that Adam and Eve are both created in the image of God:

Rabbi Jeremiah ben Eleazar said: When the Holy One created Adam, He created him hermaphrodite (i.e., androgynous), as is said, "Male and female created He them . . . and called their name Adam" (*Gen.* 5:2). Rabbi Samuel bar Nahman said: When the Holy One created Adam, He made him with two fronts; then He sawed him in half and thus gave him two backs, a back for one part and a back for the other part."[16]

The *Kabbalists* viewed God as a unified deity who contained the characteristics of masculine and feminine in divine, ideal, and harmonious perfection. Since the divine image is understood as the human representation of God, the phrase "Let us make man in our image," was interpreted as God's original intention to create man as an earthly replica of God's androgynous (male and female) nature. But in this world, unity is elusive and man was created to be different, separated, from woman:

In the world above, there is union of male and female. When the Holy One, blessed be He, set out to create man, He wanted to make him in the following fashion: on the pattern of His own image, without separation or division, as it is said, "Let us make man in *our* image." Adam was indeed made on the pattern of the celestial image, but he made a separation there, and was separated from there.[17]

Rashi (Rabbi Solomon ben Isaac of Troyes, France, 1040–1105), the preeminent Bible commentator, explained that the "image of God" refers to our ability to understand and think, which distinguishes us from all other creatures. Maimonides explains the "image of God" means that we are created with an intellect, which is the only feature which God and human beings have in common.

Most *Kabbalists* see the "image of God" as the human soul, the divine essence of a human being, enclosed with the earthly body. According to the *Zohar,* every material thing is a casing for something spiritual:

The whole of existence consists of an inner kernel with several shells covering the kernel. The whole world is constructed according to this pattern, above and below: from the mysterious being of the highest point down to the lowest of all levels, it is all one within the other, and one within the other. One level is the shell to another, and this other the shell of another. The first point is an inner light . . . Mortal man is constructed in this image in the world: kernel and shell, soul and body, and all is for the well-ordering of the world.[18]

The divine image is also understood as the spiritual seeker in us. In commenting on the reference to "in our image, according to our likeness," the *Zohar* comments:

> With the part that he will receive from Me, the holy soul, man will leave the affairs of the world and his yearning will be for the holy, divine matters.[19]

Some *Kabbalists* see the "image (*tzelem*) of God" as the likeness of a heavenly or spiritual, although not necessarily physical, structure of the human being. *Tzelem* came to mean several things in *Kabbalah*. *Tzelem* was seen by some Jewish mystics as the *adam kadmon* or *macroanthropos*, the ideal prototype of a human being that God formed before creation and which was the model for the first created human being. This heavenly model was formed by God out of His own being, with His characteristics, as the blueprint from which He created man.

The "image of God" was also viewed as our "perfected nature," the self we can isolate within our selves, removed from our body. Shem Tov Falaquera described this as an aura that we emanate, and possibly one that can be seen by others: "I isolate myself in myself and remove my body, and it is as if I were a simple entity without a body; I see myself in the beauty and glory that remains, and I see myself as if I stand within the world of divine intellect." This image is often expressed as an "aura" that a person conveys, "a spiritual force in which the powers of the soul are imprinted in a physical but hidden manner."

Other *Kabbalists* saw the "image of God" as the "astral body," our personal angel, our spiritual double, a subtle body between our body and soul whose physical image and likeness are imprinted upon each human being at conception or birth. Just as the soul comes from without, the physical body is said to have an independent spiritual existence prior to its becoming a real body. Before birth the astral body resides in the heavenly treasury known as "the heavenly Garden of Eden." Man is born with the physical manifestation of this astral body which is sometimes described as the "image" (*tzelem*) of God. The astral body stays with man during his lifetime and becomes a garment woven from his deeds that accompanies his soul to the grave. The astral body may also hover over man and serve as a protecting angel during his lifetime.[20] In the thirteenth century, Eleazar of Worms said: "Each person has his form above who is his advocate, an angel who guides that person's destiny. And when the angel is sent below, he has the image of the person who is beneath him. Because each person has his spiritual double, it says twice: 'in our image, after our likeness . . .' "[21]

Not only is the relationship of the soul and the body analogous to that of *The Infinite* and the *Sefirot*, but the soul itself, especially the *neshamah*, originates in the realm of the *Sefirot*. The *neshamah* is the very essence of God encapsulated in human form. Through the human attainment of *neshamah*, man and God share a common nature. The union of the *Sefirot Tiferet* and *Malkhut*, masculine and feminine potencies respectively, produces the original prototype of the *neshamah*. Other mystics suggest that the *Sefirah Binah* ovulates and gushes forth souls that overflow upon *Malkhut*.[22]

Man was created as a vehicle for God's own self-fulfillment. God is a vibrant being whose masculine and feminine aspects are in a constant state of ebb and flow, now united, now separate. Man, the embodiment of the *Sefirot*, is the result of the union of the masculine and feminine in God. This reunion, however, can only be achieved by human religious acts that influence God. Therefore, the cultivation of the spiritual powers in man and the union of the masculine and feminine souls on earth are indispensable to God. Ultimately, this leads to the view that man was created as the agent for the reunification of God.

Religious actions produce ascents of the soul. When the soul acts according to the requirements of Jewish religious law, it triggers forces in the world that influence the various *Sefirot*. The correspondence and influence between the *Sefirot* and man are mutual and reciprocal. Just as the different souls represent the action of different *Sefirot*, the actions of the soul influence various *Sefirot*. Consequently, there is a perpetual and dialectical relationship between God and man through the medium of the soul. When the soul is involved in religious activity, it affects the *Sefirot*. Religious actions are primarily devoted to aligning the *Sefirot* in such a manner as to bring about the union of the masculine and feminine *Sefirot*. When this occurs, the essence of the *Sefirot* continues to flow upon the world.

For example, religious rituals are linked with the *neshamah* which is also associated with *Tiferet*, the masculine *Sefirah*. When the *neshamah* is activated, it contributes to the alignment of the masculine and feminine aspects of God. This, in turn, rains blessings upon the soul. The *Zohar* states clearly: "When the *neshamah* ascends, the desire of the feminine for the masculine is aroused and the waters pour from above to below."[23]

The emphasis on Torah as God's wisdom and the *neshamah* as the highest stage of human development raises an important question: Are non-Jews able to acquire the *neshamah* or is it restricted to Jews? *Kabbalah* reflects the nativistic stream in Judaism which subscribes to an essentialist view of Jewishness. The *Kabbalistic* view that the *neshamah* is an emanation of God's essence and comes to reside in us because of our connection with Torah leads to the restrictive idea that only Jews can acquire *neshamah*. Judaism, in this view, is the only path of ascent to God.

According to *Kabbalah*, while all humans have a *nefesh*, only Jews have a *neshamah*. This is because one can only achieve a *neshamah* through following the Torah. The following dialogue in the *Zohar* illustrates this point:

> Said Rabbi Hiyya: If this is true—that *neshamah* is acquired through following the Torah—is it so that gentiles have no *neshamah*, only the living *nefesh*? Rabbi Yohanan said: That is correct. Then, Rabbi Elazar asked: What, then, is given to Israel? Rabbi Hiyya expressed astonishment (because Rabbi Yohanan seemed to have answered the question definitively.) Rabbi Elazar responded: Come and see what was taught: "One who seeks to become pure, is given assistance" (B.T. *Shabbat* 104a). What sort of assistance is he given? That very same holy *neshamah* which serves as a pillar and which provides man with assistance in this world and the world to come. Until age thirteen, the human being is occupied with the living *nefesh*. From the age of thirteen (when a child accepts the responsibility of the Torah), if he wishes to be righteous, he is given the holy and exalted *neshamah*, hewn from the king's throne of glory.[24]

Man is created as a replica of the realm of the *Sefirot*, which is often referred to as the "throne of glory," or the "heavenly glory." Just as the essence of *The Infinite* fills the *Sefirot*, so too the *Sefirot* fill man. These *Sefirot* are present in man as he acquires each of the respective souls. When the mystics speak of man as being created in the image of God, they literally mean that man is created as a microcosm and embodiment of the *Sefirot*.

It is a fundamental axiom of Jewish mysticism that whatever exists in the world must first exist, in divine form, in the divine realm. Nothing can exist unless it has its "root" in the *Sefirot*. A human being is defined as the composite of its body and soul. Therefore, if the body is created by its father and mother, the soul must also be produced by a similar union. Since the soul comes from heaven, the "parents" of the soul must also reside in the divine realm. The father and mother of the soul are, therefore, the masculine and feminine aspects of God within the realm of the *Sefirot*:

> There is a mother and father to *neshamah* above just as there is a mother and father to the body on earth. This means that on all levels, whether earthly or divine, everything is produced by masculine and feminine.[25]

Once the *neshamah* is generated by the union of the masculine and feminine aspects of God, the prototype comes to reside in the realm below the *Sefirot*. The number of *neshamot* (pl. of *neshamah*) rapidly multiplies as the union of *Tiferet* and *Malkhut* produces further offspring. All of these come to reside in a realm of spiritual beings located intermediate between the world of the *Sefirot* and the realm inhabited by human beings. This realm contains the forms produced by the *Sefirot* with none of the matter that characterizes the world in which we live. The *neshamot* reside in a realm called the "treasury of souls" (*otzar ha-neshamot*) which is located in the heaven called *Aravot*.[26]

The *neshamah* has a rich and colored existence in "treasury of souls." It is the progeny of the *Sefirot* and it has something of their nature. It contains elements of the masculine and feminine *Sefirot* that produced it. It is both masculine and feminine in equal measure and in harmonious balance. At this stage, in the "treasury of souls," the *neshamah* is androgynous. Only later on, when the soul is ready to enter the body below, does it separate into its masculine and feminine components. The masculine half of the soul enters one body, determining that its host will be a man, while the feminine half enters another body, defining her as a woman.[27]

The birth of a human being and the formation of human character are the result of processes that begin in the realm of the "treasury of souls." The mystics believe that the original androgynous nature of the human soul is a harmonious balance between contradictory masculine and feminine forces. The unity is disturbed by the necessary descent of the soul into a human body. On one hand, birth represents a loss of the original unity of the soul that is separated from its heavenly abode. On the other hand, the soul cannot accomplish its destiny except by living in a human body.

Jewish mystics exhibit a candid and comfortable attitude towards sexuality within the strict parameters of what is permissible under Jewish law. Within these limits, the mysteries of human sexuality are seen as reflections of processes and sexuality within God. Since the mystics believe that the lower world is a reflection of the divine world, human sexuality is seen as emblematic of divine sexuality.

What is the *Kabbalistic* view of birth? When a man and woman have intercourse that leads to pregnancy, their sexual union produces a physical embryo. The embryo has the characteristics of the father and mother in equal measure. The embryo, itself, is androgynous and has no determined gender. The embryo continues to grow in the mother's womb but it is not itself a human being until the soul enters the body. Until the time the soul enters the body, the embryo is simply a physical body without life. Life does not begin until forty days after conception or close to the time of birth.

When a man and woman have intercourse and produce an embryo, their mutual arousal resonates within the realm of the *Sefirot*. Their arousal brings about the union of *Tiferet* and *Malkhut*. The coupling of *Tiferet* and *Malkhut*, in this instance, produces a soul. This soul, however, is androgynous because it possesses the characteristics of *Tiferet* and *Malkhut*—male and female—in an equal yet indeterminate manner. That unified androgynous soul descends into the "treasury of souls" where it waits to be assigned to the embryo whose parents helped to bring it about.

Sometime between the time of conception and birth, the soul is dispatched from the "treasury of souls" to its designated embryo. But before descending, the soul divides into its two component halves—male and female—in a process reminiscent of cellular mitosis. In some miraculous or unfathomable way, only one of those halves is assigned to the designated embryo below. The other half remains in the "treasury of souls," ready to be assigned to another body in need of a soul or whose parents did not produce a new soul. The half that is assigned to the waiting embryo descends, determines its gender, and initiates the cycle of life. Still, the soul that enters the body is only one half of an original unified soul. It enters the world missing a part of itself.

As the person grows through life, his or her soul yearns to reunite with its original mate and to recapture the unity of their existence prior to entering the world. Love, according to *Kabbalah*, is the longing to unite with our soul mate. Love is the yearning to restore the unity with the other half of our soul that we enjoyed prior to birth, a craving for wholeness that eludes us when we are only half of our complete self, and a longing for the unbounded consciousness that we had in the "treasury of souls."

This yearning is the highest form of human love, according to the Jewish mystics, because it is the spiritual attraction of one soul for its mate. Each soul has one specific destined mate, its soul mate or other half, with which it was once united. Only God, the architect who designed the different roads on which these souls travel, can match the destined partners correctly. Truly, these are marriages made in heaven. True love is the love between two destined "soul mates" and their reunion.

Left to our own devices, men and women may wander aimlessly in search of our destined partners. It requires the guiding hand of God to match us with our intended and unique mate. Not everyone will find their soul mate. Some of us, because of our religious and moral behavior, may not be worthy. Others may be separated from their soul mate by time, geography, or other circumstance. Sometimes, the other half of our original whole soul may be left stranded in the "treasury of souls" or assigned to a body in another time or place. Sometimes, we simply choose the wrong partner and exclude ourselves from the opportunity of finding our soul mate. But if we choose the wrong partner, it is possible to have the chance to rectify this mistake and to eventually find our true partner. Divorce, remarriage, and, even, reincarnation are legitimate strategies to realign mismatched couples with their proper soul mates.[28]

This remarkable teaching is expressed in the following passage, a description of the descent of the soul into the world:

> All the souls of the world, the handiwork of the Holy One, Blessed be He, are one in one mystery. When they descend into the world, they separate into masculine and feminine forms after once having been united as masculine and feminine together. Come and see: The arousal of the feminine for the masculine produces a *nefesh* and the desire and arousal of the masculine for the feminine and his cleaving to her also produces a *nefesh*. He encompasses the passion of the feminine and carries it so that the passion of the lower is subsumed under the higher and is made one inseparable desire. Then, the feminine carries it all and becomes impregnated by the masculine; the passion of each is indistinguishable from the other and the whole is included in each. When the souls exit the treasury of souls, masculine and feminine exit as one. Then, when they have descended to the world, they separate, each to their respective place. The Holy One, Blessed be He, rejoins them later on. The ability to join a couple together is reserved for the Holy One, Blessed be He, for He alone knows how to match a couple together properly. Happy is the man who is pure in his ways and walks the path of truth so that his soul is joined with another soul just as they were joined originally.[29]

Each soul possesses divine wisdom having been impregnated with a residue of the *Sefirah Hokhmah* in the course of their passage to this realm. All the souls in the treasury possess perfect knowledge of the Torah that is lost as they are born into the world. This notion is based on a rabbinic legend, also derived from Plato, concerning the birth of a child, which suggests that the soul knows the entire Torah before it comes into the world. At the moment of birth, it forgets what it has already learned. "As soon as it comes into the world, an angel arrives and slaps it on its mouth and causes it to forget the whole of the Torah."[30] According to this legend, an angel strikes the embryo on the philtrum, the dimple on the upper lip, which causes it to forget all the wisdom it once knew. It leaves the enabling scar, the philtrum, as a reminder of what it once knew and what it should aspire to learn. It also suggests that one never learns something new but only recalls the Torah it once knew.

The wisdom of the soul is accessible through other means as well. Dreams play an important role in the life of the soul. The soul ascends to the ream below the *Sefirot* at night and receives truths in the form of dreams during this voyage. Dreams are communication from the angel Gabriel, the angel that derives its power from the *Sefirah Malkhut*. Dreams are a form of prophecy which derives its inspiration from *Malkhut*, called the "mirror that does not shine." Dreams come from the realm below *Malkhut* and can, therefore, also contain misleading information. Therefore, the dream itself is less important than the interpretation. *Kabbalists* read dreams as they would read a text. They search for the symbolism in the dream and interpret it as they would a passage in Torah. Dreams convey a message to the soul and, therefore, "a dream not interpreted is like an unread letter":

> Come and see: The Holy One, Blessed be He, created many different levels, and they all coexist one upon the other, level upon level, one above the other. All the prophets in the world draw their sustenance from one area, "the mirror that does not shine." A dream is a sixtieth part of prophecy. Every dream has some deceitful material mingled with it. Every dream must be interpreted because speech has authority over everything. Therefore, every dream follows its interpretation. A dream not interpreted is like an unread letter.[31]

The destiny of the soul after life is one of the great mysteries that preoccupy the *Kabbalists*. Just as there is a rich preexistence to the soul prior to birth, the soul continues to live after it leaves this mortal coil. The *neshamah* alone is the immortal part of us. If we achieve *neshamah*, we are able to live on in an unbounded state of connectedness to the *Sefirot*. Death, or rather life after life, is seen as kind of mystical state. Therefore, death is described as a divine kiss, an expression of God's love for the accomplished soul. This is based on a creative rendering of the verse, "Moses died at the command of the Lord" (*Deut.* 34:5). The phrase, "at the command (*al pi*) of the Lord," could also be translated as "by the kiss of God." This led to the idea that death by a divine kiss is a sign of special divine favor.

In an elaborate parable, the *Zohar* describes the destiny of the *neshamah* in the course of life and after it leaves this world. Death is described as an opportunity for the soul to return to its original home. The *neshamah*, which originates in *Tiferet*—the masculine *Sefirah*, is described as the "king's son" sent into this world to learn the mysteries of the realm from which it came. Only when the *neshamah* has learned the mysteries of the *Sefirot* through living in the human realm, is its destiny complete. When it is time to return, its mother—the Matron, the feminine *Shekhinah*, retrieves the soul and brings it back to its original home. Natural death is not the occasion for sadness but, rather, a moment of joy for a mission accomplished. The body may die but the soul, the essence of man, endures:

> A king has a son whom he sends to a village to be educated until he shall have been initiated into the ways of the palace. When the king is informed that his son is now come to maturity, the king, out of his love, sends the Matron, his mother, to bring him back to the palace, and there the king rejoices with him every day. In this wise, the Holy One, be blessed, possessed a son from the Matron, that is, the supernal holy soul. He dispatched it to a village, that is, to this world, to be raised in it, and initiated into the ways of the King's palace. Informed that his son was now come to maturity, and should be returned to the palace, the King, out of love, sent the Matron for him to bring him into the palace. The soul does not leave this world until such time as the Matron has arrived to get him and bring him into the King's palace, where he abides forever. Withal, the village people weep for the departure of the King's son from among them. But one wise man said to them: Why do you weep? Was this not the King's son, whose true place is in his father's palace, and not with you? If the righteous were only aware of this, they would be filled with joy when their time comes to leave this world.[32]

In fact, the death of a righteous person is approached with a certain degree of anticipation on the part of the individual: "At the moment when the soul of a righteous man wants to depart there is happiness. The righteous man is confident in his death that he will receive his reward."[33]

The process of death and dying is one of gradual disengagement of the soul from the body. Changes begin to occur thirty days before a person's death. At night, his soul ascends to heaven while he is sleeping and makes tentative forays into the afterlife, "the world to come." There it is introduced to its next abode and becomes acquainted with this realm. Man begins to lose awareness and control of his soul during this period as the connection between it and the body is weakened.

During this period before death, his shadow may begin to disappear.

The shadow is equated in Jewish mysticism, as it is later in Dante's Purgatory, with the astral body (*tzelem*), the nonphysical projection of an individual's physical self. The connection between the actual body and the astral body is weakened as death approaches and the latter prepares for its separate journey.

On the day of death, the soul and the body together undergo a preliminary reckoning. On that day, God judges man according to the actions he committed while he was alive. At that moment, man is especially vulnerable to the forces of evil in the world and to great terror and anxiety about his fate. Although modern Judaism has dispensed with much of the mythology of rabbinic and medieval Judaism, the Jewish mystical tradition is replete with descriptions of heaven and hell, consuming fires, vicious snakes, and threatening demons. These mythological images are taken as real phenomena that await the sinner after death:

> Woe to those who are ignorant of and do not pay attention to the ways of Torah. Woe to them when the Holy One, Blessed be He, brings man to judgment for his actions and his body and soul stand in testimony on his account before they separate. That very day is the day of reckoning, the day on which the record books lie open and the forces of judgment stand ready. At that moment, the serpent takes his place ready to strike him and all his limbs tremble. The soul departs from the body and takes flight not knowing where it is heading or where it will land. Woe for that day, a day of anger and contention.[34]

Before a man dies he has a visionary encounter with Adam, the first man. Adam asks him why he is leaving the world and how he will depart. He replies: "Oh, it is because of your sins that I am about to depart this world." Adam then responds: "My son, I violated just one commandment and was punished for it. Look at how many sins you committed and how many commandments of your Master you have violated!"[35]

On the day of death, when the soul departs the body, man is able to experience mystical and ecstatic achievements. Although no man can have a direct vision of the *Shekhinah*, the last *Sefirah*, during his lifetime, it may occur on his dying day.[36] At the moment of death, man also sees close relatives and friends who have already died. They appear to him lifelike and inviting. If he is destined for the afterlife, they greet him cheerfully. If he is destined for perdition, they do not acknowledge him unless they themselves are condemned. In this case they utter, "Woe, Woe!" In either case, his relatives lead him to view heaven and hell once he has died and leave him at the appropriate destination.[37]

As a person is being laid to rest in the grave, he is confronted by all the deeds that he has committed in his lifetime. All human words and actions have an existence independent of man which may yet return to haunt him. The *Zohar* describes graphically how these appear alongside the coffin at the graveside of someone who has led a less than exemplary life:

> When he is being carried to his grave, (his words and deeds) appear and walk before him. Three heralds, one before him, one to his right and one to his left, announce: "This man—who rebelled against his master and against heaven, earth, the Torah and its commandments—look at his deeds, look at his words! He ought never to have been created!" Then all the dead are stirred up against him from their graves and say: "Woe, Woe—that he should be buried among us!"[38]

During the seven-day mourning period (*shivah*), the soul of the deceased travels back and forth between the grave and his earthly residence and participates as a mourner over his own body. The soul of the deceased passes through many trials before it reaches the heavens. If the soul is not worthy of the afterlife, it may be "tossed around like a rock in a sling" and reincarnated into another body.

Reincarnation, or "transmigration of souls" (*gilgul nefashot*), is the recycling of the *nefesh* from one deceased person into another body. Reincarnation was the subject of great speculation and disagreement among Jewish mystics.[39] One school of *Kabbalistic* thought maintained that reincarnation was an opportunity to repair sins committed in a previous life while a second school of thought saw it as a form of punishment. For example, sins included in the thirty-six classes of mortal sins[40] are often said to require the complete obliteration of the offending soul without the possibility of any afterlife or ultimate resurrection in messianic times. Reincarnation is then seen as an act of divine mercy that saves the soul from extinction and provides it with a second chance at perfection.[41]

A righteous individual may undergo transmigration in order to complete commandments that he did not fulfill in the previous life or to correct actions that were not according to Jewish norms. This form of reincarnation may also provide the occasion for a saint to contribute to the welfare of humanity a second time or to bring additional wisdom to the world. It is generally regarded that souls can have no more than three transmigrations, except for the righteous whose returns are not limited.

On the other hand, transmigration was also seen as a form of punishment for offenders, especially those who transgress sexual norms. A man or woman who voluntarily decides to be childless may suffer transmigration for not having fulfilled the biblical injunction to "be fruitful and multiply." Some mystics even suggested that under dire conditions a soul may be resurrected in the body of an animal.[42] The alternative to reincarnation is perdition (*gehinnom*), which is portrayed as a cleansing fire that purges and punishes but does not necessarily destroy the soul.

Closely related to the concept of reincarnation is the *Kabbalistic* "mystery of conception" (*sod ha-ibbur*). According to this teaching, the soul of another person can attach itself to the resident soul of a particular person. The attendant soul of a saint or a relative attaches itself to a soul in order to guide and assist it in accomplishing a particular task or mission. The attendant soul can come or go throughout the life of the host as necessary. It serves as a guardian which ministers to its host and helps it through the course of life.

A sinful soul that has no hope of reward may be condemned to trials of fire and purgatory. Although many Jewish theologians, such as Maimonides, objected to the idea of an inferno or purgatory for souls, and others denied that there are such beliefs in Judaism, *Kabbalists* believed in the fiery extermination of unworthy souls.[43]

Despite the favorable associations with the idea of death from natural causes, the *Kabbalists* were troubled by the idea of premature death. They explain that premature death may be an anticipation of sins that the deceased might have committed had he lived. They reject the idea of inherited sin for a child over the age of thirteen, since thirteen is the age at which a child bears responsibility for his actions. Premature death is often described as an "early gathering" that plucks the individual while his life is still in full bloom and before the flower withers on the branch. This is seen as an act of divine mercy that entitles him to reward in the afterlife that he might have been denied had he lived his full life.

The mystic path in Judaism begins with the doctrine of the soul. The *Kabbalistic* doctrine of the soul explains that the spiritual dimension of the human being can link him to the *Sefirot*. The soul is the part of man that comes from the divine realm and, therefore, leads him back to the *Sefirot*. The mystic faculty in man establishes the possibility that the mystic quest can lead him to God.

8

THE MYSTIC DRAMA
The Religious Life of the Jewish Mystic

The religious observance of Jewish mystics was not essentially different from the practice of other Jews who followed the rabbinic tradition. Jewish mystics said the same prayers, prayed in the same synagogues, and observed the same rituals (*mitzvot*) as other Jews. Although they acted like their contemporaries, the Jewish mystics approached the meaning of their religious life differently.

Jewish mystics believe that the two primary purposes of religious observance are to connect the soul to its source in the *Sefirot* and to restore the intrinsic unity within the *Sefirot* through ritual actions.[1] These two functions, the unitive and restorative, permeate every aspect of Jewish mystical approaches to religious life.

Since the mystics believe that the soul comes, indirectly, from the realm of the *Sefirot*, it naturally yearns to return there. All forms of religious observance are vehicles that transport the human soul upward through the heavens and palaces of the upper world, through the chambers of the spiritual world, to the gate of the realm of the *Sefirot*. Jewish mystics are extremely cautious on the question of how high up the soul can ascend on the chain of divine being. Most *Kabbalists* agree that the rituals are not directed at, nor does the soul ascend to, *The Infinite*. They also agree that ritual cannot affect, and the soul cannot ascend, higher than *Hokhmah*. They disagree, however, on how high the soul can ascend. Some, like Isaac the Blind, believe that the soul could unite with *Hokhmah*.[2] Others, like Nah-

manides, believe the highest station it can reach is *Malkhut*.[3] Only one Kabbalist appears to suggest that the soul can ascend to *The Infinite* itself. Isaac
of Acre, in the fourteenth century, asserts that "the soul can cleave to *The
Infinite*."[4]

With the exception of some of the modern *Hasidic* mystics, most Jewish mystics do not believe that the separate existence of the soul is annihi-
lated or that the soul is absorbed into the *Sefirot* at the moment of unity.
Because the theistic strictures of Judaism are so fundamental—the belief in
the difference between the human and divine realms—Jewish mysticism is
often constrained from pursuing absorptive and annihilative forms of mystical union. The soul may come to stand in the highest domains of the *Sefirot*,
but it never becomes a *Sefirah*. Its separate identity remains, and the human
never merges into the divine. Mystical union is called *devekut* (cleaving, or
adhesion). It does not convey the same degree of oneness as does the Latin
derivative "union." It is a communion of two separate and distinct entities
that retain their separateness.

Jewish mystics place special emphasis on attentiveness and directedness
to each specific ritual action. Rabbinic Judaism has always stressed the
importance of seriousness of purpose and willfulness while performing the
mitzvot. This is expressed in the famous aphorism: "The commandments
require intention (*kavvanah*)."[5] The mystics go further in stressing that all
ritual actions must be directed to the proper *Sefirah*. They also maintain that
knowledge of the specific effects of these actions is an indispensable feature
of mystical consciousness.

Intention (*kavvanah*, also called *re'uta*, willfulness) involves the concen-
trated effort of the heart and body in the performance of the ritual. The
Zohar explains that ritual actions directed with *kavvanah* to uniting the
Sefirot—the Holy Name—brings harmony to the universe:

> One must direct his heart and will (*re'uta*) in order to bring blessings above
> and below. One who seeks to unite the Holy Name (i.e., the *Sefirot*) but does
> not direct his heart, will and awe, in order to grace above and below with
> blessings, will have his prayers thrown out and evil will be pronounced upon
> him. But for one who knows how to unite the Holy Name properly, the
> walls of darkness are split and the King's countenance is revealed and seen
> by all. When this occurs, everything above and below is blessed.[6]

Intentional action produces an ascent of the soul through the heavens and
through the lower levels of the *Sefirot*. First, the soul arrives at the gate of

the *Sefirot*, and then it continues up to *Hesed*, *Binah*, or even *Hokhmah*. Then, the mystic draws divine illumination down upon himself in ways that are palpable and recognizable by others. The *Zohar* explains:

> The person who offers his prayer and unites the Holy Name properly draws the strand of mercy (*Hesed*) upon himself. He looks up to the heavens and the light of enlightenment, divine knowledge, shines down upon him and crowns him; all stand in awe of him. Such a man is called a son of the Holy One, Blessed be He, a member of the royal entourage.[7]

Ritual action, especially Hebrew prayer, causes the ascent of *Malkhut*, the *Shekhinah*, the last *Sefirah*, to *Tiferet*. The divine presence infused in the Hebrew letters is an essential manifestation of the *Shekhinah* whose power is released by the act of prayer. The energy of the *Shekhinah* is then released and unites with *Tiferet*, the Holy One, Blessed be He. The *Tikkunei Zohar* says: "The *Shekhinah* dwells in his prayer and through it ascends to the Holy One, Blessed be He."[8] This union is necessary for the continued flow of divine blessing and providence upon the world.

Intentional prayer produces many positive results for the world, which are called "perfections" (*tikkunim*). There is a hierarchy of the levels of human perfections. Man must first cultivate and develop the faculties of his soul, especially the *neshamah*. Then, he must work for the moral and religious improvement of society through observance of the *mitzvot*. Next, he must perform the religious rituals that will bring about the elevation of his soul to the world of the pure forms. Finally, he should strive to unite *Tiferet* and *Malkhut* and achieve communion with the *Sefirot*. The *Zohar* describes this succinctly as follows:

> The first perfection is self-fulfillment; the second is the perfection of this world; the third is the perfection of the upper world and all its heavenly hosts; and the fourth is the perfection of the divine Name.[9]

The restorative approach to ritual is based on the belief in theurgy. Theurgy is the practice of influencing God through ritual means without an act of will on God's part. Rituals affect the *Sefirot* because a mystical nexus exists between human action and specific *Sefirot*. Jewish rituals constitute a special language, a system of signs intelligible only to God, that triggers responses in God that are incomprehensible to man. The Jewish mystic, however, is able to penetrate the causal connection between the theurgic act and the divine response.

The *Sefirot* are dynamic forces that are susceptible to human manipulation. The proper alignment of the *Sefirot* is necessary in order for the divine essence to flow smoothly from *The Infinite* to *Malkhut* and on through the lower worlds. In particular, this alignment is conditional upon human rituals that may manipulate the *Sefirot* properly or improperly. If the *Sefirot* are aligned properly, it will produce divine goodness. If the *Sefirot* are misaligned, divine grace is withheld from the world. Therefore, ritual has a restorative function because it is the primary means by which the theurgic manipulation of the *Sefirot* occurs.

Jewish mystics attribute great power to religious ritual and the obligation to perform theurgic acts. Yet, Jewish mystics also lived within the norms of Jewish life and accommodated themselves to the routine of daily observance. Jewish mystics prior to the sixteenth century rarely created separate societies to practice special devotions that might be contrary to the custom of the rest of the community. When special practices were introduced, especially in the sixteenth century, they did not replace traditional ritual but rather augmented it. Most Jewish mystics were indistinguishable from other Jews because they too believed in the primacy of Jewish ritual, but they viewed it as the means to union with, and restoration of, the *Sefirot*. They did not dispense with conventional ritual in favor of other more individual and idiosyncratic paths to union and restoration.

The *Kabbalists* differed from conventional religiously observant Jews in several important ways. They believed that the traditional liturgy of daily, Sabbath, and festival prayers contain hidden mystical meanings and references to dynamic processes within the *Sefirot*. The mystical interpretation of the prayer *Shema Yisrael* as an evocative and theurgic wedding ceremony between *Tiferet* and *Malkhut* is a classic illustration of this approach.

The *Kabbalists* also believed that the words of the prayers themselves take on a life of their own. The words of prayer, once uttered, become entities unto themselves and ascend upward to the *Sefirot* with which they unite. The *Zohar* explains that the words of prayer themselves, when uttered out loud, turn into disembodied voices, take on a life of their own, take flight and rise up to God:

> All that which man thinks and every meditation of his heart is ineffective until his lips utter them out loud. That very word which he utters splits the air, going, rising and flying through the world, until it becomes a voice. That voice is borne by the winged creatures who raise it up to the King who then hears it.[10]

Daily prayer is understood to bring about the perfection (*tikkun*) of the *Shekhinah*. According to rabbinic law, certain prayers can only be recited when a prayer quorum is assembled. The minimum number that defines a quorum for a "congregation" is set at ten adult males.[11] This is based upon the biblical account in *Numbers* 14:27 where Moses called the ten scouts who explored the land of Israel at his command a "congregation" (*edah*). Rabbinic legend maintains that the *Shekhinah* dwells in the midst of a congregation of ten men who pray together.[12] In the same text, God is depicted as being angry when he comes to a congregation and does not find a prayer quorum.

The rabbinic prayer quorum (*minyan*) is a precondition for the creation of a *tikkun* among the *Sefirot*. The ten-person prayer quorum reflects and invokes the unity of the ten *Sefirot*. Just as there are ten *Sefirot*, there need to be a quorum of ten men assembled for each regularly scheduled prayer service. The *Zohar* describes the assembly of the quorum within the synagogue as analogous to the unity of *Sefirot* and the creation of the first human being:

> How precious is Israel in the sight of the Holy One, Blessed be He! In every place they dwell, the Holy One, Blessed be He, is found among them because He never takes His love from them. Blessed is the man who is among the first ten to arrive at the synagogue. Among them is completed that which ought to be completed (i.e., the reenactment of joining the ten *Sefirot* together). These are sanctified by the *Shekhinah* before any others, as has been explained. Ten should arrive at the synagogue simultaneously rather than separately so as not to delay the completion of the limbs (of the ten *Sefirot*) just as man was created by God all at once and all his limbs were perfected together.[13]

The notion that there is a correspondence between human religious actions and divine processes is axiomatic in Jewish mysticism. This is evident in the mystical approach to the synagogue itself. The earliest synagogues were established during the Babylonian Exile following the destruction of the First Temple in Jerusalem in 586 B.C.E. Later, synagogues, called the "minor sanctuary" in rabbinic literature (*mikdash me'at*), replaced the Temple, and formal prayers replaced Temple sacrifices as the authorized form of worship.[14] In mystical symbolism, the destroyed Temple still exists within *Malkhut* as the divine prototype of the earthly Temple. The synagogue, therefore, corresponds to *Malkhut* and the structure itself should reflect the enormity of the correspondence. The *Zohar* also explains that one should pray in the synagogue daily because of its significance:

> It is commanded to build a sanctuary below corresponding to the heavenly sanctuary above. One should build a synagogue and should pray within it daily and worship the Holy One, Blessed be He, for prayer is called "worship" (*Sifrei Deut.* 41). The synagogue should be constructed with great beauty and adorned with all manner of refinements because the synagogue below corresponds to the heavenly synagogue.[15]

Because of the correspondence between the earthly synagogue and *Malkhut*, the *Zohar* prefers conventional prayer said within a synagogue to prayer offered anywhere else. In fact, the *Zohar* introduced into the body of Jewish customs several new practices and rites based on mystical principles. For example, the preference for synagogue prayer over prayers said elsewhere is based on the idea that since the *Shekhinah* can only be reached by a narrow path, earthly prayers must be concentrated into a narrow channel, a fixed location, in order to ascend. The very structure of a synagogue is preferable to an open area because the former would concentrate, whereas the latter would diffuse, the ascending channel of prayer. The *Zohar* also introduces as law the custom that a synagogue must have windows so that the prayers could exit the synagogue and ascend through the narrow passage of the window.[16] The *Zohar* also states that congregational prayer is preferable to individual prayer because God scrutinizes critically the worthiness and actions of an individual who prays alone. His prayer can ascend only as far as his actions warrant. Congregational prayer, however, ascends more easily because of the aggregate merit of those assembled.[17] If, however, one cannot pray with a congregation, he should at least pray at the same time as the congregation.

According to rabbinic tradition, there are 613 commandments.[18] The specific number was not originally intended to reflect the actual number of ritual obligations of a Jew as much as it was intended to convey an ideal. The number originally represented the sum of the days of the year (365) and the supposed number of organs in the human body, which the rabbinic sages somehow calculated to be 248. It conveyed the idea that Jewish law was comprehensive and addressed all the possible actions that a human might actually perform in the course of time. Later scholars took this to be a real number, and many attempted to codify their own listing of the 613 commandments. Since there are many variations and infinite possibilities, no authoritative identification of the specific 613 commandments exists. There is, however, consensus among medieval rabbinic authorities on the specific patterns of Jewish ritual behavior that are to be followed.

Jewish mystics applied their own mystical interpretations to the meaning of individual religious actions just as they did to the general meaning of prayer and observance. The unitive and restorative approach to observance can be seen in the following principle expressed in the *Zohar*: "In every ritual action, let your effort be directed toward uniting the Holy One, Blessed be He, and his *Shekhinah* through all camps above and below."[19] As a result of this principle, *Kabbalists* would recite a formula—"For the sake of the unity of the Holy One, Blessed be He, and his *Shekhinah*"—before performing any ritual action.

The most central of all Jewish rituals, perhaps, are those related to Sabbath observance. Not only are the Jewish people called "the people who sanctify the seventh day" (*am mekaddeshei shevi'i*), but rabbinic sources clearly attest to the centrality of this day in the religious life of a Jew. The *Midrash*, for example, states that "the Sabbath, by itself, is equal to all the other observances.[20] Sabbath rituals constitute the most important of all the Jewish rituals.

Sabbath symbolism in rabbinic and mystical Jewish lore is dominated by the wedding and bridal motifs. The *Talmud* welcomes the beginning of Sabbath with the injunction, "Let us come and go out to welcome the Sabbath bride."[21] Jewish mystics develop and reinterpret the elements of the Sabbath rituals into a consistent thematic drama of the reunion of the *Shekhinah*, the Sabbath bride, with *Tiferet*, her mate.

Jewish mystics frequently draw associative connections between traditional elements of Jewish rituals and the *Sefirot*. They often express the association in a formula that states that a certain ritual, or aspect of a ritual, is "against" (*ke-neged*) a particular *Sefirah*. This means that the ritual either symbolizes, influences, or creates a link with that *Sefirah*. The association is often based on the Hebrew etymology of a term related to the ritual. For example, the association of the Sabbath with *Malkhut* is drawn, in part, because of the relationship between the word *malkah*, the Sabbath bride of rabbinic literature, and the name of the last *Sefirah*, *Malkhut*. Other associations may be based on what appear to be more tenuous interpretive links such as equivalences between the numerical values of two different Hebrew words (*gematria*). Often biblical words suggest associations. For example, a word that appears in one biblical context may suggest a connection to a different passage that contains a similar word. These links are vital to the associative and imaginative thinking of Jewish mystics who saw the biblical text as filled with hidden meanings.

The Sabbath itself is usually associated with *Malkhut* or *Yesod*. This ambiguity is rooted in the fact that in each of the two versions of the Ten Commandments, the Sabbath commandment is phrased differently. As we saw earlier, *Deuteronomy* 5:12 reads: "Keep (*shamor*) the Sabbath day," whereas *Exodus* 20:8 reads: "Remember (*zakhor*) the Sabbath day." *Shamor* is associated with *Malkhut* because it is the *Sefirah* that preserves (*shomeret*) the world. *Zakhor* is associated with *Yesod*, the masculine *Sefirah*, because the Hebrew word *zakhor* means both "to remember" and "to be masculine." Occasionally, the Sabbath is linked with the *Sefirah Binah*, which brings about the messianic age, the era in which every day is Sabbath.

The Sabbath is portrayed as a restorative ritual involving the reunion of *Malkhut* with the masculine *Sefirah Yesod* or with *Tiferet*.[22] The elaborate preparations for the Sabbath are treated as preparations for a wedding.

The restoration of harmony between masculine and feminine *Sefirot* changes the prevailing order. The *Sefirah Din*, strict judgment, presides over the weekdays with severity. The Sabbath brings a respite from the dominion of *Din* and cancels out *Din* with *Hesed*, mercy. The Sabbath is described as a "tent of peace" (*sukkat shalom*) that spreads over the Jewish people and makes them immune from the forces of evil that preside during the week. This is reflected in the following passage from *Zohar* which appears in *Hasidic* prayer books as a mystical incantation to be recited on Friday night:

> The mystery of Sabbath: Sabbath is unification through oneness, which causes the mystery of oneness to dwell upon it. Prayer, which the Sabbath raises up, unifies and perfects the holy and precious Throne through the mystery of oneness so that the divine and holy King may sit upon it. When the Sabbath begins, she is made one and separates from the other side (i.e., evil) and all the forces of severity pass away. She remains unified with the holy light and is adorned with many crowns by the holy King. All the powers of ire and forces of severity are uprooted and there is no evil dominion upon the worlds. Her face is radiant with divine light and she is adorned below with the holy people.[23]

The idea that a special soul enters the body and resides there during the Sabbath dates back to the rabbinic period.[24] The *Zohar* expands this notion and explains that the Sabbath is "the day of the soul, not the body."[25]

Most modern Sabbath observers are unaware of the extent to which Jewish mystics, particularly the *Kabbalists* of Safed in the sixteenth century, introduced new rituals into Jewish practice that reflected the mystical view of the Sabbath. For example, it was their custom to go out into the fields to greet the Sabbath. They went out dressed in white ready to join the bride as her wedding entourage. They would face the west from where the *Shekhinah* would rise as the sun set. The very order of prayers for the Friday evening service that accompanied this ritual was established by these mystics as a unitive and restorative ritual.[26] This order, including the mystical hymn *Lekhah Dodi* which was discussed above, prevails even today. The *Zohar* included certain blessings such as "who extends a tent of peace" (*ha-pores sukkat shalom*) and excluded certain prayers such as "He is merciful and acquits transgression" (*ve-hu rahum yekhapper avvon*) from the Friday evening service, to illustrate the notion that unity prevails and *Din* is annulled on the Sabbath.

The elaborate Friday evening service is not the only mystical Sabbath rite that entered normative practice. The *Zohar* explains that the head of the household must accomplish ten things at the Sabbath table, corresponding to the ten *Sefirot*.[27] Although many of these are rabbinic practices, the *Zohar* actually enumerates ten central customs and their associated symbolism as follows:

1. Light at least two Sabbath candles: The woman head of the household lights at least two Sabbath candles at the table before the onset of the Sabbath, corresponding to the two versions of the Sabbath law in the Ten Commandments. The candles symbolize *Hesed* (mercy), and the table symbolizes *Din* (severity). Symbolically, placing the candles on the table dispels *Din*.

2. Bless the cup of wine: The male head of the household recites the *Kiddush*, the Sabbath blessing over wine, at the table. The first part of the *Kiddush*, taken from the biblical description of the first Sabbath (*Genesis* 2:1–3), is associated with *Yesod*, a masculine *Sefirah*. The second section is associated with the feminine *Malkhut*. Together, the *Kiddush* symbolizes the unification of masculine and feminine *Sefirot*.

3. Perform ritual handwashing before blessing the Sabbath bread: This rabbinic law of ritual hand washing is a requirement before blessing and eating bread.[28] The *Zohar* requires that one hold a cup filled with water in the right hand, which symbolizes *Hesed*, pass the cup to the left hand, which symbolizes *Din*, and pour it first upon the right hand. Then, one should pass the cup again and

pour the water upon the left hand. This is done so that the priority of *Hesed* over *Din* on the Sabbath is emphasized.[29] This is followed by reciting the blessing for ritual hand washing.

4. Put two loaves of bread on the table: Two loaves of bread recall the double portion of manna that rained down on the Sabbath (*Exodus* 16:22–26). According to the *Zohar*, the two loaves placed together symbolize the union of *Malkhut* and *Tiferet*. The *Zohar* requires that the diners eat from the lower of the two loaves, when one is placed on top of the other, to symbolize the lower *Sefirot*, especially *Malkhut*.

5. Eat three festive meals: The major meals of the Sabbath are Friday evening, Saturday lunch, and after the late afternoon service. According to the *Zohar*, these meals ceremoniously invoke the power of *Malkhut*, *Keter*, and *Tiferet*, respectively. Special songs (*zemirot*) are sung at each of the meals, many of which were composed as hymns to the *Sefirah* associated with that meal.

6. Discuss Torah at the table: According to the rabbinic tradition, the *Shekhinah* dwells at any table where Torah is discussed.

7. Welcome poor guests to the table: Charitable concern for the poor is a feature of the social consciousness of the *Zohar*. The poor are believed to bring special merit to the table and aid in the achievement of unity.[30]

8. Perform ritual handwashing after the meal: This rabbinic custom is called "final water" (*mayyim aharonim*).[31] It is done after the meal before saying the blessing after food. The *Zohar* explains that this custom is performed in order to cleanse the hands of evil and to remove the impurities that cling to them.[32] It is also intended to wash away particles of food which are then considered a concession and nourishment to the evil forces.[33]

9. Recite the blessing after the meal: This rabbinic practice is associated, according to the *Zohar*, with the *Sefirah Hesed*.[34] The *Zohar* explains that one who says this blessing with intention will invoke *Hesed* upon the world.

10. Bless a final cup of wine: According to rabbinic tradition, a final cup of wine is blessed following the blessing after the meal.[35]

These practices illustrate the way Jewish mystics reinterpret traditional practices in light of *Kabbalistic* teachings. The Sabbath is turned into a theurgic drama that unfolds in sequence.

Jewish mystics also introduced completely new customs. For example, the *Kabbalists* of Safed added the custom of singing *Eshet Hayyil* ("*Woman of Valor*")[36] as a hymn in praise of the wife and as an allusion to the *Shekhinah*.

Ritual innovation can also be seen in the *Zohar's* approach to human sexuality. The *Zohar* considers the Sabbath the most propitious occasion for unitive and restorative mysticism through human sexual intercourse. They taught that sexual intercourse on Sabbath eve produces the special Sabbath over-soul (*neshamah yeterah*).[37] Therefore, Friday evening is the time when a man and woman should have sexual contact.

To devotees of Jewish mysticism, the Jewish holidays are unitive and restorative sacraments. They are theurgic sacraments that have the power to realign and reunite the configuration of the *Sefirot*. Since the observance of the festivals brings about perfection in the divine realm, it influences the fate of God and, consequently, of man. Religious practices are always understood to influence God on behalf of man. In Jewish mysticism, however, God does not answer man's prayer or reward him for his actions directly. Rather, human actions such as prayer and the *mitzvot* directed towards God actually cause God to respond involuntarily. God responds by either accelerating towards greater alignment or greater disalignment within and among the *Sefirot*. These responses then produce reverberations that rebound from God to man. If we cause the alignment of the *Sefirot*, divine grace will flow into the world. If we cause the disalignment of the *Sefirot*, God's grace is withheld from the world.

The dialectical influences of God and man imply a new mode of thinking in Judaism about the relationship between them. The novel element in *Kabbalistic* thinking about God and man is their mutual and reciprocal interdependence. God is not complete by Himself. He cannot be complete and perfect except when made so by human action. The unity of the various aspects of God's being depends on human actions. Humans do not benefit except when God's grace flows upon the world. Neither God nor man can act or be fulfilled except through the other.

The primary Jewish holidays are the Days of Awe—*Rosh ha-Shanah* and *Yom ha-Kippurim*—and the pilgrimage festivals—*Pesah, Shavuot,* and *Sukkot*. The Jewish mystics observed these festivals as do all other observant Jews. Occasionally the mystics introduced new theurgic rituals. Generally, the difference between a Jewish mystic and a nonmystic lies in the consciousness of the significance of the festival, not in its practice.

Rosh ha-Shanah is the beginning of the Jewish calendar year. It does not, however, mark the beginning of the liturgical or religious year. That begins with *Nisan*, the month in which *Pesah* occurs. *Rosh ha-Shanah* occurs on the first two days of the seventh month, *Tishrei*. In the time of the prophets Ezra and Nehemiah (c. fifth century B.C.E.), the holiday was observed by the Israelite people with a gathering at the newly restored Temple in Jerusalem. The Torah laws for the day were read publicly and the hollow ram's horn (*shofar*) was blown. It was a day of celebration and feasting on which the kingship of God and the supremacy of the divine rule over earthly monarchs was reaffirmed.

By the first and second centuries, new themes for the holiday were introduced. The *Mishnah* adds that this holiday marks the anniversary of the date on which man was created. According to Jewish legend, man was created and sinned on the same day. Therefore, his birth date became a day of judgment for him as well as for all his descendants.

The *Talmud* develops the theme of *Rosh ha-Shanah* as the day of divine judgment upon man. It cites a legend to the effect that three heavenly books are opened on this day—one for those whose actions mark them as unredeemably wicked, one for the completely righteous, and one for those of intermediate status. The wicked are immediately inscribed in the book of death, and their fate is tentatively decreed for the coming year. The righteous are likewise inscribed in the book of life, and their fate is assured. The fate of those who are not in these categories is deferred until *Yom ha-Kippurim* when the books are finally sealed.[38] It is customary to wish friends "a good inscription" (*gemar ketivah tovah*) before *Rosh ha-Shanah* and "a good seal" (*gemar hatimah tovah*) from the first day of *Rosh ha-Shanah* until *Yom ha-Kippurim*.

In Jewish mysticism, all of the elements of the holidays are related to the goal of influencing the *Sefirot*. Jewish mystics believe that divine judgment is aroused on *Rosh ha-Shanah* through the ascendancy of the *Sefirah Din*. The rituals of *Rosh ha-Shanah* are theurgic sacraments that mitigate the power of the *Sefirah Din* by empowering the *Sefirah Hesed*. We must stimulate God's *Hesed* to soften the effects of *Din* on *Rosh ha-Shanah*. A *Kabbalistic* guide to Jewish practice explains:

> The power of severity is awakened above on *Rosh ha-Shanah*. Therefore, every person must arouse himself below to complete repentance. For by this, merciful love is awakened above.[39]

Without self-reckoning and a genuine decision to change religious and personal behavior, *Rosh ha-Shanah* can be a day when one is exposed to all the forces of evil in existence. Repentance, however, activates the *Sefirah Hesed* and aids it in balancing the *Sefirah Din*. If left unchecked, *Din* would give strength to the destructive powers that stand ready to attack us. With repentance, *Din* is held in check and human vulnerability is protected. The *Zohar* offers a graphic and mythological portrayal of cosmic, demonic forces that stand ready to pounce on us if we do not confess and repent on *Rosh ha-Shanah*:

> On the very day of *Rosh ha-Shanah*, when seventy chambers are waiting to pronounce severe judgment upon the world, many armed avengers stand ready above. Some turn to the right in favor, and some turn to the left in contempt, recalling the sins of the world, of each and every one. Therefore, man must confess his sins, every one as they really are.[40]

The public blowing of the ram's horn also symbolizes the predominance of *Hesed* over *Din*. The horn is blown one hundred times during the *Rosh ha-Shanah* service. The blowing activates the various *Sefirot* and creates an alignment in which *Hesed* predominates. The horn itself symbolizes *Binah* and emphasizes *Hesed* since it is the *Sefirah* that precedes *Hesed*.

The Torah portions read on the two days of the holiday also symbolize the ritual elevation of *Hesed* over *Din*. In Jewish mystical symbolism, certain biblical historical figures are linked to certain *Sefirot* through various associations. For example, the patriarch Abraham is linked with the *Sefirah Hesed* because of their association within the verse, "Deal graciously (*Hesed*) with my master Abraham."[41] Abraham's son, Isaac, is associated with *Din* through the biblical phrase, "the fear (*pahad*) of Isaac."[42] Consequently, the Torah reading for the first day, which details Isaac usurping the right of primogeniture over his brother Ishmael, symbolizes the supremacy of *Din*.[43] The Torah portion for the second day narrates Abraham's willingness to sacrifice Isaac at God's command and the sudden intervention that saves Isaac and replaces him on the altar with a ram.[44] *Rosh ha-Shanah* symbolizes the ultimate predominance of *Hesed* (Abraham) over *Din* (Isaac).

Confession and repentance on *Rosh ha-Shanah* moderate *Din* with *Hesed* and ultimately bring about the union of *Tiferet* and *Malkhut* on *Yom ha-Kippurim*. The mystical objective of *Rosh ha-Shanah* is to first bring about the alignment of *Din* and *Malkhut* through repentance and the softening of *Din* in preparation for the holy wedding ceremony of the Jewish people and the *Shekhinah* on *Yom ha-Kippurim*. According to the *Zohar*:

On *Rosh ha-Shanah*, the "left side" (i.e., *Din*) is aroused in order to greet the princess (i.e., *Shekhinah*). Then the whole world is terrified by *Din*. At the same time, the whole world must be repentant in the presence of the Holy One, Blessed be He. Later, the princess arrives on the eve of *Yom ha-Kippurim* and the whole assembly celebrates and they cleanse themselves in preparation for union with the princess.[45]

On *Yom ha-Kippurim*, the *Sefirah Binah*, the source of *Hesed*, prevails and uplifts the *Shekhinah* in preparation for reunion with *Tiferet*. According to the *Zohar*, when Jews fast and repent on *Yom ha-Kippurim*, they mobilize the *Sefirah Malkhut* on their own behalf. *Malkhut* unites with *Binah* and releases the power of *Hesed* upon the world:

When Israel fasts for her sins, the *Shekhinah* atones for them because the heavenly matron (i.e., *Binah*) shines her countenance upon the princess in union with her.[46]

Yom ha-Kippurim is linked symbolically to *Binah*, which is associated with all the rituals of this awesome day. The *Kol Nidrei* prayer opens the evening service and is often described as the holiest and most awesome moment in the Jewish liturgy. *Kol Nidrei* is not really a prayer but a medieval legal formula for the annulment of certain types of vows. Although it was intended to annul past vows, the formula was changed to refer only to vows made during the coming year in order not to abrogate existing contracts. For the Jewish mystic, *Kol Nidrei* is an invocation to *Binah* to release *Tiferet* and *Malkhut* from the bonds of *Din* in order to facilitate their union. *Binah* then releases and transmits the essence of *The Infinite* to the world and brings forgiveness, grace, and illumination to us. According to the *Zohar*, the entire liturgy of the day follows this pattern of invoking *Binah* to bring grace to the world:

Today, every joy, every light, and all forgiveness in the world depend on the divine matron (i.e., *Binah*). All the springs start and draw from there. All the lights are illuminated with joy and everything becomes fragrant. Even the forces of *Din* are consumed by light and are extinguished.[47]

Yom ha-Kippurim, the tenth day of *Tishrei*, is described in the Torah as a time for "affliction of the soul.[48] Although the Torah says little else about the holiday, it has generally been understood as a day for achieving awe and contrition. The *Mishnah* interprets the affliction of the day by identifying five classes of routine activities that are prohibited on *Yom ha-Kippurim*.[49] The prohibitions include consuming food and water, washing the body, wearing cosmetics or perfume, wearing leather sandals or shoes, and having sexual relations. These activities are all forms of physical comfort and pleasure that may be enjoyed at other times. Their denial on *Yom ha-Kippurim* is not intended to punish or afflict the body but rather to promote the transcendence of physical pleasures. Despite the physical nature of these prohibitions, it is the soul, not the body, that is supposed to be afflicted as a means of spiritual conditioning on *Yom ha-Kippurim*.

The liturgy of the holiday in the rabbinic tradition has its roots in two historical phenomena, each of which has a strong mystical dimension. First, *Yom ha-Kippurim* is a vivid and symbolic recreation of the events leading up to the revelation of the Torah on Mount Sinai. According to the rabbinic tradition, Moses shattered the first set of commandments that God gave to him on the sixth day of *Sivan* (i.e., *Shavuot*) when he saw the Golden Calf. Legend has it that God gave Moses the second set of tablets on *Yom ha-Kippurim*.[50] Each of the five classes of prohibitions represents one of the actions that God either commanded or prohibited in preparation for the giving of the Torah. For example, Moses was commanded to remove his sandals at the Burning Bush the first time God addressed him.[51] Later, at Sinai, the people were commanded to remain pure, to be ready, to refrain from sexual contact, and to abstain from food and drink.[52] The prohibitions, then, are intended to prepare the congregation today for reenacting the Sinai revelation by repeating the steps taken by Moses and the Jewish people. The closing *Yom ha-Kippurim* service, *Ne'ilah*, parallels the revelation at Sinai. The Bible recounts that when the laws were given, "all the people witnessed the thunder and lightning, the blare of the horn."[53] The holiday concludes its reenactment of Sinai with one final shofar blast just as occurred at Sinai during the revelation.

Second, the holy day is a carefully crafted ritual recreation of the preparations of the high priest prior to entering the Holy of Holies in the Jerusalem Temple on *Yom ha-Kippurim*. These preparations are the subject of the *Avodah* service, which is central to the midday liturgy. The rituals surrounding the preparations of the high priest are themselves a reenactment of Moses' preparations for Sinai. The high priest alone was permitted to enter the inner sanctum only once a year after completing elaborate preparations, including taking off his sandals and other acts that recall Moses at Sinai.[54] When the high priest was ready to enter, the other priests tied a rope around him in order to pull him out in case he should die inside in ecstatic rapture.

When the high priest pronounced his benedictions, the people gathered would answer, "Blessed be the name of His glorious majesty forever."

Likewise, only on *Yom ha-Kippurim* night (*Kol Nidre*) is this phrase, which is usually said in a whisper, uttered out loud in response to the *Shema*. On *Yom ha-Kippurim*, the members of the congregation symbolically become Moses and the high priest. The burden of responsibility and the anticipation of redemption are proferred sacramentally to each participant in the holy day liturgy.

Yom ha-Kippurim is ultimately a personal and communal mystical experience based on a symbolic reenactment of the revelation of Sinai. We recapitulate, on an individual and congregational level, Moses' and the high priest's preparations for mystical union with God. The purpose of the day is to experience a mini-revelation of God, to achieve mystical oneness with the *Shekhinah*, and to unite *Tiferet* and *Malkhut*.

The drama of the unification of the *Sefirot* continues throughout the month of *Tishrei*. *Sukkot*, the feast of booths, begins on the fifteenth of *Tishrei* and lasts for seven days in Israel, eight days in the Diaspora. The holiday of *Simhat Torah*, the celebration beginning the annual cycle of Torah reading, falls on the eighth day, *Shemini Atzeret*, in Israel, and on the ninth day in the Diaspora.

Sukkot is observed in a variety of ways including the construction and use of temporary booths (*sukkot*) reminiscent of the period that Israel wandered in the Sinai desert. In addition, the ritual use of four species of vegetation (*arba'ah minim*) recalls the agricultural origins of the holiday as the fall harvest festival. The four species that are used in ceremonial ways during the holiday are a palm branch (*lulav*), willows (*aravot*), a citron (*etrog*), and myrtle (*hadas*). The willows and myrtle are bundled together with the palm branch and held in the right hand while the citron is held separately in the left hand in rituals performed at home and in the synagogue.

The construction of the booth is linked symbolically with the seven *Sefirot* from *Hesed* to *Malkhut*, each of which corresponds to one of the seven days of the holiday. The booth itself symbolizes *Binah*, the divine mother, which looks after and protects the seven lower *Sefirot*.

The *Zohar* introduced a *Sukkot* ritual that has gained wide acceptance in traditional circles even today. Because of the association between the seven lower *Sefirot* and the seven days of *Sukkot*, the author of the *Zohar* framed a ritual that symbolically invites the *Sefirah* linked with that particular day as a guest to the *sukkah* (booth). Since biblical personages were identified with each *Sefirah*, the custom of welcoming "mystical guests" (*ushpizin*) to the *sukkah* emerged. Abraham (*Hesed*), Isaac (*Din*), Jacob (*Tiferet*), Moses (*Netzah*), Aaron (*Hod*), Joseph (*Yesod*), and David (*Malkhut*) are welcomed on each consecutive day.[55] Special formulae are recited to welcome each heavenly guest and elaborate wall decorations with fanciful pictures of the patriarchs adorn many *Sukkot*. A manual of *Kabbalistic* practice explains that the *Sefirot* take on the spiritual form of the patriarchs and surround the *sukkah* celebrants through the *ushpizin* ritual:

> When you enter the *sukkah*, you ought to openly invite the divine saints to join you because they are your glory. They come in spiritual form to join you on all sides.[56]

The *lulav* and *etrog* also have symbolic associations with the *Sefirot*. The seven pieces that make up the *lulav* and *etrog* are symbolic of the seven lower *Sefirot*. The tall palm branch, which is a phallic symbol, is associated with the masculine *Sefirah Yesod*. The round citron, with feminine connotations, symbolizes *Malkhut*. The three myrtle branches suggest *Hesed*, *Din*, and *Tiferet*, and the two willow branches denote *Netzah* and *Hod*.[57] Holding the *lulav* in the right hand and the *etrog* in the left, the branches are waved in the synagogue service in six directions (east, south, west, north, up, and down) each day. Each direction corresponds to another *Sefirah*, thus symbolizing the unity of the lower six *Sefirot*.

On the last day, *Simhat Torah*, the final Torah portion of the liturgical year is concluded, and the cycle begins again. For the Jewish mystic, this holiday completes the process of the unification of *Tiferet* and *Malkhut* that began on *Rosh ha-Shanah*. The *Zohar* describes *Simhat Torah* as the culminating mystical event of a process that began with *Rosh ha-Shanah*. This process results in the unification of all the *Sefirot*, *Hesed*'s embrace of *Malkhut*, and a shower of blessings upon the world in celebration of this divine union:

> On the first day of *Sukkot*, the right side (i.e., *Hesed*) is aroused toward embracing the princess (i.e., *Shekhinah*). People ought to rejoice in many ways as she is inclined toward celebration. The eighth day, *Simhat Torah*, is the day of union, the day on which all is one, the perfection of all.[58]

If the Days of Awe and *Sukkot* are part of a process of unification, *Pesah* (Passover) is a theurgic drama of vanquishing evil and demonic forces. *Kabbalists* believed that evil was a real and powerful force in the universe. They believed that cosmic forces of evil were released as dregs, a by-product of emanation, and as the result of human behavior that brought too much *Din* into the universe.

The *Pesah* festival celebrates the divine deliverance and Exodus of the Israelites from Egyptian slavery. It begins on the fifteenth of *Nisan*, the first liturgical month, and lasts for seven days in Israel, eight in the Diaspora.[59] The holiday is observed through strict prohibitions against eating any bread or other leavened products, the injunction to eat *matzah* (unleavened bread), and the telling of the narrative of the Exodus at an elaborate table ritual, the *seder*, on the first night in Israel and on the first two nights in the Diaspora.[60]

Jewish mystics invested the holiday with special significance. For them, it symbolizes a victory over the demonic forces that prevail in the world as a result of the isolation of *Malkhut* from *Tiferet*. The absence of unity in the divine realm produces an abundance of *Din* and converts the *Sefirah Malkhut* into a source of suffering that radiates upon the world. Only the reunification of the *Shekhinah* with *Tiferet* can correct this dreadful state of affairs. The enslavement in Egypt and the eventual deliverance are the consequence of and symbolize this process.

According to rabbinic legend, wherever the Israelites went into exile, the *Shekhinah* accompanied and protected them. According to another interpretation, which stresses the idea that exile is a punishment for the religious and moral failures of the people, the *Shekhinah* herself goes into exile along with the Israelites. For Jewish mystics, the Exodus from Egypt symbolizes the redemption of the *Shekhinah* from exile and the beginning of the process of restoring her unity with *Tiferet*. Egypt is transformed from a historical place to a symbol for all the evil that plagues humanity whenever the *Sefirot* are not aligned harmoniously. Egypt is described as the abode of the "husks," or "shells" (*kelipot*), that trap the *Shekhinah* and prevent her from achieving unity.

The many rituals of *Pesah* are linked to the symbolism of redemption from evil. The paschal lamb was slaughtered in ancient times and eaten on the holiday.[61] A vestige of this practice, which was abandoned after the destruction of the Second Temple, can be found in the roasted shankbone that is placed on a special plate at the *seder* table. Jewish mystics describe the slaughter of the paschal lamb as a theurgic ritual that destroys the power of evil. They explain that the Egyptians worshipped lambs as deities. Thus, the sacrifice and burning of a slaughtered lamb is an act of annihilating the demonic power of the Egyptian deities. It is interesting to note that Jewish mystics, in this way, acknowledge the reality of other deities but characterize them as demons. They are understood as satanic and evil powers that threaten and attack the holiness of the *Sefirot*. The slaughter of the paschal lamb is the first ritual performed on the holiday and indicates that the "husks" of evil must be destroyed in order for the *Sefirot* to escape from their dominion. The lamb is eaten at night, the time when evil power is ascendant, in order to vanquish evil at the moment of its greatest strength.

Matzah, which is described in the *seder* ritual as the "bread of poverty" (*lehem oni*), refers to the bread that was prepared hurriedly in the last hours of the Israelites' enslavement. In Jewish mysticism, *matzah* refers to the *Shekhinah* in exile, impoverished due to her separation from *Tiferet*.

Leavened bread (*hametz*), which is absolutely forbidden on *Pesah*, symbolizes the power of evil. The mystics explain that leavened bread is an allegory for the power of demonic forces over good. According to Nahmanides, even a small amount of leavening, fermentation, causes food to lose its original flavor.[62] Likewise, even a little evil can cause the total corruption of a good person. According to *Kabbalah*, fermented foods are outlawed on *Pesah* because they symbolize the destruction of divine goodness.

Although leavened foods are prohibited on *Pesah*, they are permitted throughout the rest of the year. If they connote evil, should not leavened foods be outlawed entirely? The mystics' response is that leaven serves as a reminder of the defeat of the forces of evil. Without such a reminder, the consciousness of redemption might fade. Therefore, the use of leaven during the rest of the year is, paradoxically, a reminder of the holiness of the *Sefirot* to which all religious actions are directed. As the author of the *Lekhah Dodi* wrote, evil exists as a reminder of goodness for without it, there is no awareness of its opposite.[63]

The Jewish mystics had another positive use for leaven, in particular, and for evil powers, in general. They recognized that actions which begin as a result of impure instincts or drives can still lead to pure and positive results. For example, they recognize that human sexual urges—lust—may derive from evil and demonic impulses. But these instincts, when channeled properly, may lead to pure and holy consequences of sexual union which, in the mystics view, is a theurgic act of divine reunification. The author of the *Lekhah Dodi* explains: "The evil inclination is vital to the world for the purpose of proper sexual union."[64] Because evil is a throne for the good, *hametz* is permitted throughout the year except for *Pesah*.

The *seder* is a theurgic ritual designed to reunite the *Shekhinah* with *Tiferet*. It is customary to perform the *seder* while leaning to the left. This symbolizes *Binah*, which appears on the left side in all diagrams of the *Sefirot*, and which is the *Sefirah* called "freedom." The entire *seder* is associated with the *Sefirah Binah*, which is ascendant on this holiday. The three *matzot* which are placed on the table symbolize *Tiferet*, *Malkhut*, and *Yesod*. The middle *matzah*, symbolizing *Malkhut*, is broken in half to suggest that *Malkhut* is divided between the two male *Sefirot*, *Tiferet* and *Yesod*, until she is finally united with her mate, *Tiferet*, in the ultimate unity. One of the halves is hidden as the *afikomen*, which is recovered after the meal and eaten. Because it is hidden, it is linked with *Binah*, the hidden source of freedom.

The four cups of wine that are consumed during the *seder* are associated with the four *Sefirot*, *Hokhmah*, *Binah*, *Tiferet*, and *Malkhut*, and symbolize the stages in the process of uniting *Tiferet* and *Malkhut*. The bitter herbs (*maror*) suggest the bitterness that plagues *Tiferet* while it is separate from *Malkhut*. The mixture of apples, nuts, and wine (*haroset*) symbolizes the sweetness of the redemption that occurs on this evening. The *seder* ritual culminates in the reunion of *Tiferet* and *Malkhut* and the liberation of the universe from the dominion of evil.

The third pilgrimage festival, *Shavuot*, occurs on the sixth day of the month of *Sivan*, and outside of Israel, it continues on the following day. It is both the anniversary celebration of the revelation of the Torah at Sinai and the festival at the beginning of the spring wheat harvest. Aside from the observances that are part of all pilgrimage festivals, there are few rituals associated specifically with this holiday. One of the most common customs is to celebrate the holiday with festive dairy meals. This custom is based on the agricultural origins of the holiday and the affinity between grain and dairy products. It also derives from the designation of Mount Sinai as *har gavnunim*, a ragged mountain with many peaks.[65] Inventive commentators noticed the similarity between the term *gavnunim* and *gevinah*, the Hebrew word for cheese. From this association, the custom of eating dairy products on *Shavuot* gained favor.

The biblical Book of Ruth, a narrative concerning the non-Israelite Ruth and her efforts to join her fate with the Israelite people, is read on *Shavuot* for two reasons. First, the story centers on apparently random agricultural events that had decisive and profound consequences for the destiny of the Israelite people: Following a famine that brought the Israelite Naomi to Moab, she returned to Israel with her widowed daughter-in-law, Ruth, a Moabite. At the harvest, Naomi's relative Boaz met Ruth, whom he soon married. Boaz and Ruth, explains the genealogical conclusion of the book, were the great-grandparents of King David. Their meeting was consequential for it set in motion a series of events that culminated in the Davidic kingship and, ultimately, in the building of the Temple and the perpetuation of the Jewish religion. Second, the Book of Ruth narrates a tale of betrothal and marriage between Ruth and Boaz. The marriage symbolizes the enduring marriage covenant between the Jewish people and God that was established at Sinai. The holiday of *Shavuot* and the Book of Ruth are linked together by the theme of covenantal marriage.

It is not surprising that Jewish mystics understood this holiday as the culmination of the unification of *Tiferet* and *Malkhut*. *Shavuot* is celebrated, according to the Torah, on one day, as opposed to the other pilgrimage festivals, *Sukkot* and *Pesah*, which each last seven days. Jewish mystics explain that this anomaly is due to the fact that on *Shavuot* there is complete unity whereas on the other festivals there is merely the anticipation of unity. The result of the divine unity achieved on *Shavuot* is God's revelation of the Torah to Moses and the Jewish people.

According to Jewish theology, God revealed to Moses all of the Torah, including details of events that had not yet occurred. He then faithfully transcribed this in the original Torah text. At the same time, according to legend, God revealed to Moses the interpretations and hidden meanings of the Torah. These insights, called the Oral Torah (*Torah she-be-al peh*), became the basis of the collected wisdom of the ages. They were supposedly transmitted faithfully from master to disciple as the authoritative companion to the Written Torah (*Torah she-be-khtav*). Jewish mystics claim that mystical insight is embedded in the Oral Law and can be extracted only by initiation into the teachings of the mystical tradition.

Because *Shavuot* is the paradigm of unity, the Jewish mystics invented special rituals to be practiced on this day. In the guise of ancient custom, the *Zohar*, for example, introduced the practice of "Creating Perfection on the Night of *Shavuot*" (*tikkun leil Shavuot*), studying selections from the Oral Torah. In mystical symbolism, the Written Torah is associated with *Tiferet* and the Oral Torah is linked with *Malkhut*. The *tikkun* ritual is designed to hasten the divine marriage by joining *Tiferet* and *Malkhut*. The Written Torah is read during the daytime service of *Shavuot*. The Oral Torah is studied intensely the night before as a means to prepare the bride, *Malkhut*, or the Oral Torah, for her wedding in the morning. The ritual of *tikkun leil Shavuot* is conducted from midnight to dawn, the time when *Malkhut* predominates. Thus the marriage ceremony between *Tiferet* and *Malkhut* is considered complete when the Written Torah is read during the morning service. The *Zohar* introduced the practice of the all-night Torah vigil on *Shavuot* as a supposedly ancient practice:

> Rabbi Shimon used to sit and learn Torah at night when the bride joined with her spouse. It is taught: The members of the bride's entourage are obligated to stay with her throughout the night before her wedding with her spouse to rejoice with her in those perfections (*tikkunim*) by which she is made perfect. They should learn Torah, Prophets, and Writings, homilies on the verses and the secrets of wisdom, for these are her perfections and adornments. She enters with her bridesmaids and stands above those who study, for she is readied by them and rejoices in them all night. On the morrow, she enters the canopy with them and they are her entourage. When she enters the canopy, the Holy One, Blessed be He, asks about them, blesses them, and crowns them with the bride's adornments. Blessed is their destiny.[66]

Every ritual aspect of the Jewish liturgical year is related to the unification of *Tiferet* and *Malkhut* and to the restoration of divine harmony. The Jewish mystics believe that each element in Jewish observance is a divinely constructed guide to theurgic action leading to unity and restoration. In his own eyes, the Jewish mystic differs from the nonmystic practitioner of Judaism in that he performs the rituals of Judaism with a consciousness of their ultimate purpose. The Jewish mystic thereby transforms all of Judaism into an intricately woven pattern of actions that lead him to the culmination of the mystic quest.

9

RAISING THE SPARKS

Modern Jewish Mysticism

At the beginning of the eighteenth century, the largest concentration of Jews in Europe was found in Lithuania and Ukraine, which was then part of Poland. The Jews of Poland numbered about three-quarters of a million people, 3 percent of the total population.[1]

The Jews of Eastern Europe are known as Ashkenazic Jews. Actually, *Ashkenaz* is the Hebrew name for Germany. Ashkenazic Jews refers to those Jews whose ancestors came from the Rhineland and who moved eastward into Poland following the Black Plague of 1348–1350. The Jews fled Germany in the wake of attacks by Christians who blamed the Jews for causing the epidemic that decimated one-third of the entire population but left the Jews relatively unscathed.

With the decline of the German and Spanish centers of world Jewry by the turn of the sixteenth century, Poland emerged as the preeminent center of Jewish life. Lithuania was annexed to Poland in 1569, and Ukraine was colonized at about the same time. Poland was a distinct and separate kingdom until 1772, when it was conquered and divided among Russia, Prussia, and Austria.

During this period, the Jews enjoyed considerable communal autonomy and flourished as a creative and dynamic civilization. An elaborate system of communal self-taxation supported a vast network of religious, educational, welfare, and publishing enterprises. This period produced some of the great luminaries of Jewish intellectual history including Rabbi Moshe

Isserles of Cracow (1520–1572), the author of the important commentary on the *Shulkhan Arukh*, the Code of Jewish Law. The Jews were involved extensively in many phases of economic life through the award and purchase of royal franchises. In exchange for high tax revenues, they were granted charters by the kings that guaranteed them monopolies (*arenda*) on certain occupations such as the distillation, distribution, and sale of alcoholic spirits. Jews dominated the export trade and engaged heavily in many middle-class occupations including shoemaking, furs, carpentry, stonecutting, and goldsmithing. Few Jews were engaged in agriculture.

Jewish residential patterns were concentrated in market towns called *shtetlach* (singular, *shtetl*, from the Yiddish word *shtot*, town), where they were often the majority. These *shtetlach* ranged in size from small hamlets to large towns with one thousand or more Jewish residents. They were communities united by religion and the Yiddish language, a Jewish language derived from medieval German, Hebrew, and Slavic.

Many *shtetlach* were established as the Jews moved eastward and were instrumental in the Polish colonization and settlement of Lithuania and Ukraine. Here the Jews came into contact with the local population, which viewed them, and their Polish sponsors, as foreigners and intruders. Bogdan Chmielnicki (pronounced Chmyelnitzki), the father of Ukrainian nationalism, led an organized paramilitary revolt in 1648 against the Jews and, indirectly, against Polish interests. It is estimated that one hundred thousand Jews were murdered, mutilated, or massacred in three hundred towns in the Ukraine. The Jewish response to this catastrophe was different from previous episodes. There were, of course, religious works and liturgical poetry composed in commemoration of the dead and in defense of God's justice. But the most significant response appeared in the form of a powerful messianic uprising that shook the very foundations of Jewish life.

Even before 1648, messianic anticipation had sunk roots among certain segments of Polish Jewry. According to rabbinic tradition, the period of messianic redemption was to be preceded by a period of travail and turmoil in the world. The *Talmud* suggests that "in the footsteps of the Messiah, audacity (*hutzpah*) would spread."[2] This would usher in a period of chaos, known as the "travails of the Messiah" (*hevlei mashiah*), during which a precursor to the Messiah would be killed. This would be followed by the appearance of the Messiah who would usher in an era of peace. In *gematria*, the system of numerical values assigned to each Hebrew letter, the Hebrew term *hevlei mashiah* has a numerical value of 408, which is shorthand for the Hebrew calendar year 5408, or 1648 according to the Gregorian system.

The messianic upheaval after 1648 had its roots in the *Kabbalistic* mythology of the previous century. Isaac Luria Ashkenazi[3] (1534–1572), the greatest of the luminaries of Safed, wove a fascinating theory concerning the hiddenness of God. His ideas appealed to his contemporaries perhaps because of their intimate familiarity with exile and dislocation. Many of them were the children of the Spanish exiles.

Luria portrayed creation as intrinsically imperfect although man, para-doxically, was invested with the capacity to perfect the world and thus com-plete the process of creation. The perfection of God, Luria taught, was unique, and the attempt to replicate His own perfection and to embody it in creation could not be accomplished without producing disruption and chaos. In attempting to communicate something of His own essence to the world, God overwhelmed the world's capacity to serve as a vessel for divine perfection. The overload led to a fracture in the process of creation and produced a world in which pain, evil, exile, and disorder predominate. The suffering and moral failures of human life are real features of existence and not primarily the result of human sinfulness.

Luria explained the process of the beginning of all existence as the limi-tation of the infinite being of *The Infinite*. *The Infinite*, portrayed metaphori-cally as boundless light, is all that exists:

> Know that before the emanations were emanated and the created things were created, the pure, divine light filled all existence. There was no empty place resembling a void or vacuum. Everything was permeated by that sim-ple light of *The Infinite*. There was neither beginning nor end. There was just one simple light, static, in equanimity. It was called the light of *The Infinite*.[4]

The only attribute of the infinite being is His will. His will is to create some-thing other than Himself, to allow something other than Himself to exist. The purpose of allowing another existence is to make it possible for His own existence to be known. The other is created for His own sake. But since His existence is infinite, it cannot be known except through the *Sefirot*. The *Sefirot* are the finite expressions, names, and attributes of the infinite being. Luria taught that:

> God's simple will was moved to create worlds, to radiate emanations, to bring to light the perfection of His actions, names and attributes, for this was the cause of His creating worlds.[5]

The Infinite initiated the process of bringing other existences into being with an act of self-limitation called "contraction" (*tzimtzum*). How did *The Infinite* restrict His own infinite being? Luria explains the solution to this conundrum with a metaphor drawn from his knowledge of medieval geometry and physics. *The Infinite* created a void within its own boundless existence by contracting itself into a primordial point. It went from unbounded infinity to unbounded finitude. The universe that existed before the contraction was not a physical universe of space and matter. It was entirely *The Infinite*. With the contraction of infinity, the universe became finite but still unbounded in the sense that it has no edge or boundary. Physicists today would call such a phenomenon a hypersphere. Within the unbounded hypersphere, *The Infinite* created a boundary by contracting Himself into a point. The being of *The Infinite* is thus infinitely shrunken into a point that has an edge and boundary. This is what modern physics calls a singularity.

After contracting Himself into a singularity, *The Infinite* expanded away from the point to the periphery of the hypersphere. By this, He created both space and matter. He created space within the bounded universe by defining a finite center and an infinite perimeter. The unbounded perimeter must be spherical because he withdrew from the center in equal measure in all directions. The area left within the sphere is His primordial space. At the same

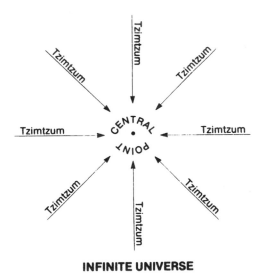

INFINITE UNIVERSE

Figure 9.1   Tzimtzum

time, since *The Infinite* has traversed from the center to the periphery, the space that He left behind is within Himself and must have a residue of His being. This is the primordial essence of God out of which all existence is formed.

Everything within the world shows traces in its being of the original essence of *The Infinite*, which withdrew in order to allow for other beings to exist. Luria explains:

> Then, *The Infinite* contracted Himself into a central point with His light in the middle. He contracted this light and then removed Himself to the sides encircling the point at the center. This left an empty place, an ether, and a vacuum around the point at the center. This contraction, equidistant all around the point at the center, formed a void in such a way that the vacuum was spherical on all sides in equal measure. It did not form a cube with right angles because *The Infinite* contracted Himself into a sphere in equal distance on all sides. He intended that the light of *The Infinite* should be in absolute equanimity. This necessitated that He contract Himself in equal measure on all sides no more on one side than any other.[6]

According to Luria, this act of contraction within and without is an act of divine self-restriction. Such a limitation gives measure and definition to the undefined and unbounded. This is described as "revealing the roots of judgment," the measure of *Din*. Luria explains that this necessary limitation is an act of *Din*. *Din* is thus necessary for creation: "The purpose of contraction is to reveal the roots of divine judgment in order to give the measure of *Din* later on to the worlds."[7]

Within this hypersphere, existence comes into being. The hypersphere appears to the human imagination as a vacuum, as empty space. This space, however, is not really a vacuum since it contains a residue of *The Infinite*, the roots of *Din*, and the potentiality of all existence. Luria explains that this vacuum is creative space:

> And after this contraction, there was only the vacuum, ether and empty space in the midst of the light of *The Infinite*. There was now place for the emanations, creations, formations and actions.[8]

The Infinite then began to create within this primordial space. He began to act directly within this vacuum to create the ideal prototypes of existence. First, He sought to radiate the ten *Sefirot* as the ten attributes of the prototype of a human being. *The Infinite* radiated His light in a straight line from one point on the periphery of the hypersphere through the point in the center to another point on the periphery. Luria describes the straight line of emanation:

> Then, one straight line descended from the light of *The Infinite* from the top to the bottom of the sphere of light. It unfolded downwards through this void. Into the space of this vacuum, He emanated, created, formed and acted upon all the worlds.[9]

A straight line, however, could not penetrate the hypersphere. Since the hypersphere is unbounded, everything within it is unbounded and has no edge. A straight line cannot traverse the space without conforming to its spherical shape. So the light of *The Infinite* was refracted from a line into a curve that formed the shape of a concentric circle within the hypersphere. The straight line, however, before it was refracted, served as a connecting link between the boundless hypersphere of *The Infinite* and the first bounded sphere within it.

> He spread the straight line bit by bit. At first, the line of light began to spread and, then, it spread out, descended and became a type of sphere round about. This sphere did not cling to the light of *The Infinite* which encompassed it. The connection and bond between the emanating sphere of *The Infinite* and the emanated sphere is that very same straight line.[10]

This first bounded sphere within the hypersphere is the first *Sefirah*, *Keter*. It is also the first aspect of the ideal prototype of man and so is called the "*Keter* of primordial man." This same process was repeated within the hypersphere. Each penetration of the straight line of the light of *The Infinite* was refracted into another concentric circle within the previous one. The straight line of emanation advances, retreats, and forms a concentric line within the previous concentric sphere. Each concentric sphere represents another stage in the unfolding of the *Sefirot* as ideal prefigurations of a human being. The straight line of emanation joins all of the concentric circles together:

> This first concentric sphere which adheres closely to *The Infinite* is called *Keter* of primordial man. Then, the straight line continues briefly, then retreats and forms another concentric sphere within the other. This sphere is called the *Hokhmah* of primordial man. That which joins all the spheres together is the subtle thin line which spreads out from *The Infinite*, traversing,

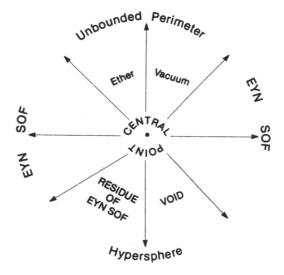

Figure 9.2   The Primordial Void

descending and joining each sphere to another until it reaches the very last. Next, the line spreads out in a straight way from the top to the bottom, from the highest point of the highest sphere to the very lowest and last of the spheres. It consists of ten *Sefirot* arranged mysteriously in the image of an upright human figure.[11]

Each concentric circle is a little less than the one that preceded it. Each emanation is less infinite than the one that preceded it. The hierarchical arrangement of concentric circles from top to bottom conveys *The Infinite* to each successive *Sefirah*. Each *Sefirah* formed in this way was a receptacle for the divine light. Without contraction, reduction, and diminution, no receptacle could have contained the divine light:

> Through the contraction and diminution of the light, it was possible for a receptacle to come into being and become apparent.[12]

As each concentric circle formed, it became more remote from the original light of *The Infinite*. Within this shrinking universe, the light remained strong although the vessel became increasingly weaker. Finally, under the impact of the powerful light of *The Infinite* the weak vessels collapsed and exploded, destroying the original prototype. This is the pivotal moment in

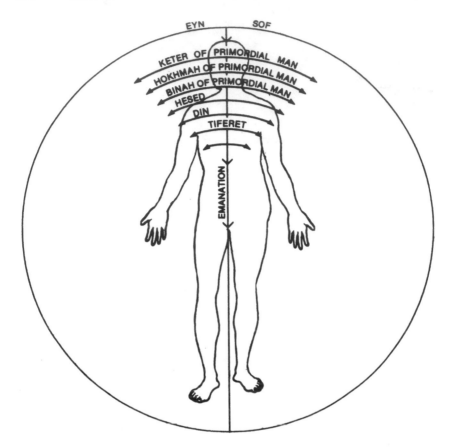

Figure 9.3   Emancipation of Primordial Man. Primordial man contains all the attributes of divinity in perfect form. He is also the blueprint for human beings. Therefore, human beings are the embodiment of the *Sefirot* in the world. Every human being is a divine microcosm.

the process of the divine emanation before creation and determines the destiny of the universe. Luria established the principle that the universe, from top to bottom, is a weak vessel incapable of containing the divine light. The vessels that were supposed to hold the divine light collapsed. Luria states this succinctly:

> When the light becomes too strong, the receptacle disintegrates due to its limited capacity to contain the powerful light.[13]

Luria describes this catastrophe as the "breaking of the vessels" (*shevirat ha-kelim*). This catastrophe undid God's involuntary plan to transmit His goodness. Was God incapable of emanating His essence? Was God powerless to replicate His goodness? Was God powerless to accomplish what He wanted? According to Luria, God was constrained from exceeding the bounds of His own infinity and crossing over into the realm of the finite. Luria proposes that not even God can surpass the nature of His own being. Consequently, the vessels imploded under the weight of the divine light. The light of *The Infinite* and the subtle vessels of the *Sefirot* were dispersed throughout the universe. On one hand, the primordial scene of creation had turned into chaos and disaster. On the other hand, the light of *The Infinite* was now diffused randomly throughout the hypersphere. The collapse of God's initial plan left the realm of the *Sefirot* in ruins and set the stage for an imperfect universe. The explosion frustrated God's effort to create a perfect world.

Within this colossal and violent explosion, the birth of the universe took place. The residue of the catastrophe provided the elemental stuff of creation. Luria describes the aftermath of this "big bang" as having produced sufficient "sparks of light" and "shards of vessels" to produce a world. The world might have been formed by dross, but it was formed from divine dross.

Next, and in spite of the cosmic collapse, *The Infinite* radiated a second and weaker light that did not overwhelm the structure. This light slowly penetrated the universe and created time, matter, and the world as we know it. The outward manifestation of the universe is chaotic and distorted. The explosion resulted in the formation of an imperfect world. In its wake, the world was shaped from the remnants and shards of the primeval chaos. The abyss between *The Infinite* and the world appears insurmountable. But because the underlying nature of the matter of the world is divine, the world is not so much devoid of divinity as it is a mask concealing divinity.

The world contains within it deeply hidden and embedded shards of divine light. The very chaotic state of the universe also inherently contains the possibility of its own perfection. All existence is paradoxical in that it appears distorted and corrupt, yet it contains the seeds of holiness. For Luria, the world contains the seeds for its own renewal. This is the possibility of restoration (*tikkun*). Luria taught that *tikkun* is the greatest tool that humans have at their disposal. Through acts of *tikkun*, it is possible for a human being to complete the work of creation that God was incapable of achieving.

Man can choose to repair the fracture that is not of his own making through theurgic rituals and acts of moral repentance. Repentance is transformed from a technique of returning to the correct and prescribed path to an active process in which God and His creation are returned to their status as it was intended before the break.

Luria also explained that this accounts for the paradoxical nature of human character. Humans contain the keys to restoring and repairing God's universe despite their own proclivity for failure, incompleteness, and sin. But Luria taught that the natural disposition of the soul to seek goodness is affected by the structure of existence. The universe is not wicked and human beings are capable of spiritual achievement. All urges, impulses, failures, and hateful thoughts are the deepest reflections within man of the fracture that permeates the world. These inclinations can themselves be repaired and restored through acts of penitence.

Luria prescribed an array of *tikkunim* as spiritual practices for his disciples. He helped them to identify "the root of their own soul," diagnosed the broken vessel which has impinged on their soul, and stipulated person-specific practices to heal the cosmic wound that is unique to them. Luria's *tikkunim* were adopted throughout the Jewish world as remedies to heal the individual soul and repair the tear in the cosmos.

Isaac Luria elevated this moral principle to a universal law. Just as repentance is the striving of the individual to return to harmony and resolution, so all existence struggles to repair the fractures and tears that are visible within the world. Repentance and restoration (*tikkun*) are as vital for the perfection of the world as they are for moral perfection. The tear that permeates existence is the cause of all pain and chaos, and yet, paradoxically, it is a necessary stage in the unfolding of divine perfection. The dichotomies of good and evil, perfection and destruction, are only apparent. In fact, all phenomena are extensions and phases of essentially divine matters. In their translation from divine perfection to worldly manifestation, something is tragically, but not hopelessly, lost.

All things proceed from God in a continuous chain of being so that good and evil are necessary and integral stages of existence. The expressions of the religious spirit of Judaism, influenced by these patterns of dislocation and restoration, are subject to oscillations of descent and ascent, growth and decay. What appears to be destructive may yet prove to be constructive. Those times that appear to be low points in the cycle of a nation's history may also serve a higher purpose.

It struck many in Poland that the catastrophe of 1648 might indicate, in paradoxical fashion, the beginning of redemption. Lurianic *Kabbalah* was deeply ingrained in Polish Jewish culture prior to 1648. Optimism was generated by the proposition that the pitiful outward appearance of life in the world contradicts the purity of the inner reality. This inspired a movement that was dedicated to spiritual and moral regeneration through penitence. Popular preachers spread the message of Lurianic penitence through missionary activities across Eastern Europe. Before and after 1648, Poland was rife with messianic expectation and ready for a popular religious revival.

The revival occurred around 1665 when Jewish missionaries began to reach Poland with the news that the Ottoman Sultan had crowned a mysterious figure as king of the Jews. Fabulous rumors spread about his miracles and great military feats. In their wake, many believers in Poland stood ready to be transported to the Land of Israel to take part in the restoration of the Jewish kingdom. Some went so far as to sell their homes, liquidate their assets, and proselytize aggressively in Christian neighborhoods.

These legends were based, in part, on real events. In 1666, Shabbetai Tzvi (1626–1676), a *Kabbalist*, was arrested and imprisoned in Gallipoli by the Ottoman Sultan.[14] Shabbetai Tzvi had begun to attract a following among Ottoman Jewish subjects who viewed him as the Messiah. He preached a version of the Lurianic *Kabbalah*, which stated that the Messiah himself will represent all the contradictions of existence within himself. The soul of the Messiah would reflect the trapped sparks of light among the husks of broken vessels. The Messiah would be able to prescribe ritual acts of penitence that would bring the travails of the world to their final resolution.

Before his arrest, Shabbetai Tzvi had attracted followers throughout the Mediterranean basin and Eastern Europe. In Eastern Europe, in particular, the combination of latent *Kabbalistic* belief and genuine messianic anticipation provided fertile ground for rumors of redemption. The early movement flourished as a force for moral regeneration and messianic anticipation.

When he arrested Shabbetai Tzvi, the Sultan had sought to restore the equilibrium among his Jewish subjects that messianism could disrupt. He challenged Shabbetai Tzvi to prove his claim, or, if he could not, he could choose between accepting Islam or death. Shabbetai Tzvi converted to Islam on September 15, 1666, and went on to justify his apostasy as part of the messianic plan implicit in the Lurianic system. The soul of the Messiah must perform the final act of restoration by uplifting the sparks of light trapped deepest in the mire of the broken vessels. This means that the Messiah must combat evil at its source and must assume the burden of descending into the deepest recesses of the world of darkness. In real terms, the final act of ingathering is a temporary descent into sin in order to conquer its power and destroy its vitality. Shabbetai Tzvi and his followers explained his apostasy as a necessary descent into the realm of evil and as a feature of the messianic process.

The followers of Shabbetai Tzvi were a strong force within Eastern European Jewry even after his apostasy. Many expected him to return to Judaism and to shortly usher in the messianic era. Few were prepared for the fact that nothing actually changed over the course of time. Those who continued to believe in him were divided. Some believed that the soul of the Messiah was in eclipse, but that he would soon complete his mission. Their task was to wait patiently with belief in their hearts. Others took an active approach to hastening his final work by assuming personal responsibility as his messianic agents. They sought to strengthen him by imitating his descent into darkness. In real terms, this meant that they violated certain norms of Jewish law in order to fulfill the messianic requirements. Many Sabbateans lived public lives of probity while committing religious transgressions in private.

The Sabbatean heresy, in both its moderate and extreme forms, swept through Poland in the years after 1666. Many respected Polish rabbis were caught up in this maelstrom, and the movement survived well into the middle of the eighteenth century. It gradually receded as a popular movement, but it left deep impressions on the Jewish population. It kindled a deep yearning for messianic redemption across all levels of Jewish society. It legitimized popular forms of religious devotion, especially penitential rites of devotion, amulets, and other folkloristic customs. It also reinforced the idea that Jews could live with a sense of inner redemption and fulfillment despite the poverty and oppression of their daily lives. The "world to come" could be realized in the present and was not restricted to the afterlife.

The Polish provinces of Galicia and Podolia, today part of eastern Poland and southern Ukraine, were deeply affected by the Sabbatean outbreak through the middle of the eighteenth century. One of the radical offshoots of Sabbateanism sprouted there in 1756. Jacob Frank (1726–1791) encouraged his Sabbatean followers to declare their faith openly. In order to "fulfill the Torah through its violation," he preached a gospel of anarchy and destruction of world order. In 1757, Frank persuaded the bishop of Kamenetz-Podolsk, a city on the Dniester River, to convene a debate between the Frankists and Jewish leaders. The Frankists charged that the Jews were guilty of murdering Christians and using their blood for ritual purposes. Later that year, these charges led to the desecration and burning of the *Talmud*. In 1758, Frank led one thousand followers in conversion to Catholicism.

Against this complex background of religious heresy, strife, and messianism, a popular religious revival of more traditional proportions emerged. *Hasidism* emerged in the Ukraine around 1735. Israel ben Eliezer, known as the *Besht*—an acronym for *Baal Shem Tov*, "one who knows how to invoke the name of God for magical and mystical purposes"—began to attract a small following of devotees. Like any great man, his reputation was a mixture of fact and fiction. He was born in 1700 in the Podolian village of Okopy, a budding but small commercial center of less than 200 Jewish families. He was orphaned as a child and became a ward of the community. His education in the Jewish elementary school was typical: he learned the holy texts by rote, memorizing long passages in a sing-song recitation in Hebrew, Aramaic, and Yiddish. Beyond these texts, nothing else was taught. He could not have been troubled by the insularity of this education, since no alternative curriculum was as yet conceivable. But he might have easily choked on the routine and memorization, at least judging from one account that said "he would learn for several days, but then he would run away from school." Evidently, he would escape to the woods outside of town to think, meditate, and converse with God.

He also served, for a time, as a *belfer*, a type of teacher's aide who escorted the younger children to school and taught them the basic Hebrew prayers. He enjoyed teaching Jewish melodies to the children and established rapport with them easily. Later, he worked as a watchman in one of the shoddy wooden synagogues in the town. But he preferred the nighttime when he could read the holy texts by candlelight, alone, with only his thoughts to accompany him. He and his wife were innkeepers who, like many Jews in Podolia, paid to lease a concession to distribute liquor from the Polish leaseholder. He later worked in the slightly larger town of Tluste as a Torah teacher, a *melamed*, for the local Jewish children.

He soon began to teach the practice of *Hasidut* (Pietism), a technique for achieving liberation from the vicissitudes of this world and achieving union with the divine. He promoted a new human ideal, the *Hasid*, as opposed to the scholar, who is intoxicated with the fullness of God and who becomes illuminated with God's presence through ecstatic prayer. He taught that only God is truly real and all the phenomena of this world are actually vessels that contain sparks of divine light. The task of the *Hasid* is to elevate the sparks, to raise everything back to its source, to transcend the partial, and seek the absolute.

The *Besht* believed that all of existence is filled with divinity and that God, in truth, is accessible to the ordinary human being. The human task is to overcome the usual barriers of earth-bound consciousness, fear, and concern with the mundane affairs of daily life and discover the divinity everywhere around us. His contemporaries, he confessed, were more preoccupied with guilt, avoiding sin, and feeling unworthy than they were infused with the joy of coming face-to-face with the presence of God everywhere around them.

In one of his famous tales, he told the story of a king who had built a glorious palace full of corridors and partitions, but he himself lived in the innermost room. When the palace was completed and his servants came to pay him honor, they found that they could not approach the king because of the devious maze. While they stood and wondered, the king's son came and showed them that those were not real partitions, but only magical illusions, and that the king, in truth, was easily accessible. The *Besht*, who saw himself as the king's son in the empire of the blind, told his listeners that anything is possible: "Push forward bravely and you shall find no obstacle!"

Hasidic teaching is strongly panentheistic. That is, it teaches that only God is truly real. All the phenomena of the world are only vessels that contain the divine light and have no independent reality of their own. This is not the same notion as pantheism, which teaches that God's being infuses all of the phenomena of the world. *Hasidic* teaching asserts that there is nothing that truly exists except God's being. The world is really a veil that, if removed, leaves only divinity.

Nothing exists in the world independent of God. Everything that exists can be elevated back to its divine source. In fact, the *Besht* suggests that there is no autonomous human will except to the extent that it is implanted in man by God. There is little room in this conception for anything but God. He says:

> One should know that everything in the world is infused with the Creator, may He be blessed. Every product of human thought is the result of His providence.[15]

The beauty of the world lies not in the things of this world but in God, the source of all beauty. The task of the *Hasid* is to elevate the sparks, to raise everything back to its source, to transcend the partial and seek the absolute.

Things in this world do not really matter except as they are the manifestations of God. Beauty does not really exist in the world other than as a concretization of divinity in human form. Everything thus is a vessel for the divine essence.

The *Besht* thought that because God fills the world, there is no place empty of him. He suggested that every human feeling, act, and thought is essentially divine, even if God's presence is not immediately evident. Even the most natural of human emotions, sexual attraction, which would ordinarily be considered taboo in Judaism, is an expression of divinity. Although we think of *Hasidism* today as puritanical, both in spirit and behavior, the *Besht* argued that every expression of the human spirit is holy. In another parable, he explained the holiness of sexual attraction:

> If one should notice a beautiful woman, he thinks: What is the cause of her beauty? Is it not true that if she were to die, she would not have this appearance? If so, her beauty comes from the divine power which suffuses her. He gives her the beauty and complexion. Thus, the source of her beauty is the divine power. Why, then, should I be drawn to the partial when I can unite with the source of the entire universe?[16]

Every *Hasid*, and not the Messiah alone, must raise the sparks. He must elevate everything to its source, must transcend the partial for the whole, must see the divine essence in every material thing. Every object that vibrates internally with the *Sefirot* must be raised back to its source. True worship of God is the pursuit of the essence within the vessel, the divine within the worldly, the spiritual within the material. For this reason *Hasidism* even suggests that there is nothing that is essentially evil. Evil is the distorted appearance of that which has not been redeemed. Levi Isaac of Berditchev (1740–1809), a revered *Hasidic* "holy man" and leader of a religious revival in Volhynia, helped to popularize the theory that we can worship God through embracing the world and finding God in the mundane realm of corporeality:

> What is the meaning of elevating the sparks? When you see something corporeal and do not find it to be evil, heaven forbid, you can worship the Creator, may He be blessed. For in this thing you can find love or awe or the other qualities (i.e., *Sefirot*) by which you can elevate it.[17]

The teachings of the *Besht* were elaborated by his most prominent disciple, Dov Baer Friedman, the Preacher (*Maggid*) of Mezritch. The *Maggid* of

Mezritch called for a further transformation in the consciousness of the ordinary Jew. The *Hasid* is privy to a mystical technique that allows him to obliterate consciousness of the world and to achieve consciousness of God to the exclusion of all else. He is able to transcend the world of corporeality and dwell in the pure consciousness of spirituality. The *Hasid* is able to disassociate himself from world-consciousness and to look behind the veil. Through prayer, the *Hasid* can achieve a state of mystical union in which he transcends consciousness of his own existence and ultimately achieves consciousness of oneness with God.

The *Maggid* introduced the technique of "annihilating existence," by which a person eradicates self-consciousness and achieves a state of absorption into God. Ultimately, nothing in the world really exists since God is the only reality. The world is really an illusion that must be overcome. *Hasidism* introduced an "acosmism," a world-denying mysticism, that is a far more radical formulation in Judaism than pantheism. Pantheism is the view that God can be found in every aspect of the world. It affirms the reality of the world and the existence of God and explains that God is found in the world. Panentheism is the view that God exists and the world appears to exist. It posits that the world is really a feature and product of God's consciousness and that the world only really exists within God. This means that only God really exists and He embraces and encompasses the world within Himself. Acosmism takes this one step further and denies the reality of the world. It suggests that the world is really illusory and nothing other than God exists. The thinking of the *Maggid* contains strong panentheistic and even acosmist tendencies. In one passage, the *Maggid* explains his acosmist view:

> Nothing in the world has any existence other than God's existence. All things which exist, existed in potentiality before creation. Then, God emanated their potentiality and gave them spiritual and material coverings. His powers vitalize them. If they were to retreat to their former state before creation, the spiritual and material coverings would not exist at all.[18]

The *Maggid* called for a transformation in the consciousness of the *Hasid*. The world exists, but the *Hasid* is privy to a mystical technique that allows him to obliterate consciousness of the world and to achieve consciousness of God to the exclusion of all else. He is able to transcend the world of corporeality (*gashmiyyut*) and dwell in the pure consciousness of spirituality (*ruhaniyyut*). The *Hasid* is able to disassociate himself from world-consciousness, since the world is essentially an illusion woven by God. He is able to look behind the veil because he knows that in fact the world is only an illusion, an obstacle to knowing God. Through prayer, the *Hasid* can achieve a state of adhesion (*devekut*) in which he transcends consciousness of his own existence and ultimately achieves consciousness of oneness with God. As one of the *Maggid*'s students explained, mystical union involves the obliteration of self-consciousness and immersion in the oneness of God's being. When we achieve this union, God receives pleasure:

> If we achieve this union, we will think about ourselves as well that we are nothing other than God who gives us life. He alone exists and there is nothing other than Him. . . . And when we realize this, that we are like nothingness in truth and nothing else exists in the world but God just as before creation, God, as it were, takes genuine pleasure.[19]

The *Maggid* introduced the technique of annihilating existence (*bittul ha-yesh*), by which the *Hasid* eradicates self-consciousness and achieves a state of absorption into God. The process begins with an understanding that the physical aspect of a human being is merely external. This can occur as one begins to pray. Meditation that precedes prayer is devoted to understanding the relationship between one's physical self and one's consciousness. For example, the power of one's physical existence is so strong that it diverts one's consciousness to physical sensations and considerations. Prayer is made difficult by stimuli that come from one's physical being and assault the consciousness. For example, thoughts of one's business, family, or relationships can intrude upon the mind during prayer. Even more intrusive are thoughts concerning the temptation to sin, especially those of a sexual nature. These thoughts contain within them the sparks of holiness that can be redeemed. This can be seen in the following statement by Jacob Joseph of Polonoye in which he quotes his teacher, the *Besht*:

> I heard a convincing argument said in the name of my teacher (the *Besht*). It concerned the strange thoughts (*mahshavot zarot*) which come to man in the midst of his prayer. They come from the mystery of the broken vessels and the 288 sparks which need to be clarified every day. They appear in order to be repaired and elevated. The strange thought which appears one day is different from that of another day. The *Besht* taught that one must pay close attention to this matter. I learned from him how to repair the strange thoughts even if they are thoughts about women. One should elevate them and make them cleave to their source, the *Sefirah Hesed*.[20]

Prayer is the meditative opportunity for man to come to terms with the range of intrusions upon his consciousness. By recognizing the power and sway over his consciousness that his physical being exercises, he is able to gain conscious control over them. Then, he is able to disassociate his consciousness from himself and gradually transcend self-awareness. This requires the total obliteration of self-awareness, which the *Maggid* characterizes as the annihilation of conscious existence (*bittul ha-yesh*). The *Maggid* introduces a profound awareness of the role of consciousness in religion. He distinguishes between self-consciousness, called "smallness" (*katnut*), and unbounded consciousness, called "greatness" (*gadlut*). Self-consciousness is an obstacle to true awareness since it is illusory. Since only God exists, all else is illusion. Mystical consciousness is the goal of *Hasidism* and prayer is the technique for its acquisition. Mystical consciousness, of course, is intermittent since the world exerts such a powerful force in the direction of false consciousness.

The task of the *Hasid* is to achieve a new and enduring consciousness that God alone is being. The process begins by recognizing that his physical self is an obstacle to true consciousness. This is called "divestment of corporeality" (*hitpashtut ha-gashmiyyut*). The *Maggid* explains that prayer is the arena in which divesting one's sense of self leads to attaining unbounded consciousness:

> The desired goal is that one must precede prayer with the act of divestment of corporeality. Man is finite and has limits but he should make himself nothingness, without limit. He can do this by directing all his effort to God alone, not to anything else, or even to himself. This is impossible unless he makes himself nothing.[21]

Hasidism teaches that observing the requirements of Jewish law and the rituals of the Torah facilitate this process. The *Hasid* becomes aware that everything he sees is really a manifestation of God. This is the process of "elevating the sparks" (*ha'alat ha-nitzotzot*). Then he thinks less about the world and only about God. He empties his consciousness of awareness of the world and thinks himself to be nothingness. This process is called "making himself nothing" (*laa'asot et atzmo 'ayyin*). It is a delicate moment of transition between two stages of consciousness. Finally, his consciousness is filled with awareness of God and nothing else. At that moment his consciousness and God's being are identical. The powerful unbounded consciousness that he achieves induces a powerful and enduring transformation.

From this point, the *Hasid* has a new orientation to the world. He can now worship God effectively in many ways. Since he possesses a new and higher level of consciousness, he is able to live in the world and recognize it for what it is. He can even worship God in a new way since he sees clearly the divinity inherent in everything. The *Hasid* is indifferent to the seductions of the world because he knows the goal to which his consciousness is directed. He keeps consciousness of God before him at all times to such an extent that he is keenly aware of the divinity in everything around him.

Although *Hasidism* presented a powerful mystical teaching and discipline, it also presented a uniquely sympathetic approach to the requirements of daily living. Many of these teachings are found in the legends of the *Hasidic* masters. Some modern scholars discount the significance and authenticity of many of the *Hasidic* legends about the *Baal Shem Tov*.[22] The *Baal Shem Tov* died in 1760, and the first tales were published in 1815, and others were published even later. The sources that are discussed above, however, are taken from homiletic literature (*derashot*) that date from the lifetime of the *Besht* and the *Maggid* and appear to be authentic. The homilies are, in the opinion of scholars, more representative of authentic early *Hasidic* teaching than the tales. The piquancy and spiritual quality of the tales may have a more immediate attraction to the modern reader than do the homilies.

Nevertheless, the tales represent the popular appeal of early *Hasidism*. For example, the *Hasidim* tell the story of a simple Jew, Zusha, who appears before heaven on the day of final judgment with fear that he has not lived up to expectations. He is afraid of being asked, "Why were you not as righteous as Abraham, Isaac, or Jacob?" But he is asked instead, "Why were you not like Zusha?" In commenting on this, Martin Buber, who brought the popular teachings of *Hasidism* to wider recognition, explained that each person's specific task in life is as unique as his specific opportunity to achieve it. *Hasidism* teaches that each situation in life presents a challenge to man and poses a problem for him to solve:

> Man should not ask what the meaning of his life is, but rather he must recognize that it is he who is asked. Each man is questioned by life and he can only answer to life by answering for his own life.[23]

The *Hasidim* offer the following parable about the nature of communal prayer. It conveys the *Hasidic* idea that human interdependence creates greater spiritual power than the individual can achieve. In fact, a lack of community cohesion has negative spiritual consequences:

> Once, in a tropical country, a certain splendid bird, more colorful than any that had ever been seen, was sighted at the top of the tallest tree. The bird's plumage contained within it all the colors of the world. But the bird was perched so high that no single person could ever hope to reach it. When news of the bird reached the ears of the king, he ordered that a number of men try to bring the bird to him. They were to stand on one another's shoulders until the highest man could reach the bird and bring it to the king. The men assembled near the tree but while they were standing balanced on one another's shoulders, some of those near the bottom decided to wander off. As soon as the first man moved, the entire chain collapsed, injuring several of the men. Still, the bird remained uncaptured. The men had doubly failed the king. For even greater than his desire to see the bird was his wish to see his people so closely joined to one another.[24]

Another parable narrates the *Hasidic* ideal of personal prayer. It explains that simplicity is a greater virtue than knowledge when it comes to prayer:

> There was once a simple herdsman who did not know how to pray. But it was his custom to say everyday: "Lord of the world! You know that if you had cattle and gave them to me to tend, though I take wages from everyone else, from you I would take nothing." Once, a rabbi was passing and heard the man pray in this way. He said to him: "Fool, do not pray in this way." The herdsman asked: "How should I pray?" Then, the rabbi taught him the *Shema* and other prayers so that he would no longer say what he was accustomed to. After the rabbi left, the herdsman forgot all the prayers and did not pray. And since the rabbi told him not to pray as he once had, he said nothing. And this was a great catastrophe.[25]

The founders of *Hasidism* had, as their goal, the attainment of mystical ecstasy, the channeling of human powers, and the drawing down of divine influence for the benefit of the community. While they taught mystical and magical interpretations of the commandments, they viewed prayer as the ultimate mystical act that can be achieved through the intense channeling of human powers. They guided their followers in mysticism, magic, ecstasy, solitariness, divesting of physicality, ego-annihilation, and soul-ascension. They created enduring institutions—"holy associations" linked with particular *Tzaddikim* ("holy rabbis"). These often developed into *Hasidic* dynasties transmitted from father to son or teacher to disciple. Each dynasty had its own unique structure, mythology, literature, lore, legacy, and melodies.

Hasidism was a blend of traditional Orthodoxy and revolutionary spirituality. When Jewish immigrants began to leave Eastern Europe after 1882, they often adapted to the new world by abandoning their Orthodoxy. But along with their emancipation and assimilation, they discarded their spiritual legacy. It was a classic case of throwing out the baby with the bath water. It is, therefore, not surprising that *Hasidism*, or at least the romance of *Hasidism*, has become attractive to a growing number of younger Jews who are part of a neo-*Hasidic* revival. Such Jewish "Seekers" are pursuing sources of deeper personal meaning and connectedness, exploring their own Jewishness, and engaging in a variety of Jewish "journeys." A growing number of Jews find this in *Hasidism* rather than in mainstream Orthodox, Conservative, Reconstructionist, or Reform Judaism. These "Seekers" crave, above all, authenticity, which to them means a faith and a way of life that are unambiguous, based on certain authority, and which is not self-conscious or temporizing. They want guides who are authentic and who do not just "talk the talk but also walk the walk." They look for a Judaism that speaks to their hearts and that provides a clear answer to those questions that matter most, how to relate to other people, how to find balance and perspective between and among the many competing claims on our time, how to create a Jewish home life, and what to believe about the presence of God in our lives. Some of them find this by joining or creating intentional communities that adopt some stylistic elements of *Hasidic* enthusiasm, chant, and dance without adopting the Orthodox lifestyle. Others select items from the menu of Judaism, including *Hasidism*, eclectically, mixing and matching from here and from there, according to taste.

On the other hand, many Jews today are repelled by the insularity and separatism of the *Hasidim*. The *Hasidim* appear to cling to an anachronistic lifestyle, which, while admirable, separates them from the mainstream culture. Their insularity is evident in their characteristic clothing and grooming styles—black gabardine suits, white shirts, wide-brimmed hats, sidelocks, and untrimmed beards for men; shape-concealing, long-sleeve and long-hemmed dresses, and wigs, scarves, or hats for women. They do not socialize outside their own society and view the surrounding culture—particularly visual media, television, movies, and advertising, as corrupting. They view other Jews with contempt or view them as lost souls who should be led patiently, but firmly, back into the traditional fold. *Hasidim* see themselves as a zealous and faithful bulwark against the disintegration of the tradi-

tional Jewish path. Many modern Jews see them as a relic of the past and
are offended by the contemptuous and patronizing ways that *Hasidim* adopt
in relation to other Jews. Modern Jews today often feel that they have
achieved too much to fall back into *Hasidic* fundamentalism, parochialism,
and an anachronistic religious lifestyle.

When *Hasidism* appeared in the 1730s, it was a dynamic, intense, and
revolutionary form of personal Jewish spirituality. It is the most radical formulation of the immediacy of individual religious experience as the essence
of the Jewish religion. It is the first and most powerful eruption of spiritual
individualism within a religion known for religious conformism. It is a mystical movement that argues that what occurred to Moses on Sinai is the
model that every individual Jew must follow: to experience an ascent of the
soul for the purpose of enlightenment. And, having gained enlightenment,
one is obligated to return to family, community, and society to work on
behalf of other people. *Hasidism* is, in its essence, a unique teaching and a
practice of mysticism and social responsibility.

The face of *Hasidism* today appears to be that of the fundamentalist
defenders of the ancient faith and practice of Judaism. But when *Hasidism*
first coalesced around the figure of the *Besht*, they saw themselves as religious revolutionaries challenging the status quo and the very definition of
Judaism as it was understood by the leading rabbis of the time. Those very
same leading rabbis saw *Hasidism* as a deviation from all Jewish norms, in
both their teaching and practice. They denounced the *Hasidim* as reformers,
ignoramuses, and deviants. They organized denunciations, boycotts, and
social and economic sanctions against them.

In its early days, *Hasidism* was a thoroughly new construct that challenged the prevailing Jewish traditions. The story of how this revolutionary
reform movement became the defender of its own new status quo, and how
it presented itself as if it always had been the guardian of true Judaism, shows
that one generation's revolution becomes another generation's fundamentalism. The fact that *Hasidism* is a modern construct also teaches us to be
cautious about all claims of exclusive Jewish authenticity.

Hasidism today has preserved only a kernel of its original dynamism.
Some say that it has degenerated into a caricature of its former self and is
today more of a fundamentalist reaction against modernity than the revolutionary revival movement that it once was. Because *Hasidism* is not what it
once was, its spiritual legacy is probably not the answer for those modern
Jews who are most avid in search of spiritual inspiration. Our immigrant
parents abandoned it and this generation cannot embrace it without surren-

dering much of our own personal autonomy. If modern Jews are to have access to our own tradition, it should not be filtered through the replica of *Hasidism* that is found around us today. We should be able to go right back to the source, to understand *Hasidic* spirituality unmediated by biased interpretation, unadulterated by a sponsor's packaging, and unembellished by modern replicas of what no longer exists. To reach the core, one needs to peel through the layers, remove the crust, to get to the heart of *Hasidism*.

The Nazis murdered more than one million *Hasidim* in Poland. What was lost in the destruction of prewar *Hasidism*? When Isaac Bashevis Singer received the Nobel Prize in 1978 and gave his acceptance speech in Stockholm in Yiddish, he explained the uniqueness of the *Hasidic* culture that was destroyed:

> The truth is that what the great religions preached, the Yiddish-speaking people of the ghettos practiced day in and day out. They were the people of the Book in the truest sense of the word. They knew of no greater joy than the study of man and human relations, which they called Torah. . . . The ghetto was not only a place of refuge for a persecuted minority but a great experiment in peace, in self-discipline, and in humanism. My father's home was a study house, a court of justice, a house of prayer, of storytelling, as well as a place for weddings and *Hasidic* banquets. The nations can learn much from those Jews, their way of thinking, their way of bringing up children, their finding happiness where others see nothing but misery and humiliation.

The mystery of *Hasidism* is a universal story that speaks to all people. *Hasidism*, however, is not the only modern mystical phenomenon in Judaism. Mysticism has persisted as one of the important strains of modern Jewish religious expression. The enduring vigor of the mystical strain in Judaism is evident in the monumental figure of Rabbi Abraham Isaac Kook, Chief Rabbi of Palestine from 1919 to 1935.[26] Rav Kook, as he is known, was educated in the great Lithuanian rabbinical academy at Volozhin. At once an Orthodox Zionist and a mystic of deep universal vision, he exhibited the complexities of intellect and spirit that characterize those religious masters whose home is Judaism but whose larger domain is human civilization.

Continuing the tradition that began with Luria and the *Hasidic* masters, Rav Kook offered an explanation of human nature. He teaches that the inner disposition of the soul to seek goodness is affected by the structure of existence. In a variation of the *Hasidic* notion of "worshiping God through corporeality," Rav Kook explains a new notion of repentance. Repentance begins with the recognition of the origin, reality, and power of human impulses. Man then proceeds to transfer and transform the passion and force of these urges to the passionate and forceful performance of the penitential act. Holiness is achieved through the freely chosen act of repentance that restores the original impulse to its intended goal.

Rav Kook's great contribution to Jewish thought may be his application of the Lurianic theory of existence to the phenomena of Jewish history. Rav Kook suggests that the long periods of exile presented the Jewish people with certain intellectual and spiritual challenges that could stimulate a national process of redefinition and, ultimately, restoration. He stated boldly, much to the chagrin of others, that atheism performed a necessary function when it confronted Judaism and challenged it to examine and redefine some of its more mythic and anthropomorphic expressions of God. In their zeal to preserve the original character of Judaism, the Orthodox assumed a defensive stance in the face of the challenge of the dominant cultural values of the period. According to Rav Kook, this only served to isolate the Jewish religion from the healthy winds of challenge while secular culture advanced alone. Moreover, the challenge persisted, and many of the best Jewish minds were alienated from the tradition. The challenge, as Rav Kook sees it, is as necessary as the endurance of the tradition.

The Zionist movement in the twentieth century was the product of a predominantly secular ideology. Many of its adherents had made the break in theory and in practice from the Jewish religious tradition. To Rav Kook, the young Zionists represented not so much a threat to traditional Judaism as a necessary challenge to the spiritual condition of Judaism. Their activism meant no less than the revitalization and restoration of Judaism through a new twist in the universal process of exile and return. Political Zionism served the highest purpose in repairing the fracture that had permeated Judaism through the periods of exile by restoring the spirit of the Jewish people to the Land of Israel, the physical base of its existence. Rav Kook elevated the secular activity of Zionism to the level of a religious obligation that performs a restorative function within Judaism.

During his tenure as Chief Rabbi, he was often criticized by his Orthodox compatriots for his extreme tolerance of the secular Zionists. In explaining his apparent liberalism, he resorted to a parable regarding the building of the Holy of Holies in the Temple. Although only the high priest was permitted to enter the inner sanctum after its completion, all classes of workmen were needed to construct the edifice. Common laborers, masons, and carpenters were needed to build the sanctuary although, ultimately, when their work was completed and the structure acquired a new character of holiness, they were prohibited from entering it. In a similar fashion, he explained, all types of Jews contributed to the construction of the new homeland and were equally vital in the process of the restoration of Judaism.

Rav Kook sought to define a mode of religious faith that reached beyond the particular and exclusive claims of Orthodox, religious Judaism in pursuit of universal values and ideals. He claimed that the highest sensibility of the Jewish soul is the quest for universality, which has been expressed in many diverse forms in Jewish history. For him, the return to Zion was the concrete manifestation of the more subtle process of gathering the dispersed forms of Jewish moral, intellectual, and spiritual expression and the reunification of the Jewish spirit with the source of its inspiration. In this venture, all bearers of the spirit, like the workmen in the tabernacle, performed an equally vital role.

Not all modern Jewish mystics follow the path of tradition. Some have drawn their inspiration from Jewish mysticism without necessarily accepting the religious behavior that had been inseparable from it. The appearance of Jewish mystics who draw their primary inspiration from *Kabbalah* but do not follow the ritual life of earlier *Kabbalists* is a modern phenomenon. Is Jewish mysticism separable from the entire culture in which it flourished? Is it possible to speak about modern *Kabbalists* who do not live according to Jewish law?

Modern Jewish mysticism rarely exists outside of traditional Jewish culture. Today, the only schools in which believers and practitioners of traditional Jewish mysticism are initiated into the *Kabbalistic* tradition are some ultra-Orthodox rabbinical seminaries in Israel. Several major research universities in Israel and North America support academic research into the history and literature of Jewish mysticism. These programs, however, produce academic scholars not mystical practitioners or believers. Other learning centers, such as the *Kabbalah* Center, blend *Kabbalistic* teaching into a potpourri of pop-culture, self-help, and commercial enterprises.

Martin Buber's writings have introduced *Hasidism* to Jewish and non-Jewish readers. His presentation of *Hasidic* ideas is highly selective and is filtered through the lens of his own philosophy. Still, Buber has done more than any other writer to popularize *Hasidic* teachings as ideas with powerful spiritual content and broad human appeal. Despite his own interpretations and interpolations, Buber has successfully opened the closed world of *Hasidism* to the outside.

The writings of Isaac Bashevis Singer portray a lost world in which mysticism was the spiritual foundation. To Singer, *Kabbalah* appears to teach, as Isaac Luria suggested, that everything is imbued with divinity. From the abstract philosophic understanding of *Kabbalah*, Singer drew imaginative but necessary conclusions. Singer's worldview was shaped in some measure by the philosophy of *Kabbalah* into which he read normal adolescent curiosity about sexuality. After all, if there are couplings and liaisons in heaven, why should humans on earth be any different? If, as the *Kabbalists* say, "even in heaven the principle of male and female prevailed," would not an adolescent infatuation with the mysteries of human sexuality follow? His fiction is replete with rich sexual fantasy and supernatural eroticism. Many of the characters in his stories suffer from confusion about gender identity. This ambiguity may, in part, derive from the androgynous nature of the human soul described in *Kabbalah*. His fanciful interpretation of *Kabbalistic* sexuality is a playful, but not incorrect, reading.

Singer's fiction is also replete with supernatural tales about demons, possessions, transmigrations, dybbuks, and evil spirits. These too, of course, derive from *Kabbalah*. Much of *Kabbalistic* and *Hasidic* demonology is actually an importation of Transylvanian, Ukrainian, and other Eastern European folklore into Jewish popular culture. Still, much of *Kabbalistic* demonology is based on the notion that there is a realm in the creation where God could not reach, a realm of darkness and evil where His light does not shine. In the *Kabbalistic* universe, there is no dead matter. Everything is alive with divinity. But since God cannot reach everywhere, Jewish mystics assume that the dark realm is equally vibrant with the power of evil. This world, for Singer, is the lowest and therefore weakest link in the chain of being.

While the occult assumes a prominent role in Singer's fiction, there is also a strong tendency to see *Kabbalah* as a source of eternal truth. The invisible world of the *Sefirot* animates all things, according to Singer's understanding of *Kabbalah*. Every bug, every book, every person vibrates internally with the power of divinity. The world is composed of the sparks of divine light that shine invisibly within all things. For Singer, the truth of *Kabbalah* is identical with the truth of modern science. The science of electricity and atomic theory, in a general sense, and the view that matter is alive and not inert seems to him to be what *Kabbalah* has been saying all along. Singer was raised in the world of *Hasidic* piety at a time when urbanization and modernization were beginning to shatter the walls of tradition. As a young boy, his faith that *Kabbalah* and modern science agree was the bridge between these two worlds.

The occult has always played a role in *Kabbalah*. The mystical belief in theurgy can easily lead to a belief in magic. If one can influence God through ritual, perhaps one should be able to bring magic to bear upon the world. For example, the legend of the *Golem* has persisted for centuries. It goes back to the *Talmudic* legends according to which the sage Rava is said to have created a kind of robot for his friend. The same legend also says that Rav Hanina and Rav Ushaya were accustomed to studying cosmology each week before the beginning of the Sabbath. As a result, they were able to create a miniature calf which they would eat.[27] This idea was further developed in the Middle Ages into the myth of the *Golem*.

The idea of the *Golem* probably originated among the *Hasidim* of Germany in the twelfth century.[28] For them, the ritual of creating a *Golem* involved a materialization of a person's astral body. The instructions for making a *Golem* are as follows: First, one begins with mastery of the occult science of cosmology found in the *Sefer Yetzirah*, with ritual purification, with dressing in clean white garments, and with two or three companions. Next, one takes virgin soil from a mountainous area and mixes it with fresh water to form a humanoid. Through invoking various magical combinations of Hebrew letters, one is able to determine the gender and duration of the *Golem's* existence.

The idea of the *Golem* as *homonculus*, that is, a robot that can serve man, developed in the seventeenth century under the influence of these earlier notions that were mixed together with magical and alchemical theories. As the legend grew, the creation of the *Golem* was attributed to the great eighteenth-century rabbi, the *Maharal* of Prague. His *Golem* would serve him six days a week but would remain inert on the Sabbath. One Sabbath, however, the *Golem* went berserk until *Maharal* deactivated him permanently.

Jacob Grimm, of the Brothers Grimm, helped to popularize this Jewish legend throughout Europe. In his version, the Jews of Poland were able to construct a *homonculus* from mud and to give him life by using the power of the divine Name. This mute automaton would perform manual tasks for its master. The legend was given special impetus by the publication of Gustav Meyrink's novel, *The Golem*, and by popular legends, many of which appear in the writings of Yiddish authors such as Isaac Bashevis Singer.

Another outstanding example of modern Jewish mysticism that appears outside of a traditional context is the artist, Yaacov Agam. Agam is noted for his three-dimensional graphic artworks that invoke possibilities of the dimension of time. An appreciation of his art requires the viewer to move around his art, to see fluid images change as one's perspective shifts. His art is transformative and involves movement on the part of the viewer as each shifting perspective creates another vision.

Agam, born in Israel in 1928, was the son of a rabbi. He was raised in the milieu of *Kabbalah* and religious orthodoxy. According to his own testimony, *Kabbalah* has been one of the guiding forces behind his artistic enterprises. He explains that the basic principle in Judaism is the reality of the infinite that does not exist except in the complete form.[29] In Judaism, God is invisible and unattainable in the abstract. He can be known, however, through His traces in the world. But human vision is too narrow to grasp the totality of God's presence in the world. Human perception is limited to partial awareness, fleeting glimpses, and occasional awareness of divinity in the world. Since all vision is partial, God simply cannot be grasped in the world. God can only be perceived in stages as one becomes increasingly aware that the infinite can be found only in the totality of the universe.

For Agam, art is the medium by which the infinite can be grasped. Art provides the vehicle for transcending the visible world and reaching new modes of perception. Since the infinite can be discovered only in the totality of the universe, art can lead one to the level of sublime awareness. God can only be perceived in stages leading to an integrated awareness of the whole. The principle of Agam's art is that forms can only be perceived in stages. His art is a vehicle through which he expresses the reality of the infinite. His art draws the viewer in, requiring that the viewer move around and about his graphic work in shifting perspectives. For Agam, the work of art, like the infinite, can exist only in the totality of fluid stages.

In his credo as an artist, Agam explains the relationship between *Kabbalah* and art:

> In Judaism, God is invisible, just as in life the essence of power is invisible. In my work I try to capture and suggest the same invisible, endless reality behind things. In any one of my works, always transformable, there are almost infinite ways of seeing it—different angles, different situations, different movements—all suggesting a basic, invisible essence, which is behind it all, and never really totally visible.[30]

Why does mysticism seem to be so foreign to Jews today? Why do Jews not know about their own mystical tradition? To many contemporary Jews, mysticism is considered to belong to the category of old wives' tales. To others who are interested in spirituality, it is often hard to find a spiritual home in Judaism Why is *Kabbalah* so hard to find in Judaism today?

Many historical factors contributed to the demise of the Jewish mystical tradition. The European Enlightenment of the eighteenth century changed the character of Judaism in Western and Central Europe. Until then, the Jews had been considered by their contemporaries as aliens who needed to be excluded from Christian society and confined to special residential districts (ghettos). Denied citizenship, frequently prohibited from taking part in productive economic activity, and subject to capricious treatment by the political authorities, the status of Western and Central European Jewry was precarious. The change and improvement in the status of the Jews in the eighteenth century was due to a series of intellectual, political, and economic factors.

The European Enlightenment brought about a profound change in the intellectual outlook of many Europeans and led to a reconsideration of the status of the Jews. The philosophies of Descartes, Voltaire, Montesquieu, and Hume evoked a reexamination of the meaning of religion. Many intellectuals began to distinguish between revealed religions and natural religion. Revealed religions are those based on the claim of historical revelation of truths directed towards a specific people. Natural religion, also called the religion of reason, is the universal truth about the nature of God and the world that any rational being can realize by observing the world around him. As Voltaire explained:

> Men are intelligent beings but such beings could not have been created by an uncouth, blind and insensible being. There is certainly a difference between (Isaac) Newton and a mule's droppings.[31]

Voltaire deduced from the order and reasonableness of nature and the world the existence of a rational deity who established the order and laws of nature. As men began to posit order in the world rather than divine intervention, religion was reexamined in light of this new philosophy. Enlightenment philosophers concluded that religion is the recognition of the order of the world and acknowledgment of the existence and providence of the deity who established nature. This understanding of the world order was not limited to the adherents of any particular religion. It could be acknowledged by any rational being despite the differences of his particular religious allegiance. This led to a new understanding of religion as the means to promote social goodness. As the British philosopher David Hume wrote: "The proper task of religion is to regulate the heart of man, to humanize his conduct, and to infuse the spirit of temperance, order and obedience."[32]

The new notion of natural religion led some liberal Christians to reconsider the status of the Jews. Perhaps the Jews were not "inherently despicable" but had become so by virtue of their history, environment, and distorted notion of religious truth. Perhaps if the Jews were made to be economically useful in the emerging mercantile economy, if they were to abandon their loyalties to the Jewish people and were to become loyal citizens of the states in which they resided, and if they were to dispense with the unenlightened aspects of their religion, Jews could be accepted. The proposition that "all men are created equal and endowed with inalienable rights to life, liberty and the pursuit of happiness" could be extended to the Jews if they changed their ways. So went the Enlightenment reasoning.

The process of Jewish emancipation was predicated on the expectation that Jews needed to bring about profound changes in their behavior and outlook. Even the Christian defenders of Jewish emancipation saw Judaism as the primary obstacle to progress towards this goal. The price of citizenship in Europe was willingness on the part of the Jews to abandon their religious teachings and supposed superstitions that conflicted with the religion of reason such as their different modes of dress, their restrictions against socializing (especially over food) with gentiles, their use of foreign languages (Yiddish and Hebrew), their belief in the return to Zion, their restrictions against intermarriage, and their belief in the existence of a separate Jewish people.

Jews were not admitted to citizenship anywhere in Europe until 1791, when two years after the French National Assembly adopted the Universal Declaration of the Rights of Man, they were emancipated in France. Although the process was fraught with setbacks, Western and Central European Jews were gradually enfranchised during the nineteenth century.

A large segment of Western and Central European Jewry attempted to respond to this challenge of emancipation by instituting changes within Judaism. Reform Judaism, which began in Germany early in the nineteenth century, attempted to preserve the rational and universal core of Judaism while removing the superstitious, nationalistic, and separatist elements of rabbinic Judaism. *Kabbalah*, which had been one aspect of the religious legacy of European Jewry, was discarded in the process.

At the same time, Lurianic *Kabbalah* and *Hasidism* continued to sink deep roots in the popular religious consciousness of Eastern European Jewry. Although modernism had greatly changed the character of Western and Central European Jewry, Eastern European Jewry was still living in the medieval world. In the early nineteenth century, *Hasidism* was growing as the predominant religious movement among Eastern European Jewry.

The European Enlightenment began to change the character of Eastern European Jewry after 1848. As the czar began to encourage the westernization of Russia, Jewish intellectuals formulated a program for Jewish emancipation. Their program, which they called *Haskalah*, the Hebrew word for enlightenment, called for reforms and modernization of Jewish religious behavior and the adoption of an enlightened educational curriculum and new social habits, styles, and language. Others pursued a similar program but argued for the use of Hebrew as the *lingua franca* of the Jewish people.

Despite the optimism of the Eastern European *Haskalah*, the Jews were not met with a welcome response. Successive czars continued to reinforce the restriction of Jewish residence to the frontier area known as the Pale of Settlement, to limit areas of Jewish economic activity, and to resist efforts to achieve emancipation. Legal emancipation came in Eastern Europe with the Russian Revolution, but even this did not bring about genuine acceptance of the Jews.

In the late nineteenth century the increase in the frequency and brutality of the pogroms led many Jews to despair of emancipation and to explore other solutions, including secularization and assimilation, socialist and communist militancy, emigration to America, and Zionism. Although a core of Eastern European Jews continued to live as they always had until the obliteration of the entire society by the Nazi Holocaust, by the late nineteenth century many Jews had already broken with tradition. With the breakdown of the traditional world of the *shtetl*, *Kabbalah* and *Hasidism* were discarded as vestiges of an earlier time.

Jewish mysticism flourished in a period when most Jews were devout practitioners of Jewish ritual. Until the time of Shabbetai Tzvi, there was little chance that a mystic would break away from traditional Jewish practice. As a result, the initiation into Jewish mysticism was quite explicit and conventional. Initiation into the mysteries of *Kabbalah* was limited to rabbis and other Jews whose mastery of rabbinic literature and practice was advanced. *Kabbalah* was simply incomprehensible to those who could not easily comprehend the Bible, *Talmud*, and *Midrash*. Since *Kabbalah* was so richly symbolic, initiation required a master teacher who could guide the novice along. There are no records of independent Jewish mystics, from the time of Ezekiel until the nineteenth century, who practiced their own forms of mysticism. The testimonies of mystics that exist are all expressed in the language of the mystical movements prevailing at that time—*Merkavah*, German *Hasidism*, *Zohar*, Lurianism, Sabbateanism, and *Hasidism*.

In the last two centuries, as Judaism ceased to hold monolithic control over Jews, independent and autonomous mysticism has appeared. Apart from the examples mentioned—Buber, Singer, and Agam, most forms of contemporary mysticism among Jews exhibit few Jewish elements. There are no significant forms of eclectic Jewish mysticism that successfully combine traditional Jewish mysticism with other forms of human spirituality.

10

MYSTICISM AND MEDITATION
The Mystic Quest

The object of the mystic quest in Judaism is the mystical encounter with God. There are many varieties of mystical experience within the Jewish mystical tradition. In this chapter, we will explore some of the varieties of Jewish mystical experiences.

In a letter to his brother-in-law and student, Gershon of Kutow, who had emigrated to Israel, the *Besht* described a mystical revelation that took place on a late summer *Rosh ha-Shanah* evening in 1746.[1] The *Besht* was transported to another world. He portrayed it as an "ascent of the soul," a well-known technique in Jewish mysticism. The letter states: "I performed an incantation for the ascent of the soul, as you know, and I saw wondrous things in a vision, which I had not seen from the day I became conscious until now."

Sitting in his small, solitary home study that served as his meditation chamber in his home, he began to focus his attention on chanting Hebrew incantations, short phrases, or whole sentences. He practiced a technique of combining Hebrew letters in his imagination so that they formed various permutations of divine names. This technique helped dissociate his conscious mind from ordinary reality and reoriented him to a different mode of consciousness. His yearning for his soul to be released from its earthly confines and to soar to a higher world was reinforced by the meaning of the sacred verses that linked together him, the holy day, the holy letters, and the sacred texts.

While his body rested in a state of earthly repose, his soul was transported out of his body and began to travel upwards. This was, for him, an active and intentional effort inspired by the reverential spirit of the holy day. It was a form of reverie, of dreaming with eyes shut but with the mind still awake. It might have looked to an observer, however, as if he were in a catatonic state of unconsciousness. Or it might have appeared that he was, at times, having epileptic seizures and, at other times, he appeared rigid, immobile, and not responsive to the world around him. He was awake, but he was not aware that he was awake, because his soul, his consciousness, was elsewhere.

He knew the roadmap his soul was about to travel from his previous reading of the ancient books and his own prior experiences. His soul would leave his body and traverse the universe; not the universe of Copernicus. In the *Besht*'s world, there were seven heavens, each of which is a sphere made of a crystalline substance, each finer than the next as you travel away from the earth, which is at the center of this universe. The planets are embedded in the surface of the first sphere; the stars in the second sphere. There are a total of seven heavenly concentric spheres that revolve one within the other at different rates. Angels and other spirits inhabit the upper spheres and God, the Unmoved Mover, dwells in the seventh heaven.

This was Ptolemy's universe, which the Jews had been familiar with since antiquity. The Jews, however, gave each of the heavens a different Hebrew name and assigned specific functions to each heaven. There were heavens that contained winds, rains, souls, spirits, and angels. One of the upper heavens, called a "palace" or "Paradise," was where the Messiah waited. It was to this palace that the *Besht*'s soul ascended on this night.

He knew the dangers. This ascent came at a time of persecutions directed against Jews in the region. Although some Jews converted to Christianity to avoid the attacks, they were murdered anyway. The *Besht* felt the burden of protecting Jews from persecutions. This is what impelled him to embark on the ascent of the soul on this day. Like Jewish mystics before him, the soul's ascent to heaven—Paradise—was an opportunity to ask questions, receive answers, and solve problems. As soon as he launched on this journey, he sensed the threatening presence of Satan, "the other side," who tracked his every movement on this ascent, ready to destroy him. "The evil one ascended to attack me with great, unparalleled joy and performed his acts; I was horrified and I literally put my life in jeopardy." So, on that night, he was accompanied by another traveler, the soul of the biblical prophet *Ahiyah* the Shilonite: "I asked my teacher and rabbi to go with me because it is very dangerous to go and ascend to the upper worlds."

The *Besht* continued on the ascent until he arrived at the heavenly Paradise—the palace of the Messiah. "I went up step by step until I entered the palace of the Messiah." In Paradise, the Messiah waits until the time for his advent into the world is right. While he waits, he studies the inner meanings of Torah along with the heavenly Jewish saints of antiquity. There, the Messiah learns Torah with all of the ancient sages and the righteous and also with the "seven shepherds—" Adam, Seth, Methusaleh, Abraham, Jacob, Moses, and David. At the moment of this epiphany, he confesses: "I felt exceedingly great joy and I don't know the reason for this joy. I thought this joy was—God forbid—over my departure from this world."

The heavenly saints charged him with the mission of spreading his new spiritual teachings. They told him that the future of the Jewish people, and the coming of the Messiah, depended on the dissemination of the *Besht*'s "Torah"—the teaching and practice of a new way of being Jewish. The world was waiting for him, and heaven was counting on him. The future of the world, they told him, depended on his teaching others to understand the presence of God in the world, the unity of heaven and earth, and the path that joins them together. And these teachings, they reinforce, are not only his but also theirs from time immemorial, and not some modern innovation: "They informed me," wrote the *Besht*, "that I was not leaving yet because in the upper spheres they derive pleasure when I perform unity down below by means of their holy teachings." Thus, the *Besht* was reinforced in his mission to his people, validated by heaven. "So I asked the Messiah, 'When will the master (i.e., the Messiah) come?' And he answered me, 'Once your Torah will have spread throughout the world.' And I prayed there over why God did thus."

Although the *Besht* soon returned from this ascent, his testimony is remarkable. It is one of the rare examples of an explicit Jewish mystical testimony that has survived. There are relatively few personal Jewish mystical testimonies that describe the mystical experience in such personal terms. Most of what has been preserved are abstract statements of the insight, knowledge, or revelation that was gained. In what follows, therefore, we will present the varieties of Jewish mystical experiences rather than testimonies of the experiences themselves.

The Jewish mystical encounter with God involves a transformation of consciousness. The most popular form of *Kabbalistic* mysticism is the practice of "raising the sparks" by recognizing the presence of God within all animate and inanimate objects. Lurianic *Kabbalah* taught that sparks of holiness are scattered throughout the universe within the shards of the broken vessels. Our task is to recognize the presence of God hidden within the world. One early Lurianic Kabbalist wrote that raising the sparks is the essence of Judaism:

> It should be the aim of every Jew to raise these sparks from where they are in this world and to elevate them to holiness by the power of your soul![2]

Rabbi Abraham Isaac Kook explained that the presence of God is a dynamic force that courses through every aspect of existence. His assertion that this vitality is present in every human emotion, every thought, and every nation was a bold and universal affirmation of Lurianism. If the divine force is present in every emotion and every thought, there is no such thing as a bad desire or an impure thought. What appears to be a sinister feeling, a dark desire, or an impure thought is only a reflection of the fractured order of the universe. A *Kabbalist* is a healer who recognizes the divine within every feeling, desire, and thought. He then isolates the holy spark within the feeling, desire, and thought and elevates it by embracing the holy spark rather than the broken shard of the feeling, desire, and thought in which it appears. Rav Kook also applies this principle to humanity and affirms that the divine force lives within all nations, not just the Jewish people. Rav Kook wrote:

> One feels the divine force coursing the pathways of existence, through all desires, all worlds, all thoughts, all nations, all creatures . . . You sense creation not as something completed, but as constantly becoming, evolving, ascending. This transports you from a place where there is nothing new to a place where there is nothing old, where everything renews itself, where heaven and earth rejoice as at the moment of Creation.[3]

There is no human activity that is too mundane to be treated as an opportunity to raise the sparks. Isaac Luria himself explained that the divine sparks are present in both animate and inanimate objects. The simple act of eating can be elevated to a mystical sacrament of raising the sparks:

> Sparks of holiness intermingle with everything in the world, even seemingly inanimate objects. You can elevate the cosmos by anything you do—even eating. Do not imagine that God wants you to eat for mere pleasure or to fill your belly. No, the purpose is elevating the sparks.[4]

A nineteenth-century *Kabbalist* explained that our physical pleasures also stem from the sparks concealed within the broken vessels. He rejected the ascetism of many mystics who believed that the material world is antithetical to spiritual attainment. On the contrary, this *Kabbalist*, like many before him, stated that God can be found wherever we look for Him. He wrote that the source of human pleasure is the divine sparks. Pleasure is, therefore, desirable:

> When you eat and drink, you experience pleasure. Arouse yourself at every moment to ask in wonder, "What is this enjoyment and pleasure?" Answer yourself, "This is nothing less than the holy sparks within the food and drink."[5]

The *Kabbalist* who raises the sparks is able to transform his own consciousness and repair the tear that permeates the cosmos. This can be practiced by any individual regardless of whether or not he understands the intricate ways in which the *Sefirot* are manipulated by his actions. "Raising the sparks" is the most universal, egalitarian, and democratic form of mystical activity spawned by *Kabbalah*. It has even entered the popular imagination today in a nonmystical sense, through the popular concept of "restoration" (*tikkun olam*). What began as a *Kabbalistic* concept—repair of the universe through raising the sparks through acts of conscious living—has evolved into the modern variant of repairing the world through social justice.

There are a variety of forms of mystical union with God in Judaism most of which are known as forms of "adhesion" or "cleaving" (*devekut*). But the term means something different to various *Kabbalists*. Some *Kabbalists* were less focused on their own personal mystical experience than on the theurgic task of uniting the various *Sefirot* in harmony and union. For theurgic *Kabbalists*, cleaving to God meant directing one's religious actions in such a way that they influence the divine, align the *Sefirot* in a particular way, and restore harmony within the divine realm. It is not the mystic himself who achieves "adhesion" to God, but rather his actions that bring about unity within God. The theurgic mystic is concerned with understanding the dynamics by which he can influence God for his own benefit. He quests for knowledge of the patterns of God's inner life more than for a direct encounter with the divine.

Other *Kabbalists* searched for ecstatic experience that leads to union with God. They often described their "cleaving" as the integration of their own soul into the realm of the *Sefirot*, in general, or with an individual

Sefirah, in particular. Most of these ecstatic *Kabbalists* sought union with *Malkhut* or *Tiferet* while the more radical *Kabbalists* sought annihilation of their own self within *The Infinite*. They seek to become "absorbed," "integrated," or "one" with God, to obliterate their sense of self, and to lose themselves within the ocean of divine being.

The issue at stake was not just the difference between theurgic and ecstatic *Kabbalists*. The real issue was how far a mystic thought it was possible to transcend the theological limits of normative Judaism. In theistic religions, such as Judaism, which believe in the existence of a transcendent God, there are serious strictures against achieving complete mystical union. These limitations are based on the belief that the differences between the human being and the transcendent God cannot be readily overcome. The character of theistic mysticism is predetermined, to a great extent, by the theist's belief that God and man are separated by an unbridgeable abyss. Theistic mysticism, therefore, rarely becomes the kind of absorptive mysticism in which the mystic becomes completely undifferentiated from God.

The ecstatic mystics within Judaism challenge the traditional assumptions of theism. When a Jewish mystic claims to have been "absorbed," "integrated," or "one" with God, he has defied the conventional wisdom that God is in heaven and man is on the earth and that man can never become God. The ecstatic mystic who believes that he can become God believes that his human existence is either an illusion or transient and can be obliterated, releasing the God within himself or abolishing the barrier that conceals the God within.

Unification *(yihhud)* is one of the fundamental categories of mystical union in *Kabbalah*. A theurgic activity that elevates the routine performance of a ritual to the status of a cosmic action results in a "unity" *(yihhud)*. This is an indirect form of mystical union because it is the *Sefirot* that are united by mystical intention and their union produces grace which flows down to benefit the mystic.

One example of a unitive ritual is marriage according to Jewish law. Abraham Abulafia, a thirteenth-century *Kabbalist*, proposed a causal hierarchy of unitive acts—marriage, procreation, birth, learning, and grasping the divine, that is, the *Sefirot*. Everything that an individual must do in the course of his life must serve the cause of uniting the *Sefirot*.

> The purpose of the marriage of a woman and a man is union. The purpose of union is fertilization. The purpose of fertilization is giving birth. The purpose of birth is learning. The purpose of learning is to grasp the divine. The

purpose of grasping the divine is that the one who grasps should endure along with the joy of his achievement.[6]

The general term in *Kabbalah* for uniting with one of the *Sefirot* is "cleaving" *(devekut)*. The Kabbalist who acquires a mystical consciousness and masters the theurgic rituals is trained in the topography of the divine world. He will have perfected his *neshamah*, including his mystical intellect. At the least, he will cleave to the *Shekhinah*. One example of this is found in Nahmanides' Torah Commentary. He explains *devekut* as a state in which the mystic cleaves to the *Shekhinah* yet continues to operate in the world:

> Such a man may be talking to other people but his heart is not with them since he is in the presence of God. And it is further plausible that those who have attained this rank, do, even in their earthly life, partake of eternal life, because they have made themselves a dwelling place of the *Shekhinah*.[7]

Some *Kabbalists* claim that their *devekut* can cause them to ascend to *Binah* or, even, to *Hokhmah*. Rabbi Azriel of Gerona writes that it is possible for human "thought to cleave to *Hokhmah*, so that they become one entity."[8]

In rare instances, *Kabbalists* state their conviction that it is possible to unite with *Keter* or *The Infinite*. Rabbi Nahman of Braslav, one of the most mercurial figures in the history of *Hasidism*, describes the total blending of the mystic and God. He teaches that man can ultimately ascend the ladder beyond the *Sefirot* to *The Infinite*. The mystic ceases to be aware of himself when he prays or learns Torah. When he prays, it is God praying through him. When he learns Torah, it is God revealing Torah through him. As Nahman explains:

> When one finally is integrated in *The Infinite*, his Torah is the Torah of God Himself, and his prayer is the prayer of God Himself . . . We thus find that there exists a Torah of God and a prayer of God. When a person merits to be integrated in *The Infinite*, his Torah and prayer are those of God Himself.[9]

In *Hasidism*, *devekut* was not always the ultimate destination but, rather, the starting point for the Jewish mystic. The *Besht* stated repeatedly that a *Hasid* must fix his thought on God constantly and never turn aside from *devekut*. To fall out of *devekut*, to not focus on God, was even considered a sin. In *Hasidism*, *devekut* meant concentration on God to the exclusion of all else.

Hasidic *devekut* also referred to the occult practice of vocalizing, over and over, the Hebrew letters that make up the divine name, *YHVH*. It also involved meditating upon the Hebrew letters until one begins to hallucinate and envision that the divine essence contained with the letters is released. The mystic concentrates on the Hebrew letters until he sees the divine light contained in the letters. The light is released and envelops the *Hasid* who is bathed and absorbed in the enveloping light.

A very high level of *devekut* is characterized as "erotic union" (*zivvug*). In this state, the mystic sublimates his natural eroticism and transfers it to union with the *Shekhinah*. This type of mystical activity requires special training and is generally reserved for the exceptional saint who is able to fully control his own sexuality. *Zivvug* entails the performance of specific rituals such as waking at midnight to study prescribed sections of the Torah, reciting the *Shema* ("Hear O Israel, the Lord our God, the Lord is One"), or greeting the Sabbath with an intense consciousness of the possibility of union with the *Shekhinah*. This type of "cleaving" is portrayed in erotic terms in which the mystic is joined to the *Shekhinah* as a bridegroom is to his bride. This is a special state of transitory transcendence for which one must possess mystical consciousness and training in theurgic rituals. The mystic experiences erotic union with the *Shekhinah* as he brings about the union of *Tiferet* and *Malkhut*.

The release of the soul from its bodily constraints through mystical practices can result in the immersion of the soul back into the *Sefirot*. This act of transcending individuality and reincorporation of the soul into God is called "integration" (*hitkallelut*).

The *Maggid* of Mezritch taught that each person must annihilate his sense of himself as a separate individual. The correct spiritual orientation is to dissociate one's self from the world of mundane experience. Forget yourself, your individuality, totally. This can be done when the mystic thinks of himself as an incarnation of God and then dissociates from one's carnal self. Each person should try to consider himself without the body as pure essence. He should then think of himself as indistinct, undifferentiated, boundless. The *Maggid* says:

> Think of yourself as Nothing and forget yourself totally. Then you can transcend time, rising to the world of thought, where all is equal: life and death, ocean and dry land. Such is not the case if you are attached to the material nature of this world. If you think of yourself as something, then God cannot clothe himself in you, for God is infinite. No vessel can contain God, unless you think of yourself as Nothing.[10]

Hasidism also connected *devekut* to the mystical state of "extinction" (*bittul*). In this state, the mystic loses awareness of himself as a separate being, extinguishes his self-awareness, and is absorbed within God. He ceases to exist, temporarily, as a separate self; he exists only to the extent that he is absorbed within God while still alive. The *Maggid* of Mezritch describes this as follows:

> Man must separate himself from any corporeal things to such an extent that he will ascend through all the worlds and be in union with God until his existence will be annihilated.[11]

The most radical formulation of *devekut* is Rabbi Shneur Zalman of Liady's explanation of complete absorption and immersion of the soul in God called "swallowing" (*beli'ah*). The mystic in the state of union is swallowed up by God:

> And this is the true cleaving, as he becomes one substance with God into whom he was swallowed, without being separate from him to be considered a distinct entity at all.[12]

Meditation has been a Jewish practice since before the rabbinic period. The *Talmud* mentions that the earliest pietists, probably from before the first millennium, would meditate for one hour prior to the start of synagogue services. The *Talmud* states: "The early pietists would sit still for one hour before each prayer service."[13] The *Kabbalists* transformed meditation from a simple act of intentionality into a mystical ritual.

Mystical meditation can lead to a state known as "drawing down" (*meshikhah*). By following a prescribed meditative technique, the mystic is able to draw vitality upon himself from the particular *Sefirah* to which he directs his actions. This technique involves a form of concentration upon the unique power of a *Sefirah*. Azriel of Gerona, for example, proposes a visualization technique in which the *Kabbalist* imagines himself bathed in light. He sees himself sitting below three lights. Above him, to the right, is the light of the *Sefirah Hesed*. Above him, to the left, is the light of the *Sefirah Din*. Above and between them is a higher light, perhaps *Hokhmah*. The entire realm of light is based in another light, the light of *Keter* or *The Infinite*.

Azriel urges the mystic to draw on the light of *Hesed* or *Din*, depending upon his requirements. When one meditates upon a particular *Sefirah*, in this fashion, one can draw down the energy of that particular *Sefirah* and harness it in the service of personal action. When the mystic aligns his words, thoughts, and intention towards this goal, he is able to draw divine energy that gives spirit and power to his mind and body. The psychological connection between the *Sefirot* and his own attributes shows that man is ultimately an extension of divinity. Therefore, man can also reach a state of connection with the source.

Azriel illustrates this particular technique with the following instructions:

> Whatever one implants firmly in the mind becomes the essential thing. So, if you pray and offer a blessing to God, or if you wish your intention to be true, imagine that you are light. All around you—in every corner and on every side—is light. Turn to your right, and you will find shining light; to your left, splendor, a radiant light. Between them, up above, the light of the Presence. Surrounding that, the light of life. Above it all, a crown of light—crowning the aspirations of thought, illuminating the paths of imagination, spreading the radiance of vision. This light is unfathomable and endless.[14] When it is necessary to carry out an act of *din*, face the radiant splendor. When it is necessary to carry out an act of *hesed*, face the good light. Let the words of your mouth be directed toward the light above them and between them which is the light of Glory. Above this light is a crown, the light which crowns the desires of consciousness, which illumines the ways of illumination, which radiates the splendor of visions. This light is infinite and boundless. And from the Glory of its perfection blessing, peace, and goodness will come to those who preserve its unity. Those who stray from the path of light, which changes from one hidden thing to another, will receive admonition and correction. It is up to the intention of one who knows how to meditate upon the truth to create a union of his mind and will which are emanated in full strength from the Boundless. According to the power of the meditation one can draw strength to his will, will to his consciousness, imagination to his mind, power to his action, and bravery to his thought when no other thought or desire interferes with his meditation and when he is strengthened by conditioning so that it draws the influx which comes from *The Infinite*. Only then are his action, consciousness, and will fulfilled.[15]

One of the most common meditative techniques is the *shiviti* visualization exercise developed in *Hasidism*. The practitioner pictures God, in whatever imaginative form works for him, standing before him. He sees God "in front of him" (*shiviti*), and recites the biblical phrase, "I have constantly placed God (*shiviti*) before me; He is at my right hand so that I shall not falter." (*Psalm* 16:8). The *Hasid* practices a form of undivided focus on God to the exclusion of all distractions.

In the sixteenth century, the *Kabbalist* Eleazar Azikri, author of the Sabbath hymn, *Yedid Nefesh*, described a visionary meditation. It involves visualizing one's self as a target for God's emanation. The mystic pictures himself as the object of God's direct aim. The mystic sees himself as the bull's-eye and God's laser beam-like emanation as the arrow flying towards its target. By viewing himself as the target of God's emanation, the individual can visualize himself in relation to *The Infinite*. Azikri writes: "At special times, you should go off to a secluded place, where no one can see you. Lift your eyes upward to the unique King, the First Cause and Prime Mover, like a bull's-eye looking at the arrow."[16]

In his book on *Kabbalistic* meditation, Mark Verman also describes a more recent outdoor meditation in which the mystic pictures his own smallness in relation to the vastness of all that lies beyond. In telescoping fashion, he visualizes the chain of being that extends beyond the world, to the heavens, and, beyond, to God. The Piasetzna Rebbe, who lived under Nazi occupation in the Warsaw ghetto, wrote that the mystic should concentrate his vision on the stages of being beyond himself, until he visualizes God Himself:

> Look at the heavenly sky and contemplate. Concentrate your mind and think: I am standing here. Beyond each heaven is another heaven. I bless You, to whom my eyes are raised. Whether I can see You or not, I concentrate my vision and gaze upon You.[17]

Isaac of Acre, a thirteenth-century *Kabbalist*, recommends a technique for experiencing an ecstatic rapture. This technique involves the visualization of the Hebrew letters of God's name, *YHVH*. The mystic gazes at the letters and penetrates them with vision until his mind's eye pierces through the letters. Then he sees into the letters and fixes his gaze on them until he sees through them until infinity. His mind travels through the letters until he induces a hallucination of seeing infinity. This technique of intense concentration on Hebrew letters, penetration, visualization, and transportation leads the mystic to the state of absorption in boundless infinity. This is one of the most intense and enduring *Kabbalistic* meditative techniques. As Isaac of Acre explains:

> If you want to know the secret of binding your soul above and joining your thought to God—so that by means of such continuous contemplation you

attain incessantly the world that is coming, and so that God be with you always, in this life and the next—then place in front of the eyes of your mind the letters of God's name, as if they were written in a book in Hebrew script. Visualize every letter extending to infinity. What I mean is: when you visualize the letters, focus on them with your mind's eye as you contemplate infinity. Both together: gazing and meditating.[18]

Rabbi Abraham Isaac Kook believed that we must become an ear that hears what the divine voice is saying to us. The divine voice, he teaches, is constantly addressing us not only through Torah, but through nature, human activity, and all of life. The challenge is to train ourselves to become alert to what the divine voice, the pulse of existence, is constantly saying. The cultivation of attentiveness is the result of perseverance and unrelenting openness to the vitality that courses through every moment of life. When we actualize this ability to hear the divine voice, we become most fully human. When we realize that it is not us who are thinking but, rather, it is God who is thinking within us, we are transformed. The transformation involves a greater elevation of our spiritual powers. We receive revelation from God, just like Moses. As Rav Kook explains:

> When you train yourself to hear the voice of God in everything, you attain the quintessence of the human spirit. Usually, the mind conceals the divine thoroughly by imagining that there is a separate mental power that constructs the mental images. But by training yourself to hear the voice of God in everything, the voice reveals itself to your mind as well. Then right in the mind, you discover revelation.[19]

Hasidism emphasizes chanting as a meditative technique for achieving ecstasy and self-transcendence. The chant (*niggun*), a melody sometimes with and sometimes without words, is invested with spiritual power. It can be practiced within a group, around a table during a festive meal, or during religious services. Chanting begins with a prayer-line or a biblical verse that has spiritual significance. For example, the late Rabbi Shlomo Carlebach popularized *niggunim* for many verses including: "One thing I ask of the Lord, only that do I seek: to live in the house of the Lord all the days of my life, to gaze upon the beauty of the Lord, and to frequent his sanctuary" (*Psalm* 27:4).

These techniques represent the different strategies that *Kabbalists* and other Jewish mystics used to achieve a state of "cleaving" to God. They include theurgic and ecstatic techniques and epitomize the range of perspectives about the ultimate goal to which a mystic might aspire. But they are all consistent with the characteristics of mysticism described at the beginning of this book.

CONCLUSION

What is the possibility of a contemporary Jewish mysticism? It is unlikely that there will be a revival of Jewish mysticism in its traditional form. The teachings of Jewish mysticism are too rooted in the medieval way of thinking for them to appeal to the modern mind. But mysticism is an enduring feature of human spirituality that continues to hold great interest for many.

The revival of interest in Jewish spirituality in the last two decades has brought about a corresponding exploration of the Jewish mystical tradition. The popularity of institutes, books, lectures, and study groups on Jewish mysticism is strong testimony that the interest in Jewish mysticism endures. Although this interest may simply reflect a search for spirituality, it may also represent a more profound phenomenon.

Interest in religion is a persistent feature of human nature. As science has become increasingly specialized and theoretical, its theories have become so complex and symbolic that most laymen cannot follow or understand the emerging theories on the origins of the universe, the nature of consciousness, and the elementary structures of being. For many, religion is a system of axiomatic beliefs about the nature of the universe and all that is within it. Religion fills the intellectual void created by the increasing inability of science to articulate its understanding of life in lay terms. Although religion then may become a pseudoscience, it is a genuine effort to address the question of the meaning of life in a contemporary context.[20]

The resurgent interest in religion may also be attributed to other factors. Humanity inherently searches for a basis of meaning outside of itself. The mechanistic view of the world and the individual as nothing more than the results of blind biochemical forces, natural processes, and random astronomical events hardly begins to answer the questions of why the world is this way and not another. The deep human impulse to search for meaning, order, and cause has left many humanists with a deep sense that the human mind is limited in its ability to provide explanations for the mysteries of existence. Human beings yearn for explanations that transcend the state of human knowledge. Each of us strives in some way for a transcendent experience, an oceanic feeling, the sense of boundlessness or undifferentiatedness. The vehicle for these forms of human expression is religion and, often, mysticism.

Religion is also one avenue within today's society to attain a sense of community. Prayer services can provide an important form of public expression, of belonging to a community, and of affirming one's Jewishness in a social context. For many, the social aspect of formal worship in a synagogue is much more important than the meaning of the liturgy itself. The synagogue is the only institution in Jewish life where entire families can be together with other families. Although many secular contexts for expressing one's Jewishness are available through social welfare and voluntary associations, the nature of the religious community in Judaism is unique.

In a subtle way, religious rituals frequently change the psychological structures that organize, limit, select, and interpret one's normal consciousness. Traditional Jewish prayer involves surrender to a mode of consciousness quite different from routine consciousness. To the involved worshipper, attention to the service itself necessitates receptivity to stimuli not encountered anywhere else. The physical sensation of singing, the presence of unusual ritual objects, the use of the Hebrew language, the codes, signals, rituals, and the invocation of religious concepts all contribute to the transformation of routine consciousness. If this involvement is sustained over time, it can produce a feeling of awe and oneness. It is hardly surprising that many Jews report that *Yom ha-Kippurim* produces a great religious exhilaration.

Psychologists refer to this change in normal consciousness as deautomatization[21] and theologians call it transcendence. The religious experience of the synagogue worshipper often leads to the sense of oneness and being uplifted that is characteristic of mystical experiences. The "oceanic feeling" that accompanies some religious experiences is evaluated in vastly different ways by modern psychology. Strict Freudians view this type of religious experience as a form of regression to a relatively undifferentiated ego state.[22] Others see it as a necessary stage of integration of human consciousness. Erich Neumann, a Jungian thinker, viewed mysticism as an essential stage in human development. In his view, the ego develops from undifferentiatedness into distinct self-consciousness. He posits a further integrative stage in which the differentiated ego can experience individuality and undifferentiatedness.[23] This may in fact provide an important insight into the psychological value of communal prayer. Communal prayer provides the occasion for simultaneous individuality and undifferentiatedness as an advanced form of human consciousness.

The religious experiences of engaged worshippers are diverse. The common element, however, is the production of an unusual state of consciousness that is accompanied by a sense of the reality and ineffability of the experience. A synagogue worshipper cannot easily explain what it is that he experiences in prayer. He may try to describe it in terms of "a good feeling" or "being a part of community," but underlying the experience is often a change in consciousness.

Prayer can also provide the primary vehicle for an individual religious experience within a religious context that otherwise emphasizes the communal dimension. The constant reiteration in Judaism of the centrality of revelation can reinforce the notion that the mystical experience is at the heart of Judaism. Yet it is striking that the central theological theme in Jewish liturgy—revelation—is regarded as a past event and not as an invitation for every contemporary Jew to have a mystical encounter with God. As long as the central theme of Judaism is the direct and unmediated relationship between God and man, individual Jews will pursue their own individual religious experiences. As long as there are persons who take Judaism seriously, there will be Jews who take mysticism seriously.

The renewed interest in Jewish mysticism may also arise, paradoxically, out of alienation from the formal liturgical structures in Judaism. The strangeness of Hebrew and conceptual difficulty with Jewish theology make Judaism inaccessible or alien to many. Yet these same individuals who do not find a home in the traditions or the formal institutions of Judaism often yearn for a spiritual way to express their Jewishness. Many today are caught between their alienation from formal Jewish religion and a deep desire to be Jewish. They see the secular and social opportunities for Jewish communal activity without a religious or spiritual dimension as petty and trivial. For these individuals who do not find a place for themselves in the community, Jewish mysticism provides an attractive alternative. It offers the possibility of a highly individualistic spirituality that is not regulated by any external authority. Jewish mysticism may have its greatest appeal to the most alienated of modern Jews.

It is impossible, however, to predict what specific forms Jewish mysticism might assume in the future. The doctrine of the *Sefirot* will never be construed as anything more than a powerful mythology. Is it possible that the underlying philosophic content of Jewish mysticism might be convertible into a form useful to contemporary men and women?

Modern science has demonstrated that the underlying structures of existence are alive. Advances in atomic theory have caused us to rethink our notion of matter as inert. Nothing in the universe is unchanging. Everything vibrates with a myriad of divisible particles that are so infinitesimal they are hidden from our senses. There is no discontinuity in the structure of existence. The universe is composed of energy and mass, and mass is the extension of energy. All of existence is unified.

Such a construction of reality is evocative of the *Kabbalistic* theory of the *Sefirot*. The difference between infinity and the humblest person on earth is simply a matter of degree. Human life is the extension of the infinity of *The Infinite* in the world. *Kabbalah* can serve as a metaphor for evoking a religious response to the miraculous discoveries of modern physics and astronomy. Perhaps *Kabbalah* can serve as a paradigm for how we can integrate the abstract hypotheses of science into a conscious organization of our understanding of the world.

The *Kabbalistic* doctrine of the soul is one of its most distinctive elements. Contemporary philosophy and psychology have developed a coherent paradigm that does not assume the separate existence of a soul that comes from without. The psyche is a feature of the biological existence of a human being. It is assumed to have neither preexistence nor duration after death. However, recent studies by Elisabeth Kubler-Ross and others have challenged some of our notions about death, dying, and the afterlife. The demonstrable truths of psychology are still being formulated. The doctrine of the human soul may still be expanded.

Finally, the *Kabbalistic* conception of God may provide a fertile basis for contemporary Jewish theology. Many people assume that if there is a God, He is a personal god. If He is not a responsive, caring, personal God, He does not exist. These popular ideas have led to very simplistic theological ideas about God's existence and nature. The notion of God's essential hiddenness may resonate best with human experience. According to Jewish mysticism, God is essentially hidden yet becomes manifest in different ways according to the actions of humanity. What we call God is not God but His manifestations. What appears as divine cruelty or indifference, then, is not a reflection of God's actions but of ours.

Kabbalistic theology may provide a new possibility for Jewish theology. God did not permit Auschwitz or the death of a child. Humanity lives in a world in which God does not relate directly to individuals. For example, the concept of the infinite and invisible God who does not act directly in the world holds a powerful theological attraction today. In a world that has suffered through the Holocaust, it is often difficult to imagine how a good God could allow such horrors. *Kabbalah*, which posits a distant and transcendent God, teaches that it is human action rather than divine action that ultimately directs the course of the world. The idea of a transcendent God whose presence is palpable only in His absence may open doors to new meaning in theology. The simplistic notions of God as a human father or mother figure can be seen as lower orders of divinity. The abstract, unknowable God might provide a way of understanding how He can exist yet be absent from the course of human affairs.

Human destiny rests entirely in the hands of humanity. God assumes whatever form or manifestation our actions dictate. Yet, at the same time, we are bound to God by a common being that challenges us to act according to His moral attributes. Our failure to do so results in a catastrophe of our own making.

Jewish mysticism, despite its powerful theology, is deeply humanistic. It confers a noble and coherent stature upon a human being who is bound by his or her own nature to God. At the same time, only we have control over our own destiny. The power to raise ourselves to the heights or sink to the depths of the broken vessels is vested entirely in us.

Jewish mysticism probably still contains layers of meaning waiting to be peeled away. The tradition of Jewish mysticism will never recur in the traditional forms of the past. It is impossible, however, to predict how it will inspire new and creative religious ideas in the future. What is certain is that two hundred years after the last strong surge of mystical fervor in Judaism, *Kabbalah* has not lost its appeal. So, in the words of the *Besht*, "Push forward bravely and you will find no obstacle."

NOTES

INTRODUCTION

1. Rodger Kamenetz, *Stalking Elijah* (San Francisco: Harper, 1997). This book and his earlier book, *The Jew in the Lotus,* offer an important window into the Jewish Renewal movement.

2. Wade Clark Roof, *A Generation of "Seekers": The Spiritual Journeys of the Baby Boom Generation* (San Francisco: Harper, 1993). This is the definitive work on the spiritual quest of the baby-boom generation in America.

3. Bethamie Horowitz, *Connections and Journeys: Assessing Critical Opportunities for Enhancing Jewish Identity* (New York: UJA-Federation of New York, 2000).

4. Arnold Eisen, and Steven M. Cohen, *The Jew Within: Self, Family, and Community in America* (Bloomington: Indiana University Press, 2000), 2.

5. Ibid., 7.

6. Ibid., 9.

7. Ibid., 137.

8. Ibid., 36–38.

9. Ibid., 9.

10. Ibid., 153.

11. Ibid., 35.

12. Abraham Joshua Heschel, *The Insecurity of Freedom: Essays on Human Existence* (New York: Farrar, Giroux, and Straus, 1966), 215. Heschel is often the inspiration for "Seekers" who pursue the Jewish spiritual path.

13. The Great Awakenings of 1730–1750 and 1815–1850 led to the creation of many American colleges, frontier missions, and fed the abolitionist and women's rights movements.

CHAPTER 1

1. Geoffrey Parrinder, *Mysticism in the World's Religions* (New York: Oxford University Press, 1976), 8f. Parrinder presents an important survey of mystical topologies and

expressions in various traditions. His discussion on Cabbalah (*sic*) is erroneous both from a historical and conceptual point of view.

2. Joseph Campbell, *The Masks of God: Occidental Mythology* (New York: Penguin, 1976), 14, 268.

3. William James, *The Varieties of Religious Experience* (London and Glasgow: The Fontana Library, 1960), 366.

4. James, *Varieties*, 371 quoting H. F. Brown, *J. A. Symonds: A Biography* (London, 1895), 29–31. James is unaware of the existence of Jewish mysticism and, therefore, does not draw on Jewish mystical testimonies in his study.

5. James, *Varieties*, 385 and note, quoting (with variations) R. M. Bucke, *Cosmic Consciousness* (Philadelphia, 1901), 7f.

6. II *Corinthians*, 12:1–4.

7. Parrinder, *Mysticism*, 185, quoting J. N. Findlay, *Ascent to the Absolute* (London: Allen and Unwin, 1970), 164.

8. Sigmund Freud, *Civilization and Its Discontents. The Standard Edition of the Complete Psychological Works of Sigmund Freud* (London: Hogarth Press, 1961) 21:64, 65.

9. James, *Varieties*, 404 (with variations).

10. W. R. Inge, *Mysticism in Religion* (London: 1947), appendix.

11. Inge, *Mysticism*, appendix.

12. Steven T. Katz, *Mysticism and Philosophical Analysis* (New York: Oxford University Press, 1978), 25.

13. Katz, *Mysticism*, 24.

14. Katz, *Mysticism*, 25.

15. Katz, *Mysticism*. 25.

16. Katz, *Mysticism*, 27.

17. William Wordsworth, "Tintern Abbey." See the various interpretations offered by R. C. Zachner, *Mysticism Sacred and Profane* (London: Clarendon Press, 1957), 33; and Parrinder, 23.

18. Rudolf Otto, *Mysticism East and West* (New York: Macmillan, 1932), 61.

19. W. T. Stace, *Mysticism and Philosophy* (Philadelphia: Lippincott, 1960), 88.

20. G. Scholem, "Devekut, or Communion with God," in *The Messianic Idea in Judaism* (New York: Schocken Books, 1971), 224. For further discussion of the character of Jewish mysticism, see Gershom Scholem, "Mysticism and Religious Authority," in *On the Kabbalah and Its Symbolism* (New York: Schocken, 1965), 5–31. Scholem, the leading scholar of Jewish mysticism, has been the subject of several critical studies including Eliezer Schweid, *Judaism and Mysticism According to Gershom Scholem* (Atlanta: Scholars Press, 1985). Schweid's criticism centers on Scholem's underlying assumptions about Judaism and Jewish philosophy. For a thorough revisionist critique of Scholem's methodology, see Moshe Idel, *Kabbalah: New Perspectives* (New Haven, Conn.: Yale University Press, 1988). For an intellectual biography of Scholem, see David Biale, *Gershom Scholem: Kabbalah and Counter-History* (Cambridge: Harvard University Press, 1978). For a bibliography of research in *Kabbalah*, see Joseph Dan, *Gershom Scholem and the Mystical Dimension of Jewish History* (New York: New York University Press, 1987).

21. Meshullam Feibusch me-Zborocz Heller, *Sefer Derech Emet* (Jerusalem, 1952), 14.

22. Stace, *Mysticism*, 228.

23. Abraham Joshua Heschel, "The Mystical Element in Judaism," *The Jews: Their History, Culture and Religion*, ed. Louis Finkelstein (New York: Harper, 1949) 2:932–951.

24. Idel, *Kabbalah: New Perspectives*

25. Idel, 62.

26. Isaac Bashevis Singer and Ira Moskowitz, *A Little Boy in Search of God: Mysticism in a Personal Light* (New York: Doubleday, 1976), vii–viii.

27. Rudolf Otto, *The Idea of the Holy* (Oxford: Oxford University Press: 1960), 44f.

CHAPTER 2

1. II *Kings* 24:8–20.

2. *Ezekiel* 1.

3. Rachel Elior, *The Three Temples: On the Emergence of Jewish Mysticism* (Oxford: Littman Library of Jewish Civilization, 2004), 3.

4. Elior, *Three Temples*, 64.

5. Elior, *Three Temples*, 165.

6. *Ezekiel* 1. The history of Jewish mysticism between the biblical and rabbinic periods is the subject of considerable recent research. For an overview of the period, see Isaiah Gafni, "The Historical Background," in *Jewish Writings of the Second Temple Period*, ed. Michael Stone (Philadelphia: Fortress Press, 1984), 1–31. Studies in Jewish apocalypticism and gnosticism, and research on the Essenes and Qumran communities are included in that volume.

7. Gershom Scholem, *Major Trends in Jewish Mysticism* (New York: Schocken, 1941), 40–79. For more recent studies, see Dan, *Scholem*, 38–76.

8. ARN 6:15.

9. B. T. *Hagigah* 14b; see also *Tosefta Hagigah* 2:1.

10. J. T. *Hagigah* 2:1.

11. David J. Halperin, *The Merkabah in Rabbinic Literature* (New Haven, Conn.: American Oriental Society, 1980), 88f. Halperin doubts the existence of Merkavah mysticism and believes the pattern was Heikhalot mysticism. For further studies in Merkavah mysticism, see Gershom Scholem, *Jewish Gnosticism, Merkabah Mysticism and Talmudic Tradition* (New York: Jewish Theological Seminary, 1960); Ithamar Gruenwald, *Apocalyptic and Merkavah Mysticism* (Leiden: E. J. Brill, 1980).

12. M. *Hagigah* 2:1.

13. M. *Megillah* 4:10; *Tosefta Megillah* 4:34.

14. *Midrash Tanhuma, Parashah Tzav* 13.

15. Benjamin Lewin, *Otzar ha-Geonim* (Haifa, 1931), vol. 4, 13–15. Quoted in Louis Jacobs, *Jewish Mystical Testimonies* (New York: Schocken Books, 1977), 23.

16. David S. Ariel, "The Eastern Dawn of Wisdom: The Problem of the Relations between Islamic and Jewish Mysticism," in *Approaches to Judaism in Medieval Times*, ed. David Blumenthal (Chico, Calif.: Scholars Press, 1985), 149–167.

17. *Koran, Sura* 2:40, 57, 64, 122; 3:64; 4:23; 5:3, 26, 32; 29:41.

18. *Koran, Sura* 2:86; 5:70, 82; 9:29; 59:2.

19. E. Strauss (Ashtor), *Toledot ha-Yehudim ba-Mitzrayim ve-Suriah Tahat Shilton ha-Mamelukim* (Jerusalem, 1944), 1:47.

20. Ariel, "Eastern Dawn," 154.

21. Strauss, *Toledot*, vol. 1, 352f.

22. Joseph Dan, *Torat ha-Sod shel Hasidei Ashkenaz* (Jerusalem: Bialik Institute, 1968), 124f.

23. Ariel, "Eastern Dawn," 159.

24. Ariel, "Eastern Dawn," 156.

25. Scholem, *Major Trends*, 80–118; Dan, *Scholem*, 92–126. See also Ivan Marcus, *Piety and Society: The Jewish Pietists of Medieval Germany* (Leiden: E. J. Brill, 1981).

26. Isadore Twersky, "Aspects of the Social and Cultural History of Provencal Jewry," in *Jewish Society through the Ages*, ed. H. H. Ben-Sasson and S. Ettinger (New York: Schocken, 1969), 191.

27. Gershom Scholem, *Ursprung und Anfange der Kabbala* (Berlin: Walter de Gruyter, 1962), 30, 216. (For the English translation, see, Gershom Scholem, *Origins of the Kabbalah* (Philadelphia: Jewish Publication Society, 1987). See also Joseph Dan and Ronald Kiener, *The Early Kabbalah* (Ramsey, N.J.: Paulist Press, 1986).

28. I *Kings* 18:19.

29. I *Kings* 19.

30. II *Kings* 2:1–11.

31. *Malachi* 3:23f.

32. *Tanna de-Vei Eliyahu*, ed. M. Friedmann (Vienna, 1902, 1904), 27ff.

33. Scholem, *Ursprung*, 219–273.

34. Scholem, *Ursprung*, 47–54.

35. Scholem, *Ursprung*. 59–159; Dan, *Scholem*, 127–146.

36. See H. H. Ben Sasson, "Rabbi Mosheh ben Nahman: Ish be-Sivkhei Tequfato," *Molad* (n.s.), no. 1 (1967): 360–366; Scholem, *Ursprung* 360–365, 396–401.

37. M. H. Levine, *Falaquera's Book of the Seeker* (New York: Yeshiva University Press, 1976), 8.

38. On the Barcelona Disputation, see O. S. Rankin, *Jewish Religious Polemic* (Edinburgh: Edinburgh University Press, 1956), 157–176; M. A. Cohen, "Reflections on the Text and Context of the Disputation of Barcelona," *Hebrew Union College Annual* 35(1964): 157–192.

39. Scholem, *Major Trends*, 156–204; Dan, *Scholem*, 203–229.

40. Isaiah Tishby, *Mishnat ha-Zohar* (Jerusalem: Bialik Institute, 1957), 1:29ff.

CHAPTER 3

1. Scholem, *Major Trends*, 7. For a critique of Scholem's philosophy of Jewish history, see Schweid, *Judaism and Mysticism*, 25–27, 61–68.

2. *Genesis* 3:8.

3. *Genesis* 18:24–33.

4. *Exodus* 3:5.

5. *Exodus* 3:13.

6. *Exodus* 20:16–25.

7. *Pesikta de-Rav Kahana*, ed. B. Mandelbaum (New York, 1962), 3. Quoted in E. Urbach, *The Sages* (Jerusalem: Magnes Press, 1975), 1:52.

8. Found in standard editions of the *Musaf Amidah* for festivals.

9. *Eykhah Rabba*, ed. S. Buber, proem 24, 13a. Quoted in Urbach, *The Sages*, 55.

10. *Targum* on *Exodus* 12:11; 33:14–15, 20; *Numbers* 14:14,42. For a history of the concept, see G. Scholem, *Pirkei Yesod be-Havanat ha-Kabbalah u-Semaleha* (Jerusalem: Bialik Institute, 1976), 259–307.

11. *Midrash Tehillim*, ed. S. Buber, 14:1, 121. Quoted in Urbach, *The Sages*, 29.

12. B. T. *Baba Metzia* 59b.

13. B. T. *Sota* 14a.

14. M. *Avot* 3:2.

15. Urbach, *The Sages*, 38–39.

16. See Jacob Neusner, *First-Century Judaism in Crisis* (Nashville: Abingdon Press,

1975), 34ff. For a more complete analysis of the Pharisees and Sadducees, see M. Stone, *Jewish Writings*, 23–24, 27–31.

17. J. Neusner, *Understanding Rabbinic Judaism* (New York: Ktav, 1974), 13ff.

18. Neusner, *Rabbinic Judaism*, 165ff.

19. Daniel Jeremy Silver, *Maimonidean Criticism and the Maimonidean Controversy* (Leiden: E. J. Brill, 1965); A Shohat, "Beirurim be-Parashat ha-Pulmus ha-Rishon al Sifrei ha-Rambam," *Zion* 36 (1971): 27–60; Y. Shatzmiller, "Le-Temunat ha-Mahloqet ha-Rishonah al Kitbhei ha-Rambam," *Zion* 34 (1969): 126–144.

20. Moses Maimonides, *Guide of the Perplexed*, trans. S. Pines (Chicago: University of Chicago Press, 1963), II:13–31, III:17–7.

21. Maimonides, *Guide*, I:71ff.

22. Maimonides, *Guide*, I:50–61.

23. Maimonides, *Hilkhot Teshuvah* 3:7.

24. *RABaD* on *Hilkhot Teshuvah* 3:7.

25. B. T. *Yevamot* 71a. Quoted in Maimonides, *Guide*, I:26.

26. The passage appears in A. Habermann's *Shirei ha-Yihud ve-ha-Kavod* (Jerusalem: Mossad Haarv Kook, 1948), 173. See also my doctoral dissertation, *Shem Tob ibn Shem Tob's Kabbalistic Critique of Jewish Philosophy in the Commentary on the Sefirot* (Waltham, Mass.: Brandeis University, 1981), 58f.

27. *Sefer Maarekhet ha-Elohut* (Mantua, 1558), 82b.

28. *Exodus* 19:18.

29. *Sefer ha-Zohar* II:239a. Tishby, *Mishnat ha-Zohar*.

30. *Sefer ha-Zohar* I:22b. Tishby, *Mishnat ha-Zohar*, 1:119–120.

31. Azriel of Gerona, *Shaar ha-Shoel* (known as *Perush Eser Sefirot*). Printed in Meir ibn Gabbai, *Sefer Derekh Emunah* (Warsaw, 1890), 3.

32. Daniel Matt, *The Essential Kabbalah* (San Francisco: HarperSanFrancisco, 1994), p. 24.

33. Peasetzna Rebbe, *B'nai Machshavah Tovah*, *Seder Hadracha v'Klalim*, #7 quoted in Yitzhak Buxbaum, *Jewish Spiritual Practices* (Northvale, N.J.: Jason Aronson, 1990).

34. Moshe Cordovero, *Sefer Shiur Qomah*, quoted in Matt, *The Essential Kabbalah*, 24.

35. Cordovero, *Elimah Rabbati*, quoted in Matt, *The Essential Kabbalah*, 24.

36. Moshe de Leon, *Sefer Harimmon*, quoted in Matt, *The Essential Kabbalah*, 25.

CHAPTER 4

1. Moshe Cordovero, *Or Ne'erav*, ed. Yehuda Z. Brandwein, 6:1; Robinson, *Moses Cordovero's Introduction to Kabbalah*, 111–146, quoted in Matt, *The Essential Kabbalah*, 40.

2. This view was introduced by Menahem Rekanati, a fourteenth-century Italian Kabbalist. See R. J. Zvi Werblowsky, *Karo: Lawyer and Mystic* (Philadelphia: Jewish Publication Society, 1977), 200ff.

3. *Zohar* II:42b–43a; Tishby, *Mishnat ha-Zohar*, 1:126–127.

4. Moshe Cordovero, *Sefer Harimmon*, quoted in Matt, *The Essential Kabbalah*, 38.

5. I *Chronicles* 29:11.

6. Quoted in Shlomo (Mordechai) Elishov, *Sefer Hakdamot u-She'arim* (Pietrakov, 1904), 3a–4b.

7. *Zohar* I:65a; Tishby, *Mishnat ha-Zohar*, 1: 176–177.

8. A. Jellinek, *Beitrage zur Geschichte der Kabbala* 11 (Leipsig, 1852), 12–13.

9. Quoted in Ariel, *Shem Tob* 49, lines 7–11 (Hebrew section).

10. Nahmanides, *Commentary on Sefer Yetzirah*, in Gershom Scholem, "Perakim me-Toledot Sifrut ha-Kabbalah," *Kiryat Sefer* 6 (1929–1930), 402–403.

11. *Proverbs* 8:22.

12. *Bereshit Rabbah* 1:1.

13. Maimonides, *Guide*, III: 53

14. *Zohar* I:15a–b; Tishby, *Mishnat ha-Zohar*, 1:163f. The translation is from *Zohar, The Book of Enlightenment*, trans. Daniel C. Matt (Ramsey, N.J.: Paulist Press, 1983), 49–50.

15. *Tikkunei Zohar* (Mantua, 1558), introduction.

16. Nahmanides, *Commentary on Sefer Yetzirah*, in Scholem, "Perakim," 402–403.

17. *Psalms* 19:2.

18. *Sefer Yetzirah* (Jerusalem, 1965), ch. 1, 2.

19. *Bereshit Rabbah* 1:4.

20. *Proverbs* 8:22.

21. *Bereshit Rabbah* 1:1.

22. G. Scholem, "The Name of God and the Linguistic Theory of the Kabbala," *Diogenes* 79 (1972): 59–80; 80 (1972): 164–194.

23. Nahmanides, *Perush al ha-Torah*, ed. C. D. Chavel (Jerusalem: Mossad Harav Kook, 1959), introduction.

24. See H. A. Wolfson, *Religious Philosophy* (Cambridge: Harvard University Press, 1961), 217–245.

25. Maimonides, *Guide*, II:30.

26. Gershom Scholem, *Kitvei Yad ba-Kabbalah* (Jerusalem: Hebrew University Press, 1930), 208–213.

CHAPTER 5

1. *Exodus*. 25:8. For many of the sources in this chapter, see Urbach, *The Sages*, 37–65; Scholem, *Pirkei Yesod*, 259–307; and Tishby, *Mishnat ha-Zohar* 1:219–265.

2. B. T. *Sota* 14a.

3. M. *Avot* 3:2.

4. *Mekhilta de-Rabbi Yishmael*, ed. Horowitz (Frankfurt, 1931), *Massekhta de-Pisha*, 14, 51–52, quoted in Urbach, *The Sages*, 43.

5. *Mekhilta, Massekhta de-ba-Hodesh* 6, 238, quoted in Urbach, *The Sages,* 43.

6. *Pesikta de-Rav Kahana*, ed. B. Mandelbaum (New York, 1962), *Va-Yehi* 4, quoted in Urbach, *The Sages,* 51.

7. B. T. *Sanhedrin* 39a, quoted in Urbach, *The Sages,* 48.

8. *Das Buch Bahir*, ed. G. Scholem (Leipsig: W. Drugulin, 1923); no. 36.

9. Scholem, *Bahir*, no. 43.

10. Scholem, *Bahir*, no. 90.

11. Scholem, *Bahir*, no. 90.

12. *Zohar* III:290a; Tishby, *Mishnat ha-Zohar,* 1:191.

13. *Zohar* III:17a; Tishby, *Mishnat ha-Zohar,* 1:252.

14. *Zohar* III:290a; Tishby, *Mishnat ha-Zohar,* 1:191.

15. *Zohar* III:81a, quoted in G. Scholem, *Zohar, The Book of Splendor* (New York: Schocken Books, 1963), 115–116.

16. *Deuteronomy* 6:4.

17. *Zohar* II: 133b–134a; Tishby, *Mishnat ha-Zohar,* 2:312–315.

18. *Zohar* III:6a. Quoted in Scholem, *Zohar, The Book of Splendor*, 110.
19. B. T. *Shabbat* 119a.

CHAPTER 6

1. *Sefer Mar'ot Ha-Tzovaot*, 110
2. Rabbi Shabtai Sheftel Horwitz, *Shefa Tal*, quoted in Matt, *The Essential Kabbalah*, 93.
3. Shem Tov ibn Shem Tov, *Commentary on the Sefirot*, quoted in Matt, *The Essential Kabbalah*, 92.
4. *Zohar* III:152a, translation from *Zohar: The Book of Enlightenment*, 43–45. For other translations of *Zohar*, see Scholem, *Zohar, The Book of Splendor, Kabbalah* (New York: Schocken, 1963). The most important translation is the series whose first two volumes have been published: Daniel Matt, *The Zohar: Pritzker Edition* (Palo Alto, Calif.: Stanford University Press, 2004).
5. Matt, *Zohar*, xxiv.
6. *Genesis* 24:12.
7. *Genesis* 12:1–2.
8. *Bereshit Rabbah* 1:1.
9. Yehudah Aryeh Leib Alter of Gur, the Gerer Rebbe (1847–1905), *Sefer Sefat Emet*, 4:22.
10. Yissakhar Baer of Prague, *Sefer Yesh Sakhar*, (Warsaw, 1901), 66; based on *Zohar* 3:98a.
11. *Zohar* 1:8a, translated in *Wisdom of the Zohar*, ed. Isaiah Tishby. 3 vols. (Oxford: Oxford University Press, 1989), 3:1318–1319.
12. Meshullam Feibush Heller of Zbarash (1740–1795), *Sefer Yosher Divrei Emet*, ch.3.
13. *Zohar* I:31b–32a, translated by Matt, *The Essential Kabbalah*, 90.
14. Baal Shem Tov, quoted in Matt, *The Essential Kabbalah*, 193.
15. *Tanhuma, Exodus* 25.
16. Moshe Hayim Efrayim of Sudilkov (1748–1800), *Degel Machaneh Efrayim* (Jerusalem, 1995), 253.
17. *Leviticus Rabbah* 36:4.
18. Menachem Mendel of Kotsk, the Kotsker Rebbe (1787–1859), *Siah Sarfei Kodesh*.
19. Gershom Scholem, "On the Possibility of Jewish Mysticism in Our Time," *On the Possibility of Jewish Mysticism in Our Time.* (Philadelphia: Jewish Publication Society, 1997).
20. Moshe Hayim Efrayim of Sudilkov, *Degel Machaneh Efrayim*, 257.

CHAPTER 7

1. Urbach, *The Sages*, 1:214.
2. *Genesis* 2:7, quoted in Urbach, *The Sages*, 1:214.
3. I *Kings* 19:10, quoted in Urbach, *The Sages*, 1:215.
4. *Exodus* 23:9, quoted in Urbach, *The Sages*, 1:215.
5. *Job* 12:10, quoted in Urbach, *The Sages* 1:215.
6. *Sifre A Tannaitic Commentary on the Book of Deuteronomy*, ed. Reuven Hammer

(New Haven, Conn.: Yale, 1986), no. 306, 307, quoted in Urbach, *The Sages*, 1:220–221.

7. Aristotle, *On the Soul. Parva Naturalia. On Breath.* Trans. W. S. Hett (Cambridge: Harvard University Press, 1957), 2:2.

8. *Zohar Hadash* (Venice, 1658), Bereshit 18b.

9. *Zohar Hadash, Midrash Ruth* 38c; Tishby, *Mishnat ha-Zohar* 2:50–51.

10. *Sefer ha-Zohar* I:83a–b; Tishby, *Mishnat ha-Zohar,* 2:51–52.

11. *Zohar* I:83a–b.

12. *Zohar* I:62a.

13. *Zohar Hadash, Bereshit,* 27b–28a; Tishby, *Mishnat ha-Zohar,* 2:96–98.

14. *Qohelet Rabbah* 7:13; *The Book of Legends,* edited by H. N. Bialik and Y. H. Ravnitzky, translated William G. Braude (New York: Schocken, 1992), 15.

15. B. T. *Sanhedrin* 38a; Bialik and Ravnitzky, *The Book of Legends,* 14.

16. *Bereshit Rabba* 8:1; Bialik and Ravnitzky, *The Book of Legends,* 15.

17. *Tikkunei Zohar* 90b.

18. *Zohar* 1:20a

19. *Zohar Chadash* 16b.

20. Scholem, *Pirqei Yesod,* 370–373.

21. Gershom Scholem, "*Tzelem*: The Astral Body," *On the Mystical Shape of the Godhead*

22. *Zohar* I:205b; Tishby, *Mishnat ha-Zohar,* 2:53.

23. *Zohar* I:235a.

24. *Zohar Hadash, Bereshit* 18b; Tishby, *Mishnat ha-Zohar,* 2:44–45.

25. *Zohar* III:174b.

26. B. T. *Hagigah* 12b. On differences between this view and rabbinic views see Urbach, *The Sages*, 1:237–239.

27. *Zohar* I:85b; Tishby, *Mishnat ha-Zohar,* 2:627.

28. This idea of soul mates, which was introduced by Plato, is known as "Platonic love." Platonic love is not asexual love, but rather the spiritual attraction of one soul for its original mate. This conception was adopted by many medieval writers including the author of the *Zohar.* See Plato's *Symposium* f. 189, in *The Dialogues of Plato,* trans. B. Jowett (New York: Random House, 1937), 2:315–316.

29. *Zohar* I:85b.

30. B. T. *Niddah* 30b. See Urbach, *The Sages*, 1:246.

31. *Zohar* 1:183a

32. *Zohar* I:224b, quoted in Scholem, *Zohar: The Book of Splendor,* 72–73.

33. *Zohar* I:99b.

34. *Zohar* I:201a; Tishby, *Mishnat ha-Zohar,* 2:154.

35. *Zohar* I:57b; Tishby, *Mishnat ha-Zohar,* 2:159.

36. *Zohar* I:78b; Tishby, *Mishnat ha-Zohar,* 2:160.

37. *Zohar* I:218b.

38. *Zohar* III:1 26a–b; Tishby, *Mishnat ha-Zohar,* 2:162–163.

39. See Scholem, *Pirqei Yesod,* 308–357.

40. M. *Keritot* 1:1.

41. Scholem, *Pirqei Yesod,* 319–320.

42. Scholem, *Pirqei Yesod,* 334.

43. See C. D. Chavel, *Kitvei Ramban,* 2:281.

CHAPTER 8

1. Efraim Gottlieb, *Mehqarim be-Sifrut ha-Qabbalah* (Tel Aviv: Tel Aviv University Press, 1976), 38ff.

2. Gershom Scholem, *Ha-Qabbalah be-Provence* (Jerusalem: Hebrew University, 1970), appendix.

3. Tishby, *Mishnat ha-Zohar*, 2:292.

4. Gottlieb, *Mehqarim*, 45.

5. B. T. *Berakhot* 13a.

6. *Zohar* II:57a; Tishby, *Mishnat ha-Zohar*, 2:340–341.

7. *Zohar* II:57a.

8. *Tikkunei Zohar* 21; Tishby, *Mishnat ha-Zohar*, 2:342.

9. *Zohar* II:215b.

10. *Zohar* III:294a–b.

11. B. T. *Berakhot* 21b.

12. B. T. *Berakhot* 6a.

13. *Zohar* III:126a; Tishby, *Mishnat ha-Zohar*, 2:308–309.

14. B. T. *Berakhot* 26a.

15. *Zohar* II:59b; Tishby, *Mishnat ha-Zohar*, 2:307–308.

16. *Zohar* II:59b–60a; II:237b.

17. *Zohar* I:234; Yissakhar Baer of Prague, *Sefer Yesh Sakhar*, 13a.

18. B. T. *Makkot* 24a.

19. *Zohar* II:119a.

20. *Midrash Shemot Rabbah*, ed. A. Halevy (Tel Aviv: Mahbarot la-Sifrut, 1959), 25:12.

21. B. T. *Shabbat* 119a.

22. *Tikkunei Zohar* 6.

23. *Zohar* II:135a–b; Tishby, *Mishnat ha-Zohar*, 2:335.

24. B. T. *Betzah* 16a.

25. *Zohar* II:205a.

26. Scholem, *Pirqei Yesod*, 135ff.

27. *Zohar* I11:272b; see also Yissakhar Baer of Prague, *Sefer Yesh Sakhar*, 50.

28. B. T. *Hullin* 105a.

29. *Zohar* 1:53b; see Jacob Katz, *Halakhah ve-Kabbalah* (Jerusalem: Magnes, 1984), 44.

30. *Zohar* II:168b, 153b; Yissakhar Baer of Prague, *Sefer Yesh Sakhar*, 21a.

31. B. T. *Berakhot* 53b.

32. *Zohar* 18:272b.

33. *Zohar* 11:154b; Yissakhar Baer of Prague, *Sefer Yesh Sakhar*, 22a.

34. *Zohar* 11:168b.

35. B. T. *Sota* 38b.

36. *Proverbs* 31:10–31.

37. *Zohar* 1:257a.

38. B. T. *Rosh ha-Shanah* 16b.

39. Yissakhar Baer of Prague, *Sefer Yesh Sakhar*, 34a.

40. *Zohar* 10:231a; Tishby, *Mishnat ha-Zohar*, 2:550.

41. *Genesis* 24:12.

42. *Genesis* 31:42.

43. *Genesis* 21.

44. *Genesis* 22.

45. *Zohar* 111:214b.

46. *Zohar* 111:214b.

47. *Zohar* 111:69a.

48. *Leviticus* 16:30–31.

49. M. *Yoma* 8:1.

50. *Seder Olam Rabbah*, ed. Ratner (Vilna, 1897), 6.

51. *Exodus* 3:5.

52. *Exodus* 19:14–15.
53. *Exodus* 20:18.
54. M. *Yoma* 1–7.
55. *Zohar* III:103b.
56. Yissakhar Baer of Prague, *Sefer Yesh Sakhar*, 39b.
57. *Zohar* 1:220a–221a.
58. *Zohar* III:214b.
59. *Exodus* 34:25.
60. *Exodus* 12:15.
61. *Exodus* 12:1–28.
62. Nahmanides on *Exodus* 23:17.
63. Shlomo ha-Levi Alkabetz, *Brit ha-Levi* (Jerusalem, 1970), 20a.
64. Alkabetz, *Brit ha-Levi*, 19a; based on *Bereshit Rabbah* 9:7.
65. *Shemot Rabba* 2:4.
66. *Zohar* 1:8a.

CHAPTER 9

1. Simon Dubnow, *History of the Jews of Russia and Poland* (New York: Ktav, 1975).
2. M. *Sota* 9:15.
3. See Scholem, *Major Trends*, 244–286; Lawrence Fine, *Physician of the Soul, Healer of the Cosmos: Isaac Luria and His Kabbalistic Fellowship* (Stanford, Calif.: Stanford University Press, 2003). For further studies on the mysticism of Safed, see Lawrence Fine, *Safed Spirituality: Rules of Mystical Piety, The Beginning of Wisdom* (Ramsey, N.J.: Paulist Press, 1984); Solomon Schechter, "Safed in the Sixteenth Century," in *Studies in Judaism* (Philadelphia: Jewish Publication Society, 1908).
4. Hayyim Vitale, *Sefer Etz Hayyim* (Jerusalem, 1910), 11b.
5. Vitale, *Sefer Etz Hayyim*, 11b.
6. Vitale, *Sefer Etz Hayyim*, 11b.
7. Vitale, *Sefer Etz Hayyim*, 11b.
8. Vitale, *Sefer Etz Hayyim*, 11b.
9. Vitale, *Sefer Etz Hayyim*, 11b.
10. Vitale, *Sefer Etz Hayyim*, 11b.
11. Vitale, *Sefer Etz Hayyim*, 12a.
12. Vitale, *Sefer Etz Hayyim*, 13a.
13. Vitale, *Sefer Etz Hayyim*, 13a.
14. For a complete biography of this figure, see Gershom Scholem, *Sabbatai Sevi* (Princeton, N.J.: Bollingen, 1973).
15. *Sefer Tzeva'at ha-Rivash* (Jerusalem, 1973), 21. For a full discussion of this issue, see Rivka Schatz, *Ha-Hasidut ke-Mistikah* (Jerusalem: Magnes, 1968), 21–40.
16. *Sefer Tzeva'at ha-Ribash*, 23–25.
17. Levi Isaac of Berditchev, *Sefer Kedushat Levi* (Jerusalem, 1958), *Parashat Pekudei*.
18. Meshullam Feibush Heller, *Sefer Derekh Emet* (Jerusalem, 1952), 14.
19. *Derekh Emet*, 14.
20. Yaakov Yosef of Polnoye, *Toledot Yaakov Yosef* (Warsaw, 1841), *va-Yakhel*.
21. *Sefer Shemuah Tovah* (Warsaw, 1938), 79b. Quoted in Schatz, *Ha-Hasidut*, 29.
22. Gershom Scholem, *The Messianic Idea in Judaism* (New York: Schocken, 1971), 227–250.

23. Martin Buber, *Hasidism and Modern Man* (New York: Harper, 1958), 140.

24. Arthur Green and Barry Holtz, *Your Word Is Fire* (Ramsey, N.J.: Paulist Press, 1977), 25. For further studies on *Hasidism*, see Arthur Green, *Tormented Master: A Life of Rabbi Nahman of Bratslav* (New York: Schocken, 1981); Rachel Elior, *Torat ha-Elohut ba-Dor ha-Sheni shel Hasidut HaBaD* (Jerusalem: Magnes Press, 1982).

25. This tale is told in many versions including Martin Buber's *Tales of the Hasidim: The Early Masters* (New York: Schocken, 1947), 69–70.

26. See *Abraham Isaac Kook*, trans. Ben Zion Bokser (New York: Paulist Press, 1978).

27. B. T. *Sanhedrin* 65b; Scholem, *Pirkei Yesod*, 388.

28. Scholem, *Pirkei Yesod*, 395.

29. Jack Solomon, Jr., *Agam* (New York: Circle Fine Art Books, 1981), 3.

30. Solomon, *Agam*, 16.

31. Norman Hampson, *The Enlightenment* (London, Penguin, 1968), 103.

32. Hampson, *Enlightenment*, 105.

CHAPTER 10

1. Yaakov Yosef of Polnoye, *Ben Porat Yosef* (1781), Appendix.

2. Rabbi Israel Sarug, *Limmudei Atzilut*, in Matt, *The Essential Kabbalah*, 97.

3. Rabbi Abraham Isaac Kook, *Orot Hakodesh*, in Matt, *The Essential Kabbalah*, 31, 99.

4. Rabbi Isaac Luria's *Kavvanah* on Eating, in Matt, *The Essential Kabbalah*, 149.

5. Alexander Susskind, *Yesod ve-Shoresh ha-Avodah*, in Matt, *The Essential Kabbalah*, 151.

6. Abraham Abulafia, *Mafteach Hatochachot*, in Matt, *The Essential Kabbalah*, 21.

7. Nahmanides, *Commentary on Torah*, Deuteronomy 13:5, quoted in Scholem, "Devekut, or Communion with God," *The Messianic Idea in Judaism,* 205.

8. Azriel of Gerona, *Commentary on the Aggadot*, 20, quoted in Idel, *Kabbalah: New Perspectives*, 46.

9. *Likkutei Moharan* I:22, #10, quoted in Moshe Idel and Bernard McGinn, *Mystical Union in Judaism, Christianity, and Islam* (New York: Continuum, 1999), 45.

10. Maggid of Mezritch, *Maggid Devarav le-Yaakov.*

11. Idel, *New Perspectives*, 65.

12. Idel, *New Perspectives*, 71.

13. B. T. *Berakhot*, 32b.

14. Quoted in Matt, *The Essential Kabbalah*, 110.

15. Azriel of Gerona, *Shaar Hakavanah*, quoted in Gershom Scholem, *Reshit ha-Qabbalah* (Jerusalem: Schocken, 1948), 143–144.

16. Eleazar Azikri, *Sefer Charedim*, #309 in Mark Verman, *The History and Varieties of Jewish Meditation* (Northvale, N.J.: Jason Aronson, 1996), 15.

17. Piasetzna Rebbe, *Sefer Chovat Ha-Talmidim*, in Verman, *History and Varieties*, 15.

18. Isaac of Acre, *Sefer Meirat Einayyim*, 217, quoted in Matt, *The Essential Kabbalah*, 120.

19. Abraham Isaac Kook, *Sefer Orot Hakodesh*, 1:268, quoted in Matt, *The Essential Kabbalah*, 125.

20. See Paul Davies, *God and the New Physics* (New York: Simon and Schuster, 1983), 1–8.

21. Arthur Deikman, "Deautomatization and the Mystic Experience," in *The Nature*

of Human Consciousness, ed. Robert E. Ornstein (San Francisco: W.H. Freeman, 1973), 216–233.

22. Sigmund Freud, *Civilization*, 21: 64–73.

23. Erich Neumann, "Mystical Man," in *The Mystic Vision: Papers from the Eranos Yearbook*, ed. Joseph Campbell (Princeton, N.J.: Princeton University Press, 1968).

GLOSSARY

Absorptive mysticism: Type of mysticism in which the mystic becomes undifferentiated and absorbed in the object of his quest.

Acosmic mysticism: World-denying mysticism.

Aliyat ha-neshamah: Ascension of the soul to heaven.

Anthropomorphisms: Descriptions of God in bodily terms.

Anthropopathisms: Descriptions of God as having human feelings and emotions.

Attentional meditation: Restful visualization of and attention to the sequence of ideas and images that enter consciousness.

Atzilut (emanation): Hypertrophy or overflow of divine essence from Eyn Sof.

Binah (understanding): Third Sefirah.

Bittul ha-yesh: Annihilation of conscious existence.

Deautomatization: Purposely contrived effort to ensure hypnotic and other trance-like stances.

Devekut: Mystical union with the Sefirot.

Din (judgment): Fifth Sefirah.

Essentialists: Kabbalists who believe that the Sefirot are God's essence.

Eyn Sof: Infinite aspect of God.

Gashmiyyut: Corporeality.

Gedulah (greatness); also Hesed (mercy). Fourth Sefirah.

Gematria: System of numerical value assigned to each Hebrew letter.

Gilgul: Transmigration of soul; reincarnation.

Gevurah (might); also Din (judgment): Fifth Sefirah.

Golem: Homonculus, robot made from soil.

Hesed (mercy): Fourth Sefirah.

Hod (majesty): Eighth Sefirah.

Hokhmah (wisdom): Second Sefirah.

Ibbur: The state in which a guardian or attendant soul of one person attaches to another person.

Kavvanah: Intention or mystical concentration.

Instrumentalists: Kabbalists who believe that the Sefirot are the vessels through which God acts.

Kabbalah: Medieval Jewish mystical movement.

233

Keter (crown): First Sefirah.

Malkhut (kingship); also Shekhinah: Tenth Sefirah.

Meshikhah (drawing down): Concentration of the power of a Sefirah upon the soul.

Mishnah: Earliest code of Jewish law (c. 200 C.E.).

Mitzvot: Jewish rituals and commandments.

Nefesh: Life, the lowest grade of soul.

Neshamah: Soul, highest grade of soul.

Netzah (triumph): Seventh Sefirah.

Noetic: An element of insight, knowledge, intuition, or revelation.

Nonabsorptive mysticism: Type of mysticism in which the mystic remains differentiated from the object of this quest.

Oceanic feeling: A sense that the mystic is undifferentiated from the rest of reality.

Pantheism: Type of mysticism in which God is perceived to be indistinguishable from nature (nature mysticism).

Penetration mysticism: Inner voyage centered within the consciousness of the mystic.

Ruah: Breath, middle grade of soul.

Ruhaniyyut: Spirituality.

Sefirot ("Calculi"): Ten aspects of God's unknowable being (sing. Sefirah).

Shekhinah: Literally "presence of God"; in Kabbalah, the feminine aspect of God.

Shevirah: The destruction of the harmony of the divine world.

Talmud: Body of Jewish law, lore, philosophy, and ethics compiled between 200 and 500 C.E. in Palestine and Babylonia.

Theism: God as a being separate and distinct from world.

Tiferet (splendor): Sixth Sefirah.

Tikkun: The repair of the shattered world of God.

Tikkunim: Purposeful ritual actions or restorative acts.

Torah: The Five Books of Moses (Genesis, Exodus, Leviticus, Numbers, Deuteronomy). Also Torah she-be-khtav.

Torah she-be-al peh: The orally transmitted body of Jewish religious precepts.

Transportation mysticism: The subject experiences his whole being traveling on a celestial journey.

Tzelem: Astral body.

Tzimtzum: Self-contraction of God.

Yesod (foundation): Ninth Sefirah.

YHVH: The Tetragrammaton, traditional four-letter name of God, pronounced "Adonai."

Yihhud (unity): Unification among the Seprot.

Ziwag (union): Union of human soul and Shekhinah.

BIBLIOGRAPHY

Aboth de-Rabbi Nathan (1887). Ed. S. Schechter, Vienna.

Abraham Isaac Kook (1978). *The Lights of Penitence, The Moral Principles, Lights of Holiness, Essays, Letters and Poems.* Trans. and ed. B. Z. Bokser. New York: Paulist Press.

Alkabetz, Shlomo ha-Levi (1970). *Brit ha-Levi.* Jerusalem.

Ariel, D. (1981). *Shem Tob ibn Shem Tob's Kabbalistic Critique of Jewish Philosophy in the Commentary on the Sefirot.* Ph.D. dissertation. Waltham, Mass.: Brandeis University.

———. (1985). The Eastern Dawn of Wisdom: The Problem of the Relation between Islamic and Jewish Mysticism. In *Approaches to Judaism in Medieval Times,* ed. D. Blumenthal, pp. 149–167. Chico, Calif.: Scholars Press.

Aristotle (1957). *On the Soul. Parva naturalia. On Breath.* Trans. W. S. Hett, Cambridge: Harvard University Press.

Babylonian Talmud (1886). Vilna: Romm.

Ben-Sasson, H. H. (1967). Rabbi Mosheh ben Nahman: Ish be-Sivkhei Tekufato. *Molad* (n.s.) 1:360–368.

Biale, D. (1978). *Gershom Scholem: Kabbalah and Counter-History.* Cambridge: Harvard University Press.

Buber, M. (1947). *Tales of the Hasidim: The Early Masters.* New York: Schocken.

———. (1958). *Hasidism and Modern Man.* New York: Harper.

Bucke, R. M. (1901). *Cosmic Consciousness.* Philadelphia.

Buxbaum, Y. (1994). *Jewish Spiritual Practices.* New Jersey: Jason Aronson.

Campbell, J. (1976). *The Masks of God: Occidental Mythology.* New York: Penguin.

Cohen, M. A. (1964). Reflections on the text and context of the disputation of Barcelona. *Hebrew Union College Annual* 35: 157–192.

Dan, J. (1968). *Torat ha-Sod shel Hasidei Ashkenaz.* Jerusalem: Bialik Institute.

———. (1987). *Gershom Scholem and the Mystical Dimension of Jewish History.* New York: New York University Press.

Dan, J., and R. Kiener. (1986). *The Early Kabbalah*. Ramsey, N.J.: Paulist Press.

Davies, P. (1983). *God and the New Physics*. New York: Simon & Schuster.

Deikman, A. (1973). Deautomatization and the Mystic Experience. In *The Nature of Human Consciousness*, ed. R. E. Ornstein, pp. 216–233. San Francisco: W. H. Freeman.

Dubnow, S. (1975). *History of the Jews of Russia and Poland*. New York: Ktav.

Eisen, A., and S. M. Cohen (2000). *The Jew Within: Self, Family, and Community in America*. Bloomington: Indiana University Press.

Elior, R. (2004). *The Three Temples: On the Emergence of Jewish Mysticism in Late Antiquity*. London: Littman Library of Jewish Civilization.

———. (1982). *Torat ha-Elohut ba-Dor ha-Sheni shel Hasidut HaBaD*. Jerusalem: Magnes Press.

Elishov, S. (1904). *Sefer Hakdamot u-Shearim*. Pietrakov.

Fine, L. (1984). *Safed Spirituality: Rules of Mystical Piety, The Beginning of Wisdom*. Ramsey, N.J.: Paulist Press.

———. (2003). *Physician of the Soul, Healer of the Cosmos: Isaac Luria and His Kabbalistic Fellowship*. Palo Alto: Stanford University Press.

Freud, S. (1961). Civilization and Its Discontents. *The Standard Edition of the Complete Works of Sigmund Freud*. London: Hogart Press.

Gafni, I. (1984). The Historical Background. In *Jewish Writings of the Second Temple Period*, ed. M. Stone, Philadelphia: Fortress Press.

Gottlieb, E. (1976). *Studies in Kabbalistic Literature*. Tel Aviv: Tel Aviv University Press.

Green, A. (1981). *Tormented Master: A Life of Rabbi Nahman of Bratslav*. New York: Schocken.

Green, A, and B. Holtz. (1993). *Your Word Is Fire*. Woodstock, Vt.: Jewish Lights.

Gruenwald, I. (1980). *Apocalyptic and Merkavah Mysticism*. Leiden: E. J. Brill.

Habermann, A (1948). *Shirei ha-Yihud ve-ha-Kavod*. Jerusalem: Mossad Harav Kook.

Halperin, D. J. (1980). *The Merkabah in Rabbinic Literature*. New Haven, Conn.: American Oriental Society.

Hammer, R. (1986). *Sifre: A Tannaitic Commentary on the Book of Deuteronomy*. New Haven, Conn.: Yale University Press.

Hampson, N. (1968). *The Enlightenment*. New York: Penguin.

Harris, L. (1985). *Holy Days: The World of a Hasidic Family*. New York: Summit.

Hayyim Hayke of Amdur (1953). *Sefer Hayyim va-Hesed*. Jerusalem.

Heller, Meshullam Feibusch me-Zborocz (1952). *Sefer Derekh Emet*. Jerusalem.

Heschel, A J. (1966). The mystical element in Judaism. In *The Jews: Their History, Culture and Religion*, 3rd ed., vol. 2, ed. L. Finkelstein, pp. 932–951. Philadelphia: Jewish Publication Society.

———. (1966). *The Insecurity of Freedom: Essays on Human Existence*. New York: Farrar, Giroux, and Straus.

Horowitz, B. (2000). *Connections and Journeys: Assessing Critical Opportunities for Enhancing Jewish Identity*. New York: UJA-Federation.

Idel, M. (1988). *Kabbalah: New Perspectives*. New Haven, Conn.: Yale University Press.

Idel, M., and B. McGinn. (1999). *Mystical Union in Judaism, Christianity, and Islam*. New York: Continuum.

Ibn Gabbai, Meir (1890). *Sefer Derekh Emunah*. Warsaw.

Inge, W. R. (1947). *Mysticism in Religion*. London.

Jacobs, L. (1977). *Jewish Mystical Testimonies*. New York: Schocken.

James, W. (1960). *The Varieties of Religious Experience*. London: Fontana Library.

Jellinek, A. (1852). *Beitrage zur Geschichte der Kabbala*. 2 vols. Leipsig: C. L. Firtzche.

Jerusalem Talmud (1948). New York: Shulsinger.

Kamenetz, R. (1997). *Stalking Elijah*. San Francisco: Harper.

———. (1995). *The Jew in the Lotus*. San Francisco: Harper.

Katz, J. (1984). *Halakhah ve-Kabbalah*. Jerusalem: Magnes Press.

Katz, S. T. (1978). Language, Epistemology and Mysticism. In *Mysticism and Philosophical Analysis*, ed. S. T. Katz, pp.22–74. New York: Oxford University Press.

Levi Isaac of Berditchev (1958). *Sefer Kedushat Levi*. Jerusalem.

Levine, M. H. (1976). *Falaquera's Book of the Seeker*. New York: Yeshiva University Press.

Lewin, B. (1928–1962). *Otzar ha-Geonim*. 13 vols. Haifa.

Maimonides (1958). *Mishneh Torah*. 14 vols. Jerusalem: Mossad Harav Kook.

———. (1963). *Guide of the Perplexed*. Trans. S. Pines. Chicago: University of Chicago Press.

Marcus, I. (1981). *Piety and Society: The Jewish Pietists of Medieval Germany*. Leiden: E. J. Brill.

Matt, D. (1996). *The Essential Kabbalah: The Heart of Jewish Mysticism*. San Francisco: Harper.

———. (1983). *Zohar: The Book of Enlightenment*. Ramsey, N.J.: Paulist Press.

———. (2003). *The Zohar: Pritzker Edition*, Vol. 1. Palo Alto, Calif.: Stanford University Press.

Mekhilta de-Rabbi Yishmael (1931). Ed. Horowitz. Frankfurt.

Midrash Bereshit Rabba (1965). Ed. J. Theodor and H. Albeck. 3 vols. Jerusalem: Wahrmann.

Midrash Shemot Rabbah (1959). Ed. A Halevy. Tel Aviv: Mahbarot la-Sifrut.

Midrash Tanhuma (1885). Ed. S. Buber, Vilna.

Mikraot Gedolot: Torah (1958–1959).2 vols. Jerusalem: Schocken.

Nahmanides (1959). *Perush al ha-Torah*. Ed. C. D. Chavel. 2 vols. Jerusalem: Mossad Harav Kook.

———. (1963–1964). *Kitvei Ramban*. Ed. C. D. Chavel. 2 vols. Jerusalem: Mossad Harav Kook.

Neumann, Erich (1968). The Mystic Man. In *The Mystic Vision: Papers from the Eranos Yearbook*, ed. Joseph Cambell. Princeton: Princeton University Press.

Neusner, J. (1974). *Understanding Rabbinic Judaism*. New York: Ktav.

———. (1975). *First-Century Judaism in Crisis*. Nashville, Tenn.: Abingdon Press.

The New Testament: An American Translation (1948). Ed. E. J. Goodspeed. Chicago: University of Chicago Press.

Otto, R. (1923). *The Idea of the Holy*. London: Oxford University Press.

————. (1932). *Mysticism East and West*. New York: Macmillan.

Parrinder, G. (1976). *Mysticism in the World's Religions*. New York: Oxford University Press.

Pesikta de-Rav Kahana (1962). Ed. B. Mandelbaum. 2 vols. New York.

Plato (1937). Symposium. In *The Dialogues of Plato*, vol. 2, trans. B. Jowett, pp. 315–316. New York: Random House.

Rankin, O. S. (1956). *Jewish Religious Polemic*. Edinburgh: Edinburgh University Press.

Roof, W. C. (1993). *A Generation of Seekers: The Spiritual Journeys of the Baby Boom Generation*. San Francisco: Harper.

Schatz, R. (1968). *Ha-Hasidut ke-Mistikah*. Jerusalem: Magnes Press.

Schechter, S. (1908). Safed in the Sixteenth Century. In *Studies in Judaism*. Philadelphia: Jewish Publication Society.

Scholem, G. (1923). *Das Buch Bahir*. Leipsig: W. Drugulin.

————. (1929–1930). Perakim me-toledot sifrut ha-Kabbalah. *Kiryat Sefer* 6:402–403.

————. (1930). *Kitvei Yad ba-Kabbalah*. Jerusalem: Hebrew University Press.

————. (1941). *Major Trends in Jewish Mysticism*. New York: Schocken.

————. (1960). *Jewish Gnosticism, Merkabah Mysticism and Talmudic Tradition*. New York: Jewish Theological Seminary.

————. (1962). *Ursprung und Anfange der Kabbala*. Berlin: Walter de Gruyter.

————. (1963). *Zohar: The Book of Splendor*. New York: Schocken.

————. (1965). *On the Kabbalah and Its Symbolism*. New York: Schocken.

————. (1970). *Ha-Kabbalah be-Provence*. Jerusalem: Hebrew University.

————. (1971). *The Messianic Idea in Judaism*. New York: Schocken.

————. (1972). The Name of God and the Linguistic Theory of the Kabbalah. In *Diogenes* 79: 59–80; 80:164–194.

————. (1973). *Sabbatai Sevi*. Princeton: Bollingen.

————. (1976). *Pirkei Yesod be-Havanat ha-Kabbalah u-Semaleha*. Jerusalem: Bialik Institute.

————. (1987). *Origins of the Kabbalah*. Philadelphia: Jewish Publication Society.

Schweid, E. (1985). *Judaism and Mysticism According to Gershom Scholem*. Atlanta: Scholars Press.

Sefer ha-Zohar (1970). Jerusalem: Mossad Harav Kook.

Seder Olam Rabbah (1897). Ed. Ratner, Vilna.

Sefer Maarekhet ha-Elohut (1558). Mantua.

Sefer Tzevaat ha-Ribash (1973). Jerusalem.

Sefer Shemuah Tovah (1938). Warsaw.

Sefer Yetzirah (1965). Jerusalem.

Shatzmiller, Y. (1969). Le-Temunat ha-Mahloqet ha-Rishonah al Kitvei ha-Rambam. *Zion* 34:126–144.

Shishah Sidrei Mishnah (1952–1956). Ed. H. Albeck and H. Yalon. 6 vols. Jerusalem: Bialik Institute.

Shohat, A. (1971). Beirurim be-Parashat ha-Pulmus ha-Rishon al Sifrei ha-Rambam. *Zion* 36: 27–60.

Silver, D. J. (1965). *Maimonidean Criticism and the Maimonidean Controversy.* Leiden: E. J. Brill.

Singer, I. B., and I. Moskowitz. (1976). *A Little Boy in Search of God: Mysticism in a Personal Light.* Garden City, N.Y.: Doubleday.

Solomon, J. (1981). *Agam.* New York: Circle Fine Art Books.

Sperling, H., and M. Simon. (1931–1934). *The Zohar.* London: Soncino Press.

Stace, W. T. (1960). *Mysticism and Philosophy.* Philadelphia: Lippincott.

Steinsaltz, A. (1980). *The Thirteen-Petalled Rose.* New York: Basic Books.

Strauss (Ashtor), E. (1944). *Toledot ha-Yehudim ba-Mitzrayim ve-Suriah Tahat Shilton ha-Mamelukim.* 2 vols. Jerusalem.

Tanakh: A New Translation of the Holy Scriptures According to the Traditional Hebrew Text (1985). Philadelphia: Jewish Publication Society.

Tanna de-Vei Eliyahu (Seder Eliahu Rabba and Seder Eliahu Zuta and *Pseudo-Seder Eliahu Zuta)* (1902, 1904). Ed. M. Friedmann, Vienna.

Tikkunei Zohar (1558). Mantua.

Tishby, I. (1957–1961). *Mishnat ha-Zohar.* 2 vols. Jerusalem: Bialik Institute.

Twersky, I. (1969). Aspects of the Social and Cultural History of Provencal Jewry. In *Jewish Society through the Ages,* ed. H. H. Ben-Sasson and S. Ettinger, pp. 185–207. New York: Schocken.

Urbach, E. E. (1975). *The Sages.* 2 vols. Jerusalem: Magnes Press.

Verman, M. (1996). *The History and Varieties of Jewish Meditation.* New Jersey: Jason Aronson.

Vitale, H. (1910). *Sefer Etz Hayyim.* Jerusalem.

Werblowsky, R. J. Z. (1977). *Karo: Lawyer and Mystic.* Philadelphia: Jewish Publication Society.

Wolfson, H. A. (1961). *Religious Philosophy.* Cambridge, Mass.: Harvard University Press.

Yaakov Yosef of Polnoye (1781). *Ben Porat Yosef.*

———. (1841). *Toledot Yaakov Yosef.* Warsaw.

Yissakhar Baer of Prague (1901). *Sefer Yesh Sakhar.* Warsaw.

Zaehner, R. C. (1957). *Mysticism Sacred and Profane.* London: Clarendon Press.

Zohar: The Book of Enlightenment (1983). Trans. D. Matt. Ramsey, N.J.: Paulist Press.

Zohar Hadash (1658). Venice.

INDEX

sonal nature of, 43–44, 58–63, 67, 70–71, 84, 218; Pharisees and, 52–54; prayer and, 18, 50, 159; rabbinic Judaism and, 45–54, 56; remoteness of, 44–52, 56–63, 96–97, 98–100, 110–11, 208, 218; Sadducees and, 52; in *Sefer ha-Bahir*, 37; *Sefirot* and, 59, 60–61, 66–72, 85, 97–101, 110–11; sexuality and, 101; *Shekhinah* and, 47, 49–57, 95–97; sin and, 46–47; soul and, 19, 135–39; as *Tiferet*, 101; Torah and, 17, 44–54, 113–16, 124–25, 169; transcendent nature of, 47, 51, 61–62, 208, 218–19; unity and, 10–11, 18, 63, 70, 71, 137, 159, 187, 207–11; universe and, 121–22; unknowability of, 65, 75. See also *The Infinite*
Golem, 197
good, 77, 167
governance, 86
Great Awakenings, 221n13
greatness, 77
Grimm, Jacob, 197
Guide of the Perplexed, 54–55

hadas, 164, 165
Hai Gaon, 28–30, 32, 74
Ha-Kadosh Barukh Hu, 95, 117
Halperin, David J., 223n11
handwashing, 157–58
harmony: God and, 17–18; *Malkhut* and, 123; masculinity and, 82; *Midrash* and, 122–23; Sabbath and, 156; *Sefirot* and, 100, 156; sin and, 101; soul and, 20–21, 133; *Tiferet* and, 78–79, 82, 123; Torah and, 122–23; unity and, 101; *Zohar* on, 100
Hasidism: Buber, Martin, and, 189, 195; chanting in, 214; community and, 189–91; consciousness and, 186–89; culture and, 191; demise of, 200–201; *devekut* and, 209–11; divinity and,

184–85; evil and, 185; in Germany, 32–34, 197; God and, 10–11, 33–34, 58–59, 183–89; individualism and, 33, 189–90; Jewish Renewal and, xviii–xix; meditation and, 187–88, 212–15; modern, 191–93; Orthodox Judaism and, 191; prayer and, 33, 187–88, 189–91; primordial light and, 125–26; Rav Kook and, 193–94; repentence and, 193–94; rituals and, 188; Sabbath and, 156; Seekers and, 191; sexuality and, 185, 187; sin and, 184; Torah and, 121–22; in Ukraine, 183–91, 192; vessels and, 183–85
Haskalah, 201
Havurah, xviii
"Hear, O Israel," 102–4
hearing, 214
heavenly limbs, 103–4
Hebrew: *devekut* and, 209–10; divine language and, 89–93; Enlightenment and, 201; *Hokhmah* and, 118; Judaism and, 217; meditation and, 203, 213–14
hell, 146–47, 148
Hellenism, 131–32
hermeneutics, 119
Heschel, Abraham Joshua, xiv–xv, 11, 221n12
Hesed: Abraham and, 117, 161; *Din* and, 78, 82, 133, 156, 157–58, 160–62; emanation and, 76–77, 79; *Hokhmah* and, 77–78; *Lekhah Dodi* and, 109, 110; love and, 81; masculinity and, 77; meditation and, 211–12; *nefesh* and, 133; *Netzah* and, 79; overview of, 76–78; *Rosh ha-Shanah* and, 160–62; Sabbath and, 156, 157–58; selflessness and, 81; soul and, 151; *Sukkot* and, 165; *Yom ha-Kippurim* and, 162
history, 1, 23–42, 55–56, 171–202
hitkallelut, 210
Hod, 79, 165

ABOUT THE AUTHOR

David Ariel is president of the Laura and Alvin Siegal College of Judaic Studies in Cleveland. He is the author of the best-selling book *What Do Jews Believe? The Spiritual Foundations of Judaism,* and *Spiritual Judaism: Restoring Heart and Soul to Jewish Life.* Ariel lives in the Cleveland area.